Our Maryland

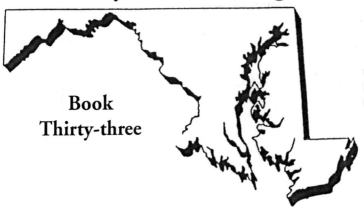

Book
Thirty-three

The
Griffith
Families

William N. Hurley, Jr.

HERITAGE BOOKS
2008

HERITAGE BOOKS

AN IMPRINT OF HERITAGE BOOKS, INC.

Books, CDs, and more—Worldwide

For our listing of thousands of titles see our website
at
www.HeritageBooks.com

Published 2008 by
HERITAGE BOOKS, INC.
Publishing Division
100 Railroad Ave. #104
Westminster, Maryland 21157

International Standard Book Numbers
Paperbound: 978-0-7884-2073-3
Clothbound: 978-0-7884-7223-7

OUR MARYLAND HERITAGE

Book 33

THE GRIFFITH FAMILIES

Being Principally the Descendants of
William Griffith, Died c.1699

Through More Than 300 years and
Twelve Generations, In Male and Female Lines

Primarily of
Montgomery & Frederick Counties
Maryland

But Including Numerous References to
the Family found in Other Counties and States

ALSO BY W. N. HURLEY, JR.

Available from the publisher: Heritage Books, Inc.

Neikirk-Newkirk-Nikirk, Volume 1, Revised
Neikirk-Newkirk-Nikirk, Volume 2
Hurley Families in America, Volumes 1 & 2, Revised
John William Hines 1600, And His Descendants, Revised
Maddox, A Southern Maryland Family
Pratt Families of Virginia and Associated Families
Lowder Families in America
Genealogical Gleanings of Montgomery County, Maryland
1850 Census of Montgomery County, Maryland
1860 Census of Montgomery County, Maryland
1870 Census of Montgomery County, Maryland
1880 Census of Montgomery County, Maryland

1900 Census of Montgomery County, Maryland
Winner 2001 Norris Harris Prize, Maryland Historical Society
"Best compilation of genealogical source records of Maryland"

Our Maryland Heritage Series:

Book 1:	Fry	Book 18:	Young
Book 2:	Walker	Book 19:	Bowman and Gue
Book 3:	Fulks	Book 20:	Trundle and Allied
Book 4:	Watkins	Book 21:	Fisher and Beckwith
Book 5:	King	Book 22:	Davis
Book 6:	Burdette	Book 23:	Etchison
Book 7:	Soper	Book 24:	Holland
Book 8:	Brandenburg	Book 25:	Ricketts
Book 9:	Purdum	Book 26:	Trail
Book 10:	Perry	Book 27:	Rabbitt
Book 11:	Stottlemyer	Book 28:	Baker
Book 12:	Browning	Book 29:	Selby
Book 13:	Miles	Book 30:	Ward
Book 14:	Lewis	Book 31:	Hays and Gott
Book 15:	Warfield	Book 32:	Waters
Book 16:	White		
Book 17:	Mullinix/Mullineaux		

INTRODUCTION

This is the Thirty-third in our series of families having their origins in Maryland, with descendants now found in all parts of the United States. This study of the Griffith families has been limited somewhat to those members of the families found primarily in Anne Arundel, Frederick and Montgomery Counties, Maryland, although others will be mentioned as they are found elsewhere.

As will be discussed, there have been at least a few rather extensive studies prepared or published relative to the probable Welsh ancestry of the Griffith family, and the immigrants who arrived in Virginia and Maryland very early during our history. But, as has been the case in other families, all too often, the reports of the early Colonial period either conflict, or have been interpreted differently by the various individuals conducting the studies. The thread is there, however, strong enough to indicate some truth to each study, although the arrangement of dates and individuals sometimes differs. It seems clear that the ancestors of the Griffith families in the area under study probably did arrive from Wales, either direct to Maryland, or by first landing in the Virginia Colony, and over time moving into areas that either were originally, or later became, part of the Maryland Colony; and from there, to the western reaches of the settlement.

We strongly recommend that the serious researcher study each of the studies discussed so that they might draw their own conclusions as to the earlier ancestry of the families.

We also found one rather interesting little tidbit in the Griffith family folder file at the library of the Montgomery County Historical Society in Rockville. It was contained in three pages of family information submitted by Lilly C. Stone in 1958, apparently without documentation, but of interest. We quote: *Professor Edward Dowden, fellow of Trinity College, Dublin, notable Shakespearian scholar and author now in this country says in an interview, a curious, and to students of heredity, an important discovery, has been made by the antiquarians who are at work upon the family history of Stratford's greatest son. It is now regarded as sufficiently proved that Shakespeare's paternal grandmother was a*

Griffith, a member of a race (Celtic) in South Wales. There is a strong strain of the Griffith blood in the Shakespeare family.

The *Baltimore Sun* of February 12, 1905 carried an article titled Maryland Heraldry, primarily devoted to the Griffith family. The first sentence reads: *There is a current saying in Maryland that the Griffith family contributed more soldiers to the War of the American Revolution than any other family in the State, and no one familiar with the records of the Griffith family would question that statement.* The article is quite lengthy, and carries genealocial data in extensive detail through several generations of the family descending from the original immigrant. Many of them are not covered here, in that we are limiting our study primarily to those found in Montgomery and Frederick Counties. The article is in the family folder file at Rockville, and probably available in major libraries in Baltimore as well.

As colonists continued to arrive, seven original counties were formed in Maryland under the Colonial Governor: Anne Arundel, Charles, St. Mary's, and Calvert on the Western Shore of the Chesapeake Bay; and Somerset, Kent, and Talbot on the Eastern Shore. As settlers moved steadily westward, and took up new lands, it was necessary to form new centers of government to serve them and, over time, sixteen new counties were formed from the original seven, as well as the City of Baltimore. The researcher must be familiar with this formation, in order to know the sources of information for any given time-frame. The following tabulation demonstrates the formation of each of the counties of Maryland:

Formation of the Counties of Maryland

Name of County	Formed	Source County or Counties
Allegany	1789	Washington
Anne Arundel	1650	Original County
Baltimore	1660	Anne Arundel
Calvert	1654	Original County
Caroline	1773	Dorchester & Queen Anne's
Carroll	1837	Baltimore & Frederick
Cecil	1674	Baltimore & Kent
Charles	1658	Original County
Dorchester	1669	Somerset & Talbot
Frederick	1748	Prince George's & Baltimore
Garrett	1872	Allegany
Harford	1773	Baltimore
Howard	1851	Anne Arundel
Kent	1642	Original County
Montgomery	1776	Frederick
Prince George's	1695	Calvert & Charles
Queen Anne's	1706	Dorchester, Kent & Talbot
Somerset	1666	Original County
St. Mary's	1637	Original County
Talbot	1662	Original County
Washington	1776	Frederick
Wicomico	1867	Somerset & Worcester
Worcester	1742	Somerset

SOURCE REFERENCES

In the library of the Montgomery County Historical Society in Rockville, we found a zerox copy of *Genealogy of the Griffith Family; the Descendants of William and Sarah Maccubbin Griffith*, by R. R. Griffith of Baltimore, 1892. Without documentation, that book first states that "Came William Griffith, from London, England, and settled on the Severn River in Anne Arundel County,

Province of Maryland." William is generally accepted as the progenitor of most, if not all, of the Griffith family in Maryland. This particular book is a series of family group entries, with birth, marriage and death dates, but little information as to geographic locations, or family color. With entries spaced throughout a rather thick book, it is a bit difficult to assemble an entire family together.

We have in our personal library copies of *Anne Arundel Gentry*, in two volumes, by Harry Wright Newman, reprinted by Family Line Publications of Westminster, Maryland. The late Mr. Newman, who died in 1983, was the author of more than a dozen studies of Maryland history and genealogy, including such monumental works as *Mareen Duvall of Middle Plantation*, widely respected as the definitive source relative to that family and associated families. Although there is no specific section in that work to the Griffith families, Newman covers the earliest members of the Griffith families, with numerous references in other families. In his typical fashion, he includes voluminous notations to his sources and the basis for conclusions that can not otherwise be supported by hard data. The serious student of this and related families is urged to refer to that extensive study, available in most historical society libraries. Newman also generally prepared his data in sequential family groupings, more or less by generations, also a bit difficult to follow. He is, however, prolific with source references, local color, geographic locations and other personal details.

Also in my library, I have a copy of *The Founders of Anne Arundel and Howard Counties, Maryland*, by J. D. Warfield, 1905. It contains numerous references to members of the Griffith family, as well, and their frequent intermarriages with the Warfield, Riggs, Dorsey, and other powerful and influential families of Maryland. Mr. Warfield presented his information in a rather rambling fashion requiring the reader to move through a mass of informaiton in order to assemble a family. He appeared much more interested in the details of life during the period studied, and the social and financial positions of his subjects.

We also found considerable information in biographies of some prominent Griffith family members contained in works by Scharff, T. J. C. Williams and others published about 1900. Much of that information follows the early reports found in other references, as well as extant records of the Colonial period in Maryland from archival sources.

Our study is principally concerned with the Griffith family as they appear primarily in records of Montgomery County, with some overlap into Frederick, which is unavoidable. The early base appears rather complete up to about 1892, and we propose to continue, and build upon some of those earlier works, the combination of material found in the three works mentioned above providing a very interesting picture of the early families, when taken in total.

It quickly became evident, however, that we must include sufficient information from the early years in Anne Arundel and Prince George's Counties, in order to establish background lineage, and interrelationships. Our goal here is to assemble all available data from census records, family folder files in the Montgomery County Historical Society library, will records of the counties, and other reference sources of the library. It will be first necessary to establish relationships with the families discussed by Newman, Warfield and Griffith in order to place later families in proper perspective.

We repeat much of the information preceding as we found it in the various studies to which we have referred, without verification by personal research. Therefore, the reader is cautioned to use that data with care. The references discussed each contain far more information than that included here, and the reader is encouraged to investigate each of those studies further for additional data, and extensive discussions of the sources and relative merits of various elements of their reports.

A WORD OF CAUTION

The data contained in this report is not intended to be an all-inclusive genealogy of the families under study. It was prepared from information found in a variety of sources, including records found at the library of the Montgomery County Historical Society, such as family files, census returns, church and cemetery records, obituary collections, and the published books and abstracts held by the library in their research collection. We have not confirmed all of the data by personal examination of contemporary records, and can not, therefore, vouch for its accuracy in all cases. Others are, of course, just as prone to making mistakes as we are, but the information reported is as accurate as we could make it from the records studied.

We recognize that it is virtually impossible to report such an extensive amount of data without an error creeping in some place. Occasionally, we may have reported a date of birth, which is in reality the date of christening, or vice versa. Some reported dates of marriage are probably the date a license was issued, as reported in the public records, but should be reasonably close. In some cases, we will report dates as approximate, but they should lead you to the general time frame, so that you may distinguish between individuals with the same name. Throughout the text, I have used terms which should caution the reader: such as, apparently; may have been; reportedly; about; possibly; could be; and similar terminology, to indicate that the information given has either not been verified by extant contemporary records, or appears to fit a given set of circumstances which, of themselves, are believed to be correct.

Our goal has been to gather all of the available material into one convenient package, which should be accurate enough to provide the casual reader with an insight into their family history. The serious researcher should verify the material with independent research. Good luck, and please forgive our occasional error.

AND A WORD OF APPRECIATION

Thanks to Pat Anderson, librarian for the Montgomery County Historical Society for her constant encouragement and assistance. Without Pat and the volunteers at the library, the work could not have been completed.

As a result of their continued assistance, from the outset the commitment was made that with publication of each of the books in the series, all royalties derived are paid directly to the account of the Montgomery County Historical Society, for use of the library.

CONTENTS

xi

Arrangement of the Principal Chapters

William Griffith
died 1699
The Immigrant
Chapter 2

Orlando Griffith
1688

Charles Griffith
1693
Chapter 3

Sarah Griffith
1730
(md Azel Warfield)

Anne Warfield
1762
Chapter 12

Henry Griffith
1720
Chapter 4

Greenberry Griffith
1727
Chapter 9

Hezekiah Griffith
1752
Chapter 10

Howard Griffith
1757
Chapter 11

Henry Griffith, Jr.
1744

Samuel Griffith
1752
Chapter 7

Philemon Griffith
1756
Chapter 8

Henry Griffith
1767
Chapter 5

Nicholas Griffith
1771
Chapter 6

CHAPTER 1

Early Griffith Family Records
Maryland

As discussed in the introductory material, we intend to confine our basic study primarily to the Griffith families of Montgomery and Frederick Counties, Maryland. However, considering the pattern of county formation in Maryland, it is necessary to research some of the earliest family members in Anne Arundel, Baltimore, Calvert, Charles and Prince George's; at least sufficiently to determine the lineage. Keep in mind that Anne Arundel, Calvert and Charles were among the original counties of Maryland. Baltimore was formed from Anne Arundel in 1660; Prince George's from part of Calvert and Charles in 1695. In 1748, Frederick was formed from parts of Prince George's and Baltimore; and finally, in 1776, Montgomery was carved out of Frederick.

Beginning with the next chapter, our study will demonstrate rather conclusively that the principal Griffith families of Frederick and Montgomery Counties are descended from one William Griffith who died in Anne Arundel County about 1699. He was reportedly born in Wales, and came to Maryland from London in 1675. If we assume that he was an adult of about twenty-one years, he could have been born c.1654 or so (just conjecture, to set a time frame).

He was not the only representative of his name in Maryland, however, nor in the Colonies; nor perhaps the first to arrive. Further, they appear to have been persons of quality, as opposed to indentured servants, and over time, by industry and labor, became quite wealthy and influential members of society. For example, in *Original Lists of Persons of Quality 1600-1700*, by John Camden Hotten, there is a report of one Edward Griffith, aged 33 years (born c.1602) who sailed from London to Virginia about October 24, 1635, on board the *Abraham*, John Barker, Master. In the same ship, we found Alexander Maddox, born c.1613, whose descendants have been researched by this author. His widow Eleanor, and her second husband William Bosman moved from Northampton County, Virginia, to Somerset County, Maryland, which was not

1

uncommon for the time; Edward could have done the same thing. This early Edward Griffith may or may not be a progenitor of the families under discussion, but he demonstrates two important points: one, the Griffith families were represented in the Colonies quite early, and two, they were persons of quality, as opposed to indentured servants.

In the course of research, we have found numerous references to Griffith family members in the early probate records of the Maryland Colony, and in other sources. They demonstrate that there were other lineages of the family in the Colony, ever earlier than the immigrant William Griffith, of whom we report. Found on both sides of the Chesapeake Bay, they could have moved up from the Virginia Colony by land on either side, or arrived by transport up the Bay, with landfall in Talbott or Kent on the eastern shore, or at the Annapolis port on the western shore. Some of them were:

Samuel Griffith
died 1741

This Samuel Griffith appeared as early as March 30, 1685 when he was named as an heir of Philip Soones, although the county was not specified. In Anne Arundel County, Faith Gongo left a will dated February 23, 1693, in which she named Samuel as Overseer of her estate. Samuel Griffith was also Executor of the will of John Whipps, dated December 10, 1716 in Calvert County. He died there, leaving a will dated October 2, 1741, probated November 2, 1741, naming his children:
1.   Samuel Griffith, Jr., who inherited land in Baltimore County. He died in Baltimore County about 1746, when administrative bond was posted by Mary Griffith and others. He was owner of 168 acres of *Leaf Jenifer*; 119 acres of *Refuge*; 100 acres of *Phillips' Swamp*; 39 acres of *William's Hope*; 182 acres of *Abbott's Forest*; and 50 acres of *Hope's Addition*. He was witness to wills in Calvert County for Patrick Dew July 17, 1716; and for Richard Leaf December 2, 1716. In the latter will, Patrick Dew was Executor, identified as father-in-law. Samuel Griffith, Jr. had children, identified in his will:

2

a. Luke Griffith, born c.1729. Married January 13, 1757 to Mrs. Blanche Hall, widow of Parker Hall.
b. Sarah Griffith, born September 11, 1734
c. Samuel Griffith, born April 7, 1737
d. Mary Griffith, born September 25, 1739
e. Elizabeth Griffith.
f. Isaac Griffith, born September 4, 1743, died March 20, 1743
g. Avarilla Griffith, a twin, born November 23, 1744
h. Priscilla Griffith, a twin, born November 23, 1744
2. Lewis Griffith, inherited the land where he then lived half the land where brother John lived. Lewis may have been married twice; first to Alice, who died March 10, 1733, and had a son, and second August 5, 1739 to Mary Johnson. Child:
a. Thomas Griffith, born February, 1731.
3. John Griffith, inherited one half the land where he then lived.
4. Benjamin Griffith, inherited the land called *Clark's Skin*, which had belonged to the testator's grandfather, thus inferring a much earlier family member in the Colony.
5. Ann Griffith, with her sisters inherited the dwelling plantation.
6. Rebecca Griffith.
7. Bathsheba Griffith.

Benjamin Griffith
died 1736

Benjamin Griffith left a will in Kent County, dated March 26, 1736, styling himself as a "taylor" (or tailor). Probated April 17, 1736, the will left his wife her thirds, without naming her, and various properties to his children as follows:
1. Jackson Griffith, received part of *Eastern Neck* and one half the lot at Town, being that half next to the wharf.
2. Nathaniel Griffith, received the other half of *Eastern Neck* and the tract called *Calfpen*.
3. Cooter Griffith, or Coother, received the other half at Town; and *Spring Garden*.
4. Jonas Griffith, received the tract called *Batchelor's Choice*.
5. Mary Griffith, received certain personalty at age eighteen.

3

Miscellaneous Entries

The following chronological listing is simply a sampling of some of the older references found probate records of the Maryland Colony, meant to demonstrate the presence and distribution of Griffith family members very early in the colonial period.

- *1648*, January 17: William Griffith inherited personalty under the will of John Harrison in Anne Arundel County.
- *1665*, April 20: Thomas Griffith left a will probated June 25, 1666. County not stated; wife Lucy received 1,000 acres located on Susquehanna River for life, being part of: *Mt. Ararat*, part of *Atrup*, and part of *Island*. After her death, to other named beneficiaries (apparently no children).
- *1665*: Will of Edmund Joy, county not stated. Witnessed by Samuel Griffith.
- *1675*, June 24: Talbot County. Will of Robert Martin. Witness was Elizabeth Griffith.
- *1675*, December 9: Kent County. Will of Richard Moy. Legatee was his Godson, Richard Griffith.
- *1676*, October 26: Calvert County. Will of Dr. Owen Griffith. Bequests to several named individuals, do not appear to be his children. No wife mentioned.
- *1680*, April 10: George Griffith left a will at Hunting Creek in Calvert County, probated July 31, 1680. Wife not named; daughter Sarah received personalty; son-in-law Robert Rouse received residue of estate, real and personal.
- *1703*, May 19: Baltimore County. Will of Thomas Capell. Witness was Francis Griffith.
- *1704*, November 30: Talbot County, St. Paul's Parish. Will of Matthew Read. Witness was Edward Griffith.
- *1708*, February 22: Dorchester County. Will of Henry Griffith probated August 9, 1709. Wife received all property during her widowhood; not named. Youngest son Samuel Griffith received 100 acres; son John Griffith, 100 acres; and son Abraham Griffith, 125 acres; all being part of home plantation. Daughter Sarah Griffith received personalty at death of mother.

- *1711*, June 1: Anne Arundel County. Will of John Stephens, probated June 11, 1711. Witness was Edward Griffith.
- *1712*, August 3: Prince George's County. Will of Guy White, witness was Samuel Griffith, Jr.
- *1713*, March 10: Kent Island. Will of John Wells, Queen Anne County. Witness was Mathew Griffith.
- *1715*, February 25: Kent County. Will of Samuel Berry probated February 21, 1724. Bequest to George Griffith, "son of present wife Martha" the plantation with 100 acres and half the personal estate at the death of his mother. Apparently a second marriage for mother of George Griffith.
- *1718*, June 30: Will of Thomas Smyth, Kent County. Probated August 4, 1719. Reference to 100 acre tract where John Griffith "is now seated." Bequeathed to John Griffith and wife Mary during their lives.
- *1718*, December 16: Calvert County. Will of Elizabeth Griffith, wife of Samuel Griffith, deceased. Makes son Samuel Griffith lawful heir of her part of husband's will. Deed of gift next day to son Samuel Griffith, subject to payment by him of personalty to other named heirs (apparently not children).
- *1723*, February 29: Dorchester County will of Frances Fisher witnessed by Thomas Griffith.
- *1724*, September 1: Will of Edward Griffith, Gentleman, of Annapolis, probated September 15, 1724. Wife Sarah Executrix and heir to 400 acres *Griffith's Adventure*, north side of main falls of Patapsco River. 200 acres in Dorchester County to be sold to settle estate. Daughter Mary *Griffith's Park* between lower and upper falls of Potomac in Prince George's County; 200 acres of *Maiden Head* on Deer Creek in Baltimore County. Mary was then under sixteen years of age.

5

William Griffith
died 1699
The Immigrant
Chapter 2
*
*
* * * * * * * * *
*
*
* * Orlando Griffith 1688
*
*
* * Sophia Griffith 1691
*
*
* * Charles Griffith 1693......................Chapter 3
*
*
* * William Griffith, Jr. 1697

6

CHAPTER 2

William Griffith
died 1699

William Griffith was reportedly born near Cardigan, in Wales, and came to Maryland from London in 1675. He settled on the Severn River in Anne Arundel County, and married Sarah Maccubbin, who died April 22, 1716, daughter of John Maccubbin of Scotland, said to be descended from Kenneth, II, first king of Scotland.

John Maccubbin came with the Howard family to the Maryland Colony, and settled on *Timber Rock* along the Severn River in Anne Arundel County. He was twice married, and had children by both marriages. His second wife was Eleanor who, after his death in 1686, became the second wife of John Howard, without issue. As Eleanor Howard, she left a will in Anne Arundel County dated November 10, 1705, probated August 4, 1711, in which she left all of her personal estate to her grandchildren: Orlando, Sophia, Charles and William Griffith, who are hereafter shown to be children of the subject of our study; and apparently their only children. The will of Eleanor Maccubbin Howard named Sarah Reynolds as Executor. She was Sarah Maccubbin Griffith Reynolds, daughter of Eleanor and remarried widow of William Griffith, the immigrant; and the mother of the four grandchildren named in Eleanor's will.

John Howard, Sr. also left a will in Anne Arundel County, dated December 30, 1695, probated May 13, 1696. He there named his wife Eleanor as Executrix, and made certain bequests to his son John Howard and his unnamed heirs. He made a specific bequest of the residue of a 200-acre tract on the Little Falls to his grandson (actually his step-grandson) Orlando Griffith, and in event of his death, the land to pass to his mother Sarah Griffith, and her heirs.

William Griffith, the immigrant, left a will in Anne Arundel County, dated August 31, 1699, and probated October 23, 1699. To his wife Sarah, he left the dwelling plantation and personalty. His son Charles and daughter Sophia received the tract called *Griffith's Lot*, to share equally. Son Orlando received personalty. There was no mention in the will of a son William, but he appears to be a son of this family. After the death of William, the father, his widow Sarah was married secondly to Thomas Reynolds, High Sheriff of Anne Arundel County, by whom she had children. William and Sarah Griffith had children, born in Anne Arundel County, Maryland:

1. Orlando Griffith, born October 17, 1688, of whom more as Child 1.
2. Sophia Griffith, born April 27, 1691, died April 19, 1730, and inherited one-half of *Griffith's Lot* from her father. Married c.1713 to Benjamin Duvall, born c.1684, youngest son of Mareen Duvall, the immigrant in that line, and the subject of *Mareen Duvall of Middle Plantation*, by Harry Wright Newman, 1952. Benjamin Duvall inherited 200 acres of *Howerton's Range* in Calvert County under the will of his father, and was one of the signers of the petition to create Frederick County in 1748. Their descendants are treated in detail beginning at page 472 of *Middle Plantation*, to which the reader is referred.
3. Charles Griffith, a Captain, born January 20, 1693, of whom more in Chapter 3.
4. William Griffith, Jr., born April 15, 1697, and of whom more as Child 4.

CHILD 1

Orlando Griffith
1688-1757

This son of William Griffith, the Immigrant (died 1699) and his wife Sarah Maccubbin, was born October 17, 1688, died c.1757, and received personalty under the will of his father, and of his mother. Married June 6, 1717 at Annapolis to Katherine Howard, who died February, 1783, only daughter of Captain John Howard and Katherine (Greenberry) Ridgely. From her father, she reportedly inherited the tract called *Howard's Luck* at Huntington. John Howard of Anne Arundel County left a will probated February 23, 1703, in which he left to his daughter Katharine the 360 acres tract called *Owing's Contrivance* on the Bush River, which may be the same Katharine Howard who married Orlando Griffith.

The estate of John Howard was appraised August 18, 1753 in Anne Arundel County at 173 pounds, 4 shillings, 9 pence, and distribution made to the heirs. Among them was Catherine (sic), wife of Orlando Griffith, who received the negroes Simon and Ned. They made their home at *Griffith's Adventure* on a branch of the Patapsco River, where their children were apparently born. Orlando left a will in Anne Arundel County, dated April 8, 1753, probated April 26, 1757. He mentioned his wife Katherine, and eight children, sons and daughters. He also made reference to the Patapsco River, placing the family home location. Various tracts of land were mentioned, including: *Marly Run, Ward's Care Enlarged, Howard's Luck, Rich Neck, Griffith's Adventure,* and *Polecat Forest.* Son Henry Griffith was named Administrator of the Estate. The estate of Orlando Griffith was appraised by Joshua Hall and Thomas Sappington and reported to the court February 2, 1758, at a value of 271 pounds, 9 shillings, 5 pence. Next of kin were listed as Greenberry Griffith and Joseph Griffith; Executor was Henry Griffith. The children, not necessarily in birth order, included:

1. Sarah Howard Griffith, born May 13, 1718, died September 1, 1794. Married to Colonel Nicholas Dorsey of *Long Reach,* the son of Colonel Edward Dorsey. Colonel Edward left a will in Baltimore County, dated October 26, 1704, probated December 31, 1705, naming numerous children, among them his son Nicholas, who received 100 acres of *Long Reach* and personalty, upon his reaching the age of sixteen years. Nicholas was therefore born between 1688 and 1704. *Early Families of Southern Maryland,* Volume 1, by Elise Greenup Jourdan list the parents of Colonel Nicholas Dorsey as Nicholas Dorsey and Frances Hughes, who married in Anne Arundel December 20, 1709. Further, she states that Colonel Nicholas was born c.1712 and died 1780 in Baltimore County. That may be correct, based on his will in Baltimore County probated May 28, 1780, but conflicts with other reports naming the Colonel as son of Colonel Edward Dorsey who, as we note above, also named a son Nicholas in his will. In any event, Colonel Nicholas Dorsey and his wife Sarah lived at Eldersburg, Carroll County, and had children, including:

9

a. Rachel Dorsey, born c.1737; married to Anthony Lindsey, born c.1736, died c.1801 in Scott County, Kentucky.

b. Lydia Dorsey, born c.1740; married Charles Dorsey, son of Edward Dorsey, and moved to Kentucky.

c. Nicholas Dorsey, born c.1741, died c.1796. Married February 24, 1765 to Ruth Todd, born c.1741, died February, 1816, and had at least ten children. See *Early Families of Southern Maryland*, Volume 1, by Elise Greenup Jourdan, page 207.

d. Catherine Dorsey, a twin, born c.1744 married to Wood.

e. Charles Griffith Dorsey, a twin, born c.1744, died September 12, 1814; married to Catherine Welsh according to some reports. However, *Early Families of Southern Maryland*, Volume 1, by Elise Greenup Jourdan assigns the marriage to Nancy Dorsey, died September 30, 1806, daughter of Michael Dorsey and Ruth Todd. Six children, reported by Jourdan in her book, which see.

f. Henry Dorsey, born c.1745, died November 2, 1808. He was reportedly married to Martha and had three children, with descendants in western Virginia and Ohio, but not proven. See *Early Families of Southern Maryland*, Volume 1.

g. Sarah Dorsey.

h. Vachel Dorsey.

i. Achsah Dorsey, married July 25, 1785 to Bela Warfield, son of Seth Warfield (1723) and Mary Gaither. They had nine children, discussed in *Our Maryland Heritage, Book Fifteen, The Warfield Families*, which see.

j. Lucretia Dorsey, born June 4, 1754; married as his second wife to John Welsh, IV and had one child.

k. Frances Dorsey, married Chapman and second on February 17, 1792 to Elie Warfield, son of Seth Warfield (1723) and Mary Gaither. They had eight children, discussed in *Our Maryland Heritage, Book Fifteen, The Warfield Families*, which see.

l. Orlando Griffith Dorsey, inherited the homestead and was married second to Mary Gaither, daughter of Henry and

Martha Ridgely. At least nine children, listed in *Early Families of Southern Maryland*, Volume 1.

2. Nicholas Howard Griffith, died young; not in his father's will.
3. Henry Griffith, born February 14, 1720, of whom more in Chapter 4.
4. Greenberry Griffith, born December 31, 1727, of whom more in Chapter 9.
5. Joshua Griffith, born January 25, 1730, died 1799; a Lieutenant in the Continental Army, and Tobacco Inspector at the Elk Ridge Landing, as well as Deputy Surveyor in 1759. Married November 2, 1758 to Ann Hall and had children, including:
   a. Dennis Griffith, born November 9, 1759, died 1805, Lieutenant, 3rd Co., 7th Battalion, Continental Army. He surveyed the state in 1794 and the map can still be found in library collections. Married January 20, 1785 to Elizabeth Ridgely, born December 25, 1766, died 1834, daughter of Greenberry Ridgely and Lucy Stringer. At least these children:
      (1) Rachel Griffith, born February 13, 1786; married Henry Gassaway, son of Brice John Gassaway of Brookeville, Montgomery County. Henry moved from Baltimore to Cincinnati. At least two sons:
         (a) Henry Charles Gassaway, married Elizabeth Allen, daughter of the Reverend Ethan Allen.
         (b) Stephen Griffith Gassaway, an Episcopal minister who died in a steamboat accident on the Mississippi River.
      (2) Lucy Griffith, born April 3, 1788
      (3) Stephen Griffith, born February 19, 1790 served in the US Army as a Lieutenant.
      (4) David Griffith, born August 21, 1791, single
      (5) Ann Hall Griffith, born March 27, 1793
      (6) Dennis Griffith, Jr., born December 8, 1794
      (7) Peter Griffith, born March 17, 1796 died young
      (8) Elizabeth Griffith, born July 22, 1798 and died young
      (9) Elizabeth Greenberry Ridgely Griffith, born May 8, 1800

b. Rachel Griffith, born September 16, 1761, married to John Sprigg Belt, Captain of Fourth Company, First Regiment, Maryland Line, Continental Army. He was born September 10, 1752, a son of Jeremiah Belt (1724) and Mary Sprigg (1723).

c. Ann Griffith, born August 12, 1763. Married to Captain Edward Spurrier of the Continental Army, who served for seven years.

d. William Pitt Griffith, born April 11, 1766, reported as lost at sea

e. Joshua Griffith, Jr., born October 22, 1769, single

6. Benjamin Griffith, born November 22, 1732; moved to Poplar Springs, Maryland. Married November 27, 1755 to Mary Riggs, born September 24, 1732, the daughter of John Riggs, Jr. (1687) and Mary Davis (1702). Eight children, including:

a. Betsy Griffith, born August 25, 1756

b. Elisha Griffith, born March 25, 1758; perhaps the same of that name married in Frederick County by license dated August 27, 1781 to Catherine Woolf.

c. Ann Griffith, born December 5, 1759, married as his second wife to Aquilla Dorsey, born March 23, 1729, son of Charles and Anne Dorsey. Believed to have had children:

   (1) Aquilla Dorsey, born c.1789

   (2) Ann Dorsey, born December 10, 1797

d. Mary Griffith, born November 22, 1761, married in Anne Arundel County c.1774 to Richard Stringer.

e. Katey Griffith, born July 18, 1765

f. Orlando Griffith, born November 24, 1767

g. Charles Greenberry Griffith, born July 11, 1771

7. Lucretia Griffith, born February 5, 1739; married December 15, 1759 at Christ Church, Queen Caroline Parish, to Caleb Davis, born April 10, 1731, son of Richard Davis (1697) and Ruth Warfield (1707). They had at least one daughter. Lucretia was married second to Azel Waters, born about 1744, son of Richard Waters (1715). Azel had also been previously wed, on October 15, 1805 to Cassandra Williams, and some of the Waters children listed following may have been born to that union. Azel Waters served as Quartermaster of Colonel James

Johnson's battalion of Militia, raised in Fredericktown. He also later served as Deputy Sheriff under Thomas Beatty. Azel lived in Frederick County, in possession of part of *Monocacy Manor*, where he was killed by a highwayman in 1794. His father's will was written shortly after that, in which 60 acres of *Timber Neck* on Ten Mile Creek was left to the first three listed daughters of Azel, deceased. His widow Lucretia left a will in Frederick County dated November 10, 1817, probated December 18, 1817, recorded in liber HS 2 at folio 131, in which she named several daughters and a granddaughter. Two of the daughters were reportedly married to Fleming, but the given names are not stated. The will of Lucretia was witnessed by Samuel Fleming, Arthur Fleming, and Joseph Fleming; and son-in-law John Fleming was named Executor. Some of these others are perhaps sons-in-law. The children included:

a.   Elizabeth Davis, born March 17, 1768, died August 25, 1837. Married by Frederick County marriage license dated April 14, 1791 to Philip Welsh, born August 7, 1765 in Anne Arundel, died there February 15, 1833, son of Captain John Welsh and Hannah Hammond. Children:

(1)   Singleton Welsh, born April 21, 1792, died single.

(2)   Upton Welsh, died young.

(3)   Philemon Welsh, died young.

(4)   Grafton Welsh, died young.

(5)   Lucretia Griffith Welsh, born September 7, 1799, of whom more

(6)   Agrippa Welsh, born 1802, died 1824, single.

(7)   Philip Welsh, Jr., died young.

(8)   Milton Welsh, born April 6, 1816, died January 6, 1853. Married September 1, 1846 Leanna Mathews, born January 16, 1821, the daughter of James B. Mathews (1791) and Catherine Griffith (1797). Children:

(a)   Elizabeth Welsh, born 1847, died 1853

(b)   Kate M. Welsh, born 1852, died 1853

b.   Amelia Waters, married in Frederick County by license dated June 23, 1804 to John Flanigan. In her mother's will and certain court papers, she appeared as Milla.

13

c. Anna Waters, married in Frederick County by license dated March 27, 1806 to Jacob Frees or Freeze.

d. Catherine Waters, married in Frederick County by license dated November 14, 1799 to Moses Hedges. Not named in her mother's will, perhaps deceased, but had at least one child named in the mother's will:
    (1) Anna Hedges.

e. Sarah Waters; married to Fleming.

f. Rachel Waters, married to Fleming.

g. Lucy Waters, married to Soper.

h. Elizabeth Waters, married to Welsh.

8. Orlando Griffith, Jr., born April 27, 1741, died single. He left a will in Frederick County dated May 1, 1774, probated August 16, 1774, recorded in liber A-1 at folio 507, and appeared to be single. He left a specific bequest of a roan mare to his brother Greenbury Griffith; and a bequest of 20 pounds to that brother's daughter, Lydia. He then provides that the residue of his estate is to be left to his *'five brothers'*, naming them in the will. It is important here to note that there was a brother Greenbury, and a brother Charles Greenbury named in the will as two of the five brothers included there. In *The Founders of Anne Arundel and Howard Counties, Maryland*, by J. D. Warfield, 1905, the brother Greenbury Griffith is not named.

9. Charles Greenberry Griffith, born May 17, 1744, died August 12, 1792; Colonel of the First Baltimore Flying Camp in 1776. He was a Justice of the County Court in 1777, and a member of the House of Delegates from Montgomery County in 1781 and 1782. Married Sarah Ridgely, born November 14, 1745, daughter of Colonel Henry Ridgely and Elizabeth Warfield. At least one daughter:

a. Elizabeth Ridgely Griffith, born August 10, 1764, of whom more following.

Elizabeth Ridgely Griffith
1764-1824

This daughter of Charles Greenberry Griffith (1744) and Sarah Ridgely (1745), their only child, was born August 10, 1764, and died January 31, 1824. Married to General Jeremiah Crabb, born c.1760, died c.1800; Fourth Battalion, Continental Army. He was Representative in Congress from Maryland in 1789-1791 and 1795-1796. Children:

1. Nancy Crabb; married to Dr. R. Orme and had children:
   a. Elizabeth Orme, born September 24, 1801
   b. Sarah Griffith Orme, born March 22, 1804
   c. Jeremiah C. Orme, born 1806
   d. Charles Orme.
   e. James Orme, born July 19, 1808
   f. Nancy Crabb Orme, born February 22, 1815
2. Charles Crabb; married July 3, 1811 to Mary Summers, born June 23, 1792, daughter of Zadock Summers. No children.
3. Elizabeth Ridgely Crabb. Married March 26, 1807 to Thomas W. Howard and had a child:
   a. Emily Howard, born February 2, 1812
4. Richard Crabb.
5. Sarah Griffith Crabb, born January 27, 1793, died April 27, 1862 in Baltimore; buried in the Griffith family cemetery on Derwood Road, Montgomery County. Married as his second wife to Philemon Griffith, born March 22, 1794 (son of Samuel Griffith of 1752), and had first been married to Sarah Hammond Riggs (1797) and was then the father of two children, born to that marriage. Philemon was head of household in the 1850 census of Montgomery County for the Rockville District, listed as owning six slaves. He then had $3,750 in real estate and his wife and three children were at home; Mortimer, Emeline and Philemon. He was head of household in the 1860 census of the Fourth District, Forest Oak Post Office, living alone with his wife Sarah, next door to the newly formed household of his son Philemon C. Griffith. The elderly Philemon was listed as a tobacco inspector, with $6,000 in real estate and $5,600 in personal property. Philemon died

October 8, 1873 and was buried in the family cemetery on Derwood Road in Montgomery County. The children of Philemon from his marriage to Sarah Griffith Crabb were:

a. Emeline Griffith, born December 10, 1829; infant death.
b. Mortimer Crabb Griffith, born July 8, 1831, died December 22, 1891. Married on November 15, 1859 to Mary Jane Cassell and had children. Head of household in the 1870 census of the Fourth District, we read his name as Mortimer E. Griffith, apparently incorrectly. He was a farmer, with $5,000 in real estate and $1,000 in personal property. His wife was there, with four children. Also living with him was his brother Philemon and his son Alfred. Mortimer was head of household in the 1880 census of the Fourth District of Montgomery County, with his wife Mary, and seven children. She was there reported as born c.1840. Children:
   (1) Philemon Griffith, born September 13, 1860
   (2) Mortimer Crabb Griffith, Jr., born October 8, 1863
   (3) Samuel C. Griffith, born April 17, 1867
   (4) Mary R. Griffith, born February 2, 1870
   (5) Alice Griffith, born November 13, 1873
   (6) Emory Griffith, born June 24, 1876; in the census of 1880, this child is listed as Emily, born c.1877, and a female.
   (7) Sarah Griffith, born c.1879
c. Alfred Griffith, born July 10, 1832, a twin.
d. Emeline C. Griffith, born July 10, 1832, a twin. Married in Montgomery County (or Frederick County ?) by license dated July 27, 1858 to Walter A. Orme. They were not found in census records of Montgomery County.
e. Philemon Crabb Griffith, born c.1835, died July 18, 1885; buried in the family burying ground near Derwood, Montgomery County. His obituary in the *Sentinel* stated that he left a son and a daughter, and that his wife died "some years ago"; buried in the family burying ground near Derwood, Montgomery County. Married June 6, 1857 to Elizabeth Anderson, born November 12, 1834, died May 25, 1868, daughter of Doctor John W. Ander-

son and Mira C. Magruder (married February 15, 1831). Head of household in the 1860 census for the Fourth District of Montgomery County, Forest Oak Post Office, with his wife Elizabeth, living next door to the household of his parents. In the 1870 census of the Fourth District, he was living in the household of his brother Mortimer, with a son Alfred. In the 1880 census of the county for the Fourth District, Philemon was living in the household of Chandler Keys (1805), with both his children with him. They were:

(1) Alfred Charles Griffith, born May 27, 1864, died November 10, 1921 in Baltimore; buried Rockville Cemetery, apparently single. (*Sentinel* obituary). In birth records of Christ Episcopal Church in Rockville, the name of this child is reported as Alfred Crabb Griffith, probably correct.

(2) Sarah Crabb Griffith, whose date of birth is questionable. Family file records in the library report February 22, 1868; records of Christ Episcopal Church in Rockville report February 27, 1865; tombstone reads February 14, 1866, died April 21, 1900. In the 1870 census of the county for the Fourth District this child was living in the household of Thomas Anderson (1805), there listed as Sallie Griffith. In the 1880 census of the Fourth District, she was living with Julia Anderson (1841), keeping house, and William Anderson (1850), an engineer; both single. Sarah C. Griffith (probably this individual) was married in the county by license dated October 26, 1897 to Doctor Ernest T. Fearon of Washington. In the 1900 census of the county for Rockville Town, he was listed as born November, 1869 in Pennsylvania, a druggist, a widower, with a daughter, living in the household of Mitta B. Anderson (1850), establishing a relationship. The daughter was listed as a grand-niece:

(a) Julia A. Fearon, born August, 1898; married to Clyde Stout of Rockville.

6. Matilda Crabb, born May 12, 1795
7. Emeline Crabb, born July 19, 1797
8. Lydia Ridgely Crabb, born in Montgomery County June 24, 1799, died March 20, 1864 in Texas. Married in Montgomery County August 28, 1823 to Michael Berry Griffith, born there February 26, 1796, (son of Samuel Griffith of 1752), died in Texas. The family moved to Terrell, Texas about 1839, having first had children in Montgomery County. Descendants of the family born in Texas will not be followed here. The children were:
   a. Jeremiah Crabb Griffith, born April 30, 1825
   b. A. Elizabeth Griffith, born May 23, 1827
   c. John Summerfield Griffith, born June 17, 1829. Lt. Colonel commanding, 6th Texas Cavalry, CSA, appointed Brigadier General of State troops by Governor Murrah in March, 1864.
   d. Joseph H. B. Griffith, born August 20, 1831
   e. Ruth Matilda Griffith, born August 20, 1835
   f. Amanda J. Griffith, born August 20, 1838, died May 7, 1852.

CHILD 4

William Griffith, Jr.
1697-1757

This son of William Griffith, the Immigrant (died 1699) and his wife Sarah Maccubbin, was born April 15, 1697 in Anne Arundel County, and moved west into the Catoctin Mountains of Frederick County, where he became a Commissioner and a Justice of the county. Married before 1720 to Comfort Duvall, born March 17, 1700 in All Hallows Parish, daughter of Captain John Duvall and Elizabeth Jones, and granddaughter of Mareen Duvall, the immigrant, of *Middle Plantation*. William Griffith died in Frederick County, leaving a will dated July 28, 1757, probated there September 1, 1757, recorded in liber A-1 at folio 111 in Frederick County Will records. He named his two sons, Orlando and William, as well as his wife Comfort, named Executrix, and also received the residue of his lands to dispose of as she sees fit "amongst her children". To son William, he left his lands located between the Blue Ridge and Catoctin Mountains, one tract of 199 acres called *The Bubby*; the other of 50 acres, called *The Nipple*. To his son Orlando, he left the tract called *Black Acre*, on which William then lived, containing 100 acres, as well as four head of sheep. Land lying on Antietam of 200 acres called *Fairly Gott* was to be sold. They had children:

1. Ezekiel Griffith, born August 5, 1720 in Anne Arundel County, and died young.

2. Orlando Griffith, born about 1722, probably in an area of Prince George's County that became Frederick in 1748; married a girl named Elizabeth, and had children. Died in Frederick County, leaving a will dated September 10, 1800, probated July 31, 1801, recorded in liber GM-3 at folio 460. The will is quite lengthy, with specific bequests to various children, all named. Wife Elizabeth was left the negro man Sam for her lifetime, and after her death to son Orlando. On July 31, 1801, Elizabeth filed a renouncement of the will, and elected to take her dower or legal share of the estate instead. Having been virtually excluded from the estate by the terms of her husband's will, one can understand her actions. The children were:

   a. Orlando Griffith, Jr.

   b. Elisha Griffith, born about 1750 in Frederick County, and died between 1832 and 1843 in Harrison County, Virginia (later West Virginia), leaving descendants there. He received five shillings and no more under his father's will. Some of his descendants are discussed in *Provincial Families of Maryland, Volume 1*, by Vernon L. Skinner, Jr., March 14, 1998, Willow Bend Books, Westminster, Maryland, which see.

   c. Zadock Griffith, born c.1756; received five shillings and no more under his father's will. Served in the Flying Camp during the Revolution, and moved to North Carolina after the war, where he had numerous descendants, spreading from there into Tennessee, Kentucky, Virginia and Missouri.

   d. Chisholm Griffith; received five shillings and no more under his father's will. Perhaps the same of that name who was married in Frederick County by license dated August 22, 1778 to Mary Ann Scott.

e. Joshua Griffith received five shillings under his father's will, as well as the English musket, all wearing apparel, and no more.

f. Elizabeth Griffith, born c.1762. Received from her father the negro girl Charity, and the rent of that part of the plantation then occupied by Matthew Hilton, so long as she remained unmarried.

g. Rachel Griffith. Received from her father the negro girl Kate, and the rent of part of the plantation then occupied by the widow Gater, so long as she remained unmarried.

h. Ann Griffith, born c.1766. Married to George Silver and under her married name, received from her father's will the negro girl named Cassy. At least one child:
   (1) Elizabeth Silver, received from her grandfather the negro girl Moll.

i. William Griffith, born c.1768; received from his father two plantations; one then in possession of William Caywood, and one in possession of Henry Griffith. The will then described the land by boundaries, referring to a line of the tract called *Black Acre*. He also received the negro woman Fanny, a cow and calf, a sow and pigs, a ewe and lamb, the feather bed and furniture now called his, and his father's rifle gun.

j. John Griffith, born July 20, 1770. After the other bequests discussed above, John received the rest and residue of his father's estate, real and personal.

3. William Griffith, moved into the Catoctin Valley of Frederick County, married to Priscilla, and had at least one child:

a. Sarah Griffith, born March 8, 1749

William Griffith
died 1699
The Immigrant
Chapter 2
*
*
Charles Griffith
1693
Chapter 3
*
*

* * * * * * * * *
*
*
* * William Griffith 1718
*
*
* * Charles Griffith, Jr. 1719
*
*
* * Mary Griffith 1721
*
*
* * John Griffith 1728
*
*
* * Sarah Griffith 1730
*
*
* * Catherine Griffith 1732

CHAPTER 3

Charles Griffith
1693-1771

This son of William Griffith, the Immigrant (died 1699) and his wife Sarah Maccubbin, was born January 20, 1693, died October 6, 1771. He was a Captain, and lived on the north side of South River about six miles from Annapolis in Anne Arundel County. Charles left a journal, or a Pocket Book, in which he entered the names and dates pertinent to his two marriages, and the birth of his children. He was married twice, but outlived both his wives nearly forty years. Married first August 29, 1717 to Mrs. Mary (Wolden) Mercer, widow of Jacob Mercer, and had three children. She died February 18, 1721, about a month after the birth of her third child. Married second c.1727 to Catharine Baldwin, born c.1705, died May 13, 1733, daughter of John Baldwin and Hester Larkin. Charles lived on the north side of South River about six miles from Annapolis, and left a will in Anne Arundel County, dated October 4, 1767, probated October 17, 1771. He named his children, William, Charles, Mary White, John, and Catherine Worthington. Properties mentioned in the will included parts of the tracts called *Richardson's Joy, Narrow Neck, Hickory Neck, Orphans' Inheritance, Norwood's Fancy, Jones' Inheritance, Griffith's Lott*, and an island in the Severn River. The children were:

1. William Griffith, born August 15, 1718, died September, 1793 and inherited *Griffith's Island* in the Severn River. Married Priscilla Ridgely and made his home near the head of the Severn River as early as 1752. Children:
   a. Sarah Griffith, born March 8, 1749.
   b. Charles Griffith, named in his grandfather's will.
   c. Catherine Griffith, named in her grandfather's will.
2. Charles Griffith, Jr., born March 5, 1719, of whom more as Child 2, following.
3. Mary Griffith, born January 16, 1721; married to Joseph White, and settled on *Wincopin Neck*, near Savage between

the branches of the Patuxent River, which he purchased from Mrs. Henry Ridgely.

4. John Griffith, born December 16, 1728 to the second marriage, lived on the Severn River and married the widow of Benjamin Williams. She was married next to Thomas Rutland.
5. Sarah Griffith, born August 30, 1730 to the second marriage, and of whom more as Child 5.
6. Catherine Griffith, born May 31, 1732 to the second marriage; married to Colonel Nicholas Worthington, born March 29, 1733, died c.1793, the son of Thomas Worthington and Elizabeth Ridgely. Both were named in the will of her father, as well as four of their children, although there were reportedly at least two others:
   a. Catherine Worthington.
   b. Elizabeth Worthington.
   c. Charles Worthington.
   d. John Griffith Worthington.

CHILD 2

Charles Griffith, Jr.
1719-1803

This son of Captain Charles Griffith (1693) and his first wife, Mrs. Mary Wolden Mercer, was born March 5, 1719 in Anne Arundel County, died c.1803, and married to Ann Davidge, daughter of Robert Davidge and Rachel Warfield. He inherited *Griffith's Island* on the Severn River and lived near Stoner's Mill in Anne Arundel. They had children:

1. Charles Griffith, born c.1758. Married in Montgomery County by license dated May 26, 1799 to Elizabeth Green, born c.1769 and had children. His descendants lived primarily in Anne Arundel and Howard Counties.
2. John Griffith.
3. Robert Griffith.
4. Basil Griffith, born June 6, 1759, died May, 1841 at *Fairview* in Montgomery County. Married c.1795 to Ruth Gartrell of Montgomery County, and had children:

a. Charles A. Griffith, born c.1796, died August, 1855, single.
b. Sarah Griffith, born 1802, died November, 1882, single. She was head of household in the 1860 census of the county for the First District, listed next door to her brother John. She then had $5,125 in personal property, and had one black farm hand listed in the household. She left a will in Montgomery County, dated January 12, 1880, probated November 28, 1882 and recorded in liber RWC 6 at folio 311. Most of her bequests were to the descendants of her sister Ann Griffith (next) through the Clark and Holland lineages.
c. Ann Griffith, born c.1804, of whom more.
d. Davidge Griffith, born 1806, died 1859, single.
e. John Griffith, born 1808, died 1886, single. He was found as head of household in the 1850 census of Montgomery County for the First District, but there reported as born c.1810. However, we identify him by the fact that he then had living with him his brother Charles, reported as born c.1796; his brother Davidge, reported as born c.1798 and listed as insane; and his sister Sarah, reported as born c.1805. All of them appeared to be single, and John then owned six slaves, and was listed in the agricultural census as owning 240 acres of improved land and 40 acres unimproved, valued at $5,200 in total. He owned 4 horses, 10 milch cows, 2 working oxen, 3 other cattle, and 16 swine. In the last year, he had produced 300 bushels of wheat, 500 bushels of Indian corn, 200 bushels of oats, 100 bushels of Irish potatoes, 10 bushels of buckwheat, 800 pounds of butter, 20 tons of hay and 2 bushels of clover seed. He was next found as head of household in the 1860 census of the county for the First District, living alone, with $7,500 in real estate and $4,600 in personal property. He was then listed next door to his sister Sarah, also single. John was head of household in the 1870 census of the First District, with his sister Sarah and four black servants. John was head of

household in the 1880 census of the county for the Eighth District, with his sister Sarah living with him, both single.
   f. Rachel Griffith, died single
   g. Philip Griffith, died single
   h. Basil Griffith, Jr., died young.
5. Rachel Griffith; married C. Ridgely.
6. Anne Griffith.
7. Mary Griffith.
8. Henrietta Griffith.
9. Eleanor Griffith, married September 23, 1786 as his second wife to Vachel Warfield, son of Samuel Warfield and Sarah Welsh, and lived at Crown Point, Anne Arundel County. Children included:
   a. Charles Griffith, single.
   b. Vachel Warfield, Jr., married December 17, 1819 Achsah Marriott.
   c. William Griffith, married Sarah Jane Merryman.
   d. Henrietta Warfield Griffith, married April 30, 1818 in Baltimore County to Joshua Marriott
10. Margaret Griffith.
11. Sarah Griffith, married to John Boone, son of Captain John Boone.

Ann Griffith
1804-1876

This daughter of Basil Griffith and Ruth Gartrell was born c.1804 in Montgomery County, and died there February 27, 1876. Her name may have been Nancy Griffith, or perhaps Nancy Ann Griffith. Married in the county by license dated February 16, 1832 Charles Holland, born c.1796, and died 1850, son of James Holland (1764) and Hannah Hammon Welsh (1770). Head of household in the 1850 census of Montgomery County, First District, Charles was listed as born c.1804 (probably earlier) in Maryland, and then owned $8,000 in real estate, and six slaves. His wife was Ann, born c.1804 in Maryland. *Genealogy of the Griffith Family*, by R. R. Griffith of Baltimore, 1892, reports the first son of Charles Holland and Ann Griffith as being James F. Holland, with the proper birth date; the name is actually James Thomas Holland, as reported following. Records of family cemetery at Prospect Hill, Brookeville, where other family members are buried, includes what was transcribed as Nance Holland, born c.1805, died February 28, 1876, which is probably Nancy Ann Griffith Holland. The same records include a listing for Charles Holland, born c.1796, died April 29, 1850, which may be our subject here, with an error in the birth date, either in burial records or census records. In the agricultural census of 1850, Charles was listed with 200 acres of improved land and 30 acres unimproved. He owned 5 horses, 10 milch cows, 2 working oxen, 15 other cattle and 15 swine. In the previous twelve-month period, he had produced 300 bushels of wheat, 575 bushels of Indian corn, 250 bushels of oats, 10 bushels of Irish potatoes, 1,000 pounds of butter, 25 tons of hay, and 3 bushels of clover seed. Charles left a will in Montgomery County, dated April 3, 1858, probated May 4, 1858, recorded in liber JWS-1, at folio 2, in which he left to his wife, not named, a "home and support on the place where I now dwell." He left bequests to each of his three children, who were:

1. James Thomas Holland, born January 12, 1833, died July 28, 1911; buried in the family cemetery at *Prospect Hill*, Brookeville, Montgomery County, Maryland. Under his father's will, he received the home farm and all personal property subject to the rights of the widow and his sister Ann Lavinia. He was also named Executor of the estate. In the 1850 census, we mistakenly read the name as James L. Holland. The 1860 census of the First District lists James T. Holland, born c.1833 as head of household. Living with him was Ann Holland, then aged 55, his mother; and Ann L. Holland, aged 18, his sister. James was rather prosperous, being listed with $11,800 in real estate and $4,600 in personal property. We next found James T. Holland (which is apparently correct) as head of household in the 1870 census of the First District. He had a wife, Alice Warfield, born September 23, 1841, died December 1, 1891, and two children. Some reports list her as Alice Warfield Linthicum, daughter of Lloyd Linthicum. His mother Ann was still living in the household. Head of household in the 1880 census, James and Alice then had four children; his mother

27

was not listed. James Thomas appeared as head of household in the 1900 census of the Eighth District, a widower, with two sons, a daughter, and a granddaughter living with him. He had children:

a. Charles Griffith Holland, born September 16, 1867 at Brookeville, died August 5, 1955; buried at Rockville new cemetery with his wife. Married to Florence Clark, born 1870, died October 3, 1961. No children. He was the second mayor of the city of Rockville in its recorded history, serving from 1924 to 1926. His obituary credits him with opening Commerce Lane in Rockville as a business street, and he was a partner in the implements firm of Holland and Clark. No children.

b. Lloyd Walter Holland, born November 17, 1869, died April 1, 1951. Buried Rockville new cemetery. In the 1900 census, living at home with his father, and listed there simply as Walter Holland.

c. Annie Linthicum Holland, born December 12, 1871; married at Mt. Carmel Methodist Church November 30, 1896 to Samuel Dorsey Owings, born c.1868, died November 12, 1897, son of L. I. G. Owings of Triadelphia. His obituary in the *Sentinel* states that they had no children, but the widow Annie L. appeared in her father's household in the 1900 census with a daughter, apparently expecting the child at the time of her husband's death:

(1) Alice Dorsey Owings, born 1898. Married Guy Wood and had a son:

(a) Guy Holland Wood.

d. James Philip Holland, born May 11, 1874; married Margaret Warfield Henderson and had children. She was perhaps born c.1875, daughter of James B. Henderson (1845), a lawyer, and wife Clara S. Adamson (1846) of Rockville. The children were:

(1) Thomas Rufus Holland.

(2) Nicholas Henderson Holland.

(3) Amos Thornton Holland, born 1910, died 1993.

(4) Hester Louise Holland.

28

e. M. L. Holland, sex not stated, born September 1, 1880, died April 29, 1882; buried at Prospect Hill.

2. Ruth Hanna Holland, born October 26, 1834, died July 4, 1858. Under her father's will, she received the farm on which she and her husband were then living, together with a 10-acre wood lot purchased from William Brown. Married January 3, 1856 to Thomas William Clagett, born c.1834, son of Horatio Clagett (1807). The family of Horatio Clagett appeared in the 1860 census of the Fourth District in household #177, but was there incorrectly entered (or interpreted) as Oratio Clagett. A daughter:

a. Margaret Ann Clagett, born October 2, 1856. Married November 5, 1874 to John O. Clark, who died November 3, 1919, son of David Clark, and had three children. He had been first married to Anne Lavinia Holland (1842), sister of Margaret Ann's mother, by whom he had one son. John and Margaret appeared in the 1880 census of the Eighth District of Montgomery County. Living with them was John Griffith Clark, born c.1869, apparently from the first marriage of John O. Clark; and two children, born to Margaret. We found John Clarke (sic) and Margaret in the 1900 census of the Eighth District, with their youngest son at home. It was stated that they had been married 25 years, and that Margaret had been the mother of six children, four then living (see report of his first marriage just following). They had at least one son, whose obituary appeared in the *Sentinel*. The children included:

(1) David W. Clark, born December 29, 1875, married May 12, 1895 to Florence Griffith and had children:

(a) Isabel Clark, born July 29, 1899, married 1920 to Otis Poss.

(2) Ruth Lavinia Clark, born August 14, 1878, married December 8, 1897 to Owings Warfield. Children:

(a) John O. Warfield, born October 17, 1898

(b) Laura M. Warfield, born September 14, 1901, married January 14, 1922 to William Allen Scrivnor and had three children.

 (c) Thomas O. Warfield, born August 24, 1904

 (d) Gertrude Warfield, born July 12, 1906

 (e) Kennard Warfield, born March 8, 1911

(3) Ridgely Brown Clark, born c.1882, died December 29, 1883, aged sixteen months.

(4) Henry Thomas Clark, born July 29, 1893, lived at Brookeville; listed in the 1900 census with his parents as Thomas H. Clarke (sic). Married April 8, 1915 to Margaret Magruder and had a son:

 (a) Henry Thomas Clark, Jr.: January 30, 1918.

3. Anne Lavinia Holland, born May 29, 1842, died January 27, 1873. Single when her father wrote his will, she was to receive a home and support on the home farm. Additionally, her brother James Thomas was to pay to her the sum of $4,500 as part of her inheritance. Married July 31, 1867 to John O. Clark, who died November 3, 1919, son of David Clark, and had one son. After her death, he was married secondly November 5, 1874 to her niece, Margaret Ann Clagett, born October 2, 1856, by whom he had three children. Anne's son was:

a. John Griffith Clark, born June 6, 1869, died February 23, 1920. Married October 30, 1895 to Mary E. Knott, born c.1871, and had children. They appeared in the 1900 census of the Eighth District, with two children. There were at least four born to their marriage:

(1) J. Frances Clark, born July, 1896

(2) Alice L. Clark, born November, 1898

(3) Mabel Clark, born 1906

(4) Spencer Clark, born 1908

CHILD 5

Sarah Griffith
1730-1765

 This daughter of Captain Charles Griffith (1693) and his second wife, Catherine Baldwin (1705), was born August 30, 1730 in Anne Arundel County and died December 24, 1765. Married February 26, 1751 to Azel Warfield, born April 3, 1726, son of Alexander Warfield and Dinah Davidge. After the death of Sarah, Azel was married second May 19, 1768 to Susanna Magruder, by whom he had two more children, for a total of eight. He was named as a son-in-law in the will of her mother Mary Magruder, probated in Prince George's County July 13, 1774. He owned the plantation containing part of *Yate's Contrivance* and part of *Second Addition to Snowden's Manor*. Azel also held indentured servants on his plantations, as did many prosperous Colonial planters. The *Maryland Gazette* of December 24, 1760 reported that "Daniel Stephenson, in Bladensburg, Prince George's County, reports a runaway convict servant named James Fairbanks who formerly lived with Mr. Azel Warfield on Elk Ridge." Azel and Sarah had six children:

1. Charles Alexander Warfield, born December 3, 1751, died March 29, 1813 at his home. A doctor, he was married November 21, 1771 to Elizabeth Ridgely, born September 25, 1752, died September 8, 1808, daughter of Major Henry Ridgely (1728) and Ann Dorsey (1730). On March 27, 1813 in the *Fredericktown Herald*, his sons Gustavus and Charles Alexander advertised the sale of negroes at the home of their late father. Children, including:

   a. Elizabeth R. Warfield, married December 26, 1834 to Major Richard N. Snowden, son of Washington's friend, Colonel Edward Snowden of Prince George's County. Eliza won title to *Glenwood* by casting lots with her brother, Gustavus.

   b. Henry Ridgely Warfield; admitted to the Bar 1797 in Montgomery County; represented Frederick County in the House of Delegates 1797 and 1798; served in Congress during 1820. Perhaps the same Henry R. who died March 18, 1839 in Frederick County. Remained single.

   c. Walter Warfield, a doctor, served in the Revolution, and settled in Virginia.

   d. Charles Alexander Warfield, Jr., a merchant in Sykesville, married Eliza Harris and had children. They moved to New Orleans.

   e. Gustavus Warfield, a doctor. He was the builder of *Longwood,* within sight of *Bushy Park.* Married Mary Thomas of Philadelphia and had nine children.

31

f.   Ann Warfield, married in Anne Arundel County by license dated September 16, 1789 to Samuel Thomas and made their home at *Roxbury Hall.*

g.   Peregrine Warfield, a doctor, and Justice of the Peace, married May 7, 1806 in Frederick County to Harriet Lucy Sappington. He lived in Georgetown.

h.   Laura Victoria Warfield, married to Major Richard N. Snowden, widower of her sister Elizabeth.

2.   Dinah Warfield, born April 4, 1753. Married to Brice John Gassaway, born c.1755, son of Nicholas Gassaway and Catherine Worthington. Nicholas Gassaway left a will in Anne Arundel County dated May 17, 1774, probated May 15, 1775, naming his wife and his children. From his father, Brice John Gassaway inherited part of the home plantation called *Partnership,* and part of *Second Addition to Snowden's Manor.* Dinah's father Azel Warfield was a witness to the will. They had at least seven children.

3.   Catherine Warfield, born April 7, 1757, died April 14, 1796. Married November 14, 1775 to Hezekiah Griffith, born November 25, 1752, died July 28, 1825, son of Greenberry Griffith (1727) and Ruth Riggs (1730). In 1777, Hezekiah was commissioned a first Lieutenant in the Montgomery County Militia. They had children:

a.   Ann Griffith, born September 27, 1776. Married to Jonas Clark and had children:

(1) Katherine Clark, born December 27, 1798

(2) Hezekiah Clark, born August 29, 1802. This is perhaps the same individual who was found at the age of 48, in the 1850 census of Berry District, Montgomery County, living in the household of James Smith (1822) and his wife Mary Ann (1823) with five Smith children. Could Mary Ann have been a daughter of Hezekiah?

(3) Sarah Clark, born July 25, 1804

(4) John Clark, born April 14, 1807

(5) Robert Clark, born November 24, 1809

(6) Mary Clark, born April 14, 1812

(7) Lydia Clark, born October 7, 1814

(8) Bazaleel Clark, born September 7, 1816
b. Sarah Griffith, born May 17, 1778, died July 10, 1839. Married in 1797 to Bazaleel Wells, and had children:
  (1) Catherine Wells, born April 17, 1798, died September, 1843. Married October 8, 1818 to John W. McDowell.
  (2) Rebecca Wells, born October 11, 1799. Married November 10, 1822 to Philander Chase.
  (3) James Ross Wells, born October 8, 1801, died October 23, 1846. Married April 17, 1834 to Ann Eliza Wilson, who died in 1868.
  (4) Samuel D. Wells, born October 8, 1803, died December 13, 1849, single.
  (5) Alexander Wells, born September 16, 1805, died January 6, 1839, single.
  (6) Bazaleel Wells, Jr., born August 6, 1808.
  (7) Hezekiah Griffith Wells, born January 16, 1811. Married to Achsah Strong.
  (8) Frank A. Wells, born September 4, 1813. Married to Jane Boggs.
  (9) Ann C. Wells, born August 28, 1813, died 1885. Married the Reverend Ezra Kellogg.
  (10) Sarah Griffith Wells, born January 11, 1818, died August 24, 1866. Married the Reverend Dudley Chase.
  (11) Mary Wells, born February 12, 1822, died March 3, 1822.
c. John Belford Griffith, born December 28, 1780
d. Walter Griffith, born February 3, 1783
e. Lydia Griffith, born December 10, 1785, died April, 1815. Married George Fetter who died in September, 1817, and had children:
  (1) Daniel Fetter, born May 31, 1807
  (2) George Fetter, Jr., born October 6, 1809
  (3) Hezekiah Fetter, born November 1, 1811
  (4) Roderick Fetter, born February 16, 1814
f. Roderick Griffith, born December 8, 1787, died May 26, 1817.

g. Hezekiah Griffith, Jr., born November 1, 1790, died August 13, 1840. Married to Lydia Mobley, who died April 16, 1874. Children:
    (1) John Griffith, born November 8, 1814.
    (2) Roderick R. Griffith, born July 21, 1816, died August 6, 1889. Married first Isabel Clark, and had three children. Married second Mary Tillman and had six children.
    (3) Anne E. Griffith, born June 15, 1815. Married to Jesse V. Bramwell.
    (4) Randolph Griffith, married Eliza J. Barfield.
    (5) Rebecca Griffith, born February 4, 1824. Married Ezra Bramwell.
    (6) Rachel Griffith, born June 13, 1827. Married to Samuel Hovens.
    (7) Catherine Griffith, born July 30, 1829, died July 24, 1851, single.
    (8) Hezekiah Griffith, 3rd, born May 2, 1832. Married to Mary Ann Stevens.
    (9) Alexander W. Griffith, born July 7, 1835
    (10) Lydia Griffith, born December 11, 1837. Married Joseph Renier.
h. Charles Greenberry Griffith, born July 3, 1792, died May 24, 1864. Married Jane Johnson and had children:
    (1) Sarah Griffith, born December 29, 1817. Married three times: A. Arnick; M. C. Maynard; and Smith Vowler.
    (2) James J. Griffith, born November 13, 1819, died November 7, 1855.
    (3) Margaret Griffith, born November 20, 1820. Married to McKeehan.
    (4) Samuel Griffith, born November 26, 1822. Married to Elizabeth Goltha.
    (5) Hezekiah Griffith, born August 19, 1824
    (6) Mary Griffith, born August 31, 1826. Married to Johnson.
    (7) Anna Griffith, born November 31, 1828, died November, 1860. Married to J. Chase.

(8) Charles Greenberry Griffith, Jr., born August 19, 1830. Married to McKeehan.

(9) Rachel Griffith, born August 10, 1832. Married to W. C. Soper.

(10) Jennie Griffith, born March 31, 1833.

i. Jane Griffith, born November 3, 1794.

4. Walter Warfield, born June 17, 1760, died March 10, 1826. He was a surgeon in the Revolutionary War. Moved to Virginia and was married to Sarah Winston Christian, niece of Patrick Henry. They moved on to Kentucky, where he received a grant of 1,000 acres on Glover's Creek in 1794. Children:

a. Anne Henry Warfield.

b. Charles Alexander Warfield, a doctor.

c. William Christian Warfield, Baptist Minister. Married Rachel Edwards, daughter of Benjamin Edwards of Montgomery County, and had children.

5. Anne Warfield, born June 28, 1762, married Ignatius Waters, son of Richard Waters (1715) and Elizabeth Williams, and of whom more in Chapter 12.

6. Zachariah Warfield, born January 6, 1765, died c.1832 in Montgomery County, single, with a will, dated March 8, 1832, probated April 3, 1832 and filed in liber S at folio 205; refiled in liber VMB 3 at folio 479. He named his sister Sarah and his brother George Fraser Warfield as his heirs. He also provided that his negro woman Bett and her son George were to be set free, provided George agreed to care for his mother.

35

William Griffith
died 1699
The Immigrant
Chapter 2
*

Orlando Griffith
1688
*

**Henry Griffith
1720
Chapter 4**
*
*

*   *   *   *   *   *   *   *   *
*
*   * Sarah Griffith 1741
*
*   * Henry Griffith, Jr. 1744
*
*   * Ruth Griffith 1747
*
*   * Rachel Griffith 1749
*
*   * Samuel Griffith 1752 .... Chapter 7
*
*   * John Hammond Griffith 1754
*
*   * Philemon Griffith 1756 .... Chapter 8
*
*   * Charles Griffith 1758
*
*   * Ann Griffith 1762
*
*   * Joshua Griffith 1764
*
*   * Eleanor Griffith 1766
*
*   * Elizabeth Griffith 1768
*
*   * Ruth Griffith 1770

CHAPTER 4

Henry Griffith
1720-1794

The eldest son of Orlando Griffith (1688) and his wife Katherine Howard, Henry Griffith was born February 14, 1720, died September 28, 1794, and was Executor of his father's estate. He acquired lands in both Howard and Montgomery Counties and was active in civic affairs. Served as Tobacco Inspector, was a Commissioner in the formation of Montgomery County, member of the Colonial Assembly from Frederick County, and numerous other activities. On June 12, 1774, a group met at Charles Hungerford's Tavern in what is now Rockville, to discuss what they perceived as a denial of their rights as Englishmen by the Crown in London. Henry Griffith was named Moderator of that meeting, which resulted in the adoption of the Hungerford Resolves, the first open protest in the Colonies leading to the Revolutionary War.

A biography appears in the *Biographical Dictionary of the Maryland Legislature, 1635-1789*, Volume I, which is recommended reading. It contains such interesting items as the fact that at the time of his first election to the legislature, he owned 6,957 acres of land in Anne Arundel and Frederick Counties. His wealth at the time of death was appraised at 4,329 pounds, 5 shillings, 2 pence, including 19 slaves, 3 ounces of plate, and an "electrical machine."

He married first April 9, 1741 at Christ Church, Queen Caroline Parish, to Elizabeth Dorsey, daughter of Edward Dorsey and Sarah Todd. Elizabeth died December 24, 1749, and he married second June 3, 1751 to Ruth Hammond, born c.1733, died January 27, 1782, buried at Laytonsville, Montgomery County, daughter of John Hammond and Ann Dorsey. He had four known children from his first marriage, and five sons and several daughters from the second marriage. Honorable Henry Griffith and his second wife Ruth, settled closer to Damascus on the road from Unity. He lived on the north side of the road from Unity to Etchison on the tract of land called *Tusculum*, and later created the *Edge Hill Farm*, which was owned by the family for several generations. The sons they sent to the Revolution, and returned, included three Colonels, one Captain, one Lieutenant, one Ensign, and a high private. He was reportedly the only local citizen invited to witness the signing of the Declaration of Independence.

Henry Griffith died September 28, 1794, and left a will in Rockville, Montgomery County, dated January 14, 1794, probated October 10, 1794, recorded in liber C at folio 152, later rerecorded in book VMB 1 at page 308 in the Register of Wills office. By any measure, he was a very wealthy man, owning more than two thousand acres specified in his will, plus other lands referred to there without designating the size of the parcels. Most of his land was located in Montgomery County along the Hawlings River, but he owned property in Anne Arundel, Frederick and Allegany Counties also. He left specific bequests to various children as noted following under their names. He also directed that the executor sell *Mill Land* and the mill, as well as part of *Tusculum* adjoining the mill, containing about 200 acres. Also they were to sell an undivided part of *Tusculum* which lay on the main road called New Design; and the lands in Anne Arundel County containing about 250 acres of *Griffith's Place*. Additionally, they were to also sell two small parcels of about 100 acres in Frederick County; and a small parcel in Anne Arundel County on Curtis Creek. The money derived from the sales was to be divided "among all my children" who were then listed, including the husbands of some of the daughters. The children were:

1. Sarah Griffith, born January 25, 1741, died before 1794; married at St. Margaret's Church to Rezin Todd, born June 24, 1743, son of John and Ruth Todd. Reference is made in her father's will to the children of Sarah Todd, but they were not named.

2. Henry Griffith, Jr., born March 1, 1744, died April 14, 1809, Colonel. He lived on *Hammond's Great Branch*, and was a member of the Committee of Observation for Frederick County. Married first November 13, 1766 to Sarah B. Warfield, born November 12, 1746, died January 21, 1776, daughter of John Warfield and Rachel Dorsey of *Warfield's Range*. Their descendants settled on *Griffith's Range* between Unity and Laytonsville, in Montgomery County. Married sec-

ond Sarah Davis, who died June 25, 1805, the daughter of Thomas Davis, Jr. (1703) and Elizabeth Gaither (1711), and had one son. Under his father's will, he received the two plantations whereon two of his sons then lived, supposed to contain about 600 acres, on the Hawlings River, either part of, or adjoining *Tusculum* and *Elk Ridge*, which would be in Montgomery County. Colonel Henry Griffith left a will dated September 8, 1806, proven at Annapolis on June 21, 1809. The children were:

a. Henry Griffith, born December 31, 1767, of whom more in Chapter 5.

b. Allen Griffith, born May 8, 1769, died August 12, 1787

c. Nicholas Griffith, born November 10, 1771, the youngest son, of whom more in Chapter 6.

d. Elizabeth Griffith, born July 22, 1773, died December 31, 1853. Married January 24, 1792 at Baltimore to James Worthington, born January 16, 1772. They had children, and descendants in Frederick County:

(1) John H. Worthington, born c.1793; died April 18, 1858; buried at Mt. Olivet Cemetery in Frederick with his wife, Ann H., born July 25, 1791, and died December 26, 1866.

(2) Ann Worthington, died single.

(3) Nicholas Griffith Worthington.

(4) Sarah Worthington, born February 9, 1800

(5) Susan Worthington, born April 26, 1803, died single

(6) Charles Worthington.

(7) Thomas Worthington.

(8) William Worthington.

(9) Mary H. Worthington.

(10) Upton Worthington, born c.1810, died October 14, 1869; buried at Urbana Episcopal Church with his wife and one daughter. Head of household in the 1850 census of Frederick County, in the New Market District, his wife Catherine was born January 19, 1810 and died April 12, 1880. Children:

(a) Achsah Worthington, born c.1836

     (b)   Lloyd Anna Worthington, born January 23, 1839, died June 12, 1920 and buried with her parents. Married to Nicholas Dorsey.

     (c)   Elizabeth Worthington, born c.1843

     (d)   Joshua D. Worthington, born c.1845

     (e)   Lavinia Worthington, born c.1847

     (f)   James Worthington, born c.1850

  (11) Elizabeth Worthington.

e. Henrietta Griffith, born April 20, 1775, an infant death

f. Thomas Griffith, died c.1838, leaving a will dated September 6, 1837, proved at Annapolis May 26, 1838. He was born to the second marriage, held the family homestead, and passed it down to succeeding generations. He married January 17, 1811 to Harriet W. Simpson. His descendants are discussed in extensive detail in an article dated February 12, 1905, appearing in the *Baltimore Sun*, which is recommended reading. It will not be repeated here, in that few, if any, of those individuals made their homes in Montgomery or Frederick County.

3. Ruth Griffith, born May 18, 1747, died September 24, 1830; married to Amon Edwin Riggs, born April 11, 1748, died March 16, 1822. Captain of the Continental Army, youngest son of John Riggs, Jr. (1687) and Mary Davis (1701). Under the will of Ruth's father, their children received the plantation known as *Griffith's Park* in Allegany County, Maryland. Amon inherited the family homestead of *Riggs Hills* in Montgomery County. Under the will of her father, the sons and daughters of Ruth and her husband Amon Riggs, received jointly the tract of land called *Griffith's Park Spring* located in Allegany County, Maryland. They had children and descendants living in Montgomery and Frederick Counties. Amon Riggs left a will in Montgomery County dated November 27, 1818, probated April 15, 1822 and recorded in liber N at folio 120; rerecorded in liber VMB 3 at page 160. It refers to a wife but does not name her. The only reference by name to children includes John Riggs, who received the plantation where he then lived, and his brother Henry, the two of them being

named Executors. Reference is also made to the children of the deceased son Charles, without naming them. Children:

a. John Riggs, the eldest son, born November 20, 1770 and married December 18, 1794 to Esther Willett, daughter of Benjamin Willett. At least a son:
   (1) Henry Riggs, the eldest son, born July 11, 1796 and married to Rebecca Mussetter, daughter of Captain Christian Mussetter of the War of 1812, and Ruth Ijams. They had children.

b. Henry Riggs, born July 23, 1772. Married November 20, 1804 to Jemima Jacob Griffith, born February 17, 1784, died November 15, 1819, daughter of Howard Griffith and Jemima Jacob, and had children. They are discussed under their mother's name, but briefly here included:
   (1) Howard Griffith Riggs, born October 17, 1805
   (2) Amon Riggs, born June 30, 1808; moved to Ohio.
   (3) Antoinette Riggs, born August 2, 1811
   (4) Lydia Griffith Riggs, born June 21, 1813
   (5) Eliza Riggs, born August 3, 1817
   (6) William H. Riggs, born November 8, 1819, an infant death.

c. Charles Riggs, born February 25, 1774, died September 10, 1802

d. Amon Riggs, Jr., born March 10, 1776

e. James Riggs, born February 27, 1779

f. Samuel Riggs, born July 31, 1781

g. Eleanor M. Riggs, born May 27, 1784, died c.1863 and is buried in the Purdum family burying ground on Watkins Road at Cedar Grove. Married April 9, 1805 to John Lewis Purdum, born September 11, 1779 in Montgomery County, Maryland, and died about 1865, a son of John Purdum (1739) and Kezia Darby (1742). John appears in the 1850 census of Clarksburg, with his wife, and one of his sons; and in the 1860 census of Clarksburg, Montgomery County, with his wife, and three of their children. The family is the subject of Chapter 7 in our earlier book, *Our Maryland Heritage, Book Nine, The Purdum Fami-*

lies, to which the reader is directed. Briefly, the children included:

(1) Mary Purdum, born c.1805
(2) Charles Riggs Purdum, born April 12,
(3) Henrietta Maria Purdum, born January 17, 1809
(4) John Riggs Purdum, twin, born December 1, 1816.
(5) Keziah Purdum, twin, born December 1, 1816, died June 24, 1900. Married December 11, 1841 to John Upton Riggs, born c.1812. She married second March 21, 1849 in Montgomery County to Joseph Woodfield, born c.1812.
(6) James W. Purdum, born March 17, 1819
(7) Eleanor Riggs Purdum, born c.1820
(8) John Rufus Purdum, born August 10, 1827

h. Mary Riggs, born January 23, 1787. Married December 13, 1809 in Montgomery County to George Washington Darby, born March 11, 1785, died 1854; believed to be a son of Samuel Darby (1760). The descendants of this couple, through several generations, are discussed in *All About Darbys*, by Rodney H. Darby, privately printed at Rockville, Maryland in 1999 (beginning at page 505). The reader is referred to that publication, available from the author, or to be found in the library of the Montgomery County Historical Society in Rockville.

i. Joshua Riggs, born April 4, 1790, died 1810.

4. Rachel Griffith, born November 28, 1749; married Samuel Welsh, son of John Welsh and Hannah Hammond. Rachel died before 1794, and in her father's will her children (not named) inherited the tract of *Sherwood Forest*. The children were:
a. Samuel Welsh.
b. Elizabeth Welsh.
c. Henry Griffith Welsh.
d. Ruth Welsh.
e. Henrietta Welsh.
f. Warner Welsh.
g. John Welsh.
h. Rachel Griffith Welsh, born 1790, died 1815. Married as his first wife January 29, 1807 to Joshua Warfield, born

September 11, 1781, died March 19, 1846, youngest son of Benjamin Worthington Warfield (1734) and Catherine Dorsey (1745). He was married second March 12, 1816 to Lydia Dorsey Welsh, born October 23, 1790 in Anne Arundel County, Maryland (in an area that later became Howard County), daughter of John Welsh and Lucretia Dorsey. Three children were born to the first marriage and two to the second; the children of Rachel being:

(1) Benjamin Warfield, died young.
(2) Nicholas Ridgely Warfield, died 1860; married Eleanor Warfield, the daughter of Elie and Frances Warfield. No children.
(3) Avolina Warfield, born May 8, 1813, died February 23, 1883. Married September 26, 1833 to Elisha Riggs, born July 6, 1810 on *Bordley's Choice* in Montgomery County, died July 16, 1883 at *Annandale,* near Florence, Howard County, son of Thomas Riggs (1772), and Mary Riggs (1776) of Elisha. Elisha lived at *Rockland* on the Patuxent River in Montgomery County, formerly owned by his father. Elisha and his wife appear in the 1850 census for the First District of Montgomery County with the first four of their children. They are also in the 1860 census for the same District, although the entry could be overlooked. Only the name of Elisha is correct; the enumerator has listed his wife as Eveline; a daughter Eve; a son Joshua; and a daughter Kate; all of whom can be identified if one knows the names. The couple appears next in the 1870 census of the First District, where he is said to be a retired farmer, with $6,000 in real estate and $500 in personal property. Only the daughter called Eva is at home, who appears to be Avolina, according to the age stated. Elisha and Avolina are buried in the Warfield cemetery at *Cherry Grove* in Howard County. Seven children:
(a) Mary Olivia Riggs, born August 7, 1834, died September 9, 1863. Married November 12,

1856 Dr. Lloyd Thomas McGill of city of Frederick.

(b) Rachel Griffith Riggs, born July 9, 1836. Married January 8, 1856 Evan Aquila Jones and had four children.

(c) Avolina Riggs, born July 7, 1838, died January 25, 1892 in Howard County. Married June 28, 1871 to Captain Festus Griffith, 8th Virginia Infantry, Co. H., CSA, born July 12, 1838 at *Edgehill* near Unity, Montgomery County, the son of Thomas Griffith and Elizabeth (Griffith) Griffith. In the 1880 census of the county for the Eighth District, they were in the household of her parents, with no children.

(d) Joshua Warfield Riggs, born March 4, 1844, private, 43rd Virginia Cavalry, (Mosby's Rangers), CSA. Married October 2, 1867 to Matilda S. Dorsey, born February 9, 1849, daughter of John A. Dorsey and Margaret Banks. Two children.

(e) George Thomas Riggs, born November 1, 1847, lived twenty-nine days.

(f) Nicholas Ridgely Warfield Riggs, born March 4, 1849, died April 22, 1849.

(g) Catherine Augusta Riggs, born June 8, 1850. Married June 8, 1870 to Humphrey Dorsey of Montgomery County.

5. Samuel Griffith, born May 7, 1752, and of whom more in Chapter 7.

6. John Hammond Griffith, born April 20, 1754, died before 1794. John predeceased his father, and his children, all being minors, were named in his father's will. He was First Lieutenant, 5th Co., 7th Battalion Regulars, Continental Army as of March, 1777. Married March 22, 1778 to Elizabeth Ridgely, and had children:

a. William Ridgely Griffith.

b. Juliet Griffith.

c. Phebe Griffith.

d.   John Griffith.
7.   Philemon Griffith, born August 29, 1756, of whom more in Chapter 8.
8.   Charles Griffith, born December 16, 1758, 2nd Lieutenant, 7th Co., 3rd Battalion Regulars, Continental Army, March 27, 1777. He was taken prisoner by the English during the Revolution, and exchanged. After the war, he went to sea and was captured by Algerian pirates, sold as a slave to the Turks, made his escape and returned to America. He lived at the home of his nephew, Colonel Lyde Griffith (1774) in Montgomery County, where he died, having fallen from an upstairs window while sleep-walking.
9.   Ann Griffith, born February 24, 1762, died May 27, 1791. In her father's will of 1794, reference is made to the children of Nicholas Hall and his wife Ann; apparently this daughter. Married June 1, 1779 to Nicholas Hall, Sr., born c.1757, died December 29, 1821; buried in the Hall-Wood family cemetery at New Market, Frederick County. The will of Nicholas, dated May 9, 1820, was probated in Frederick County, January 9, 1821. He freed many of his slaves, and named a number of his grandchildren, and his children, who were:
a.   Elizabeth Hall, born October 10, 1780, died January 27, 1830, buried with her husband. Married May 31, 1804 to the Reverend Jonathan Pitts, born c.1772, died February 7, 1821, buried in the Hall-Wood cemetery at New Market, son of Thomas Pitts and Sussanah Lusby. He served the Methodist Church in Frederick from 1804 to 1806, and then for several years, was serving in Baltimore. His will, dated June 26, 1820, was probated February 26, 1821 in Frederick County, Maryland, and named the children. They had children, with descendants in Ohio, Baltimore, and elsewhere. Briefly, the children were:
   (1)   Nicholas Pitts, died February, 1853, single. He was an attorney.
   (2)   John Lusby Pitts, born June 29, 1808, died 1843. A minister like his father, married May 18, 1829 in Woodfield, Ohio to Elizabeth Jane Hall, born No-

45

vember 1, 1810, daughter of Nicholas Hall and Ann McElfresh. At least three children.

    (3) Anne Maria Pitts, born August, 1810, died January 31, 1843; married in March, 1830 to Colonel Thomas C. Brashear, died January 15, 1851, and had at least seven children.

    (4) Thomas Griffith Pitts, born September 12, 1812

    (5) Charles H. Pitts.

    (6) William Pitts.

    (7) Susan Pitts, died young.

b. Henry Hall, born July 14, 1782, died March 27, 1788

c. Nicholas Hall, Jr., born February 21, 1784, died February 22, 1817; buried with his father.

d. John Hall, born November 20, 1785, died May 13, 1788

e. Anne Hall, born March 6, 1787. Married June 5, 1805 to Thomas Chew Shipley and had at least eight children, who primarily lived in Frederick and Baltimore Counties.

f. Eleanor Hall, born December 9, 1788, died May 6, 1805

g. Henry Griffith Hall, born September 26, 1790, died May 3, 1791

10. Joshua Griffith, born March 25, 1764. Under his father's will, he received the home dwelling plantation, supposed to contain 500 acres, on the Hawlings River, adjoining *Gaither's Spring* and the plantations bequeathed to his brothers Henry and Samuel. He also received the mulatto lad called Abraham and the negro man Ben, together with one-half the cattle, sheep and hogs on the home plantation. Married first by license dated November 1, 1783 in Frederick County, Maryland to Elizabeth Ridgely, born c.1765, the daughter of William Ridgely and Elizabeth Dorsey. They had five children, and she died in 1797. He married secondly June 10, 1798 in Maryland to a second Elizabeth Ridgely, born c.1769, daughter of Charles Greenberry Ridgely (1735) and Sarah Macgill, and had two more children, all of them being born in Maryland. About 1805, Joshua Griffith moved his family to Kentucky, where he died November 29, 1845 at Owensboro. Briefly, the children were:

a. Lydia Griffith, born November 6, 1784. Married c.1808 in Kentucky to Warner Crow, born in Maryland, and had at least eleven children.

b. Remus Griffith, born December 31, 1786

c. Ruth Griffith, born January 18, 1789

d. Elizabeth Griffith, born c.1791, an infant death

e. William Ridgely Griffith, born February 28, 1793

f. Elizabeth Ridgely Griffith, born September 7, 1799, the first child of the second marriage.

g. Mary Griffith, born July 25, 1801

11. Eleanor Griffith, born March 9, 1766. Married July 27, 1785 in Anne Arundel County to John Burgess and had at least nine children in Frederick County. He is the same John Burgess, born January 24, 1766, and died October 5, 1821, buried at New Market Methodist Church; son of Colonel John Burgess and Sarah Dorsey. The children were:

a. Eleanor Burgess, married in Montgomery County by license dated April 6, 1808 to John McCann.

b. Nancy Burgess, married to Henry Stier.

c. Charlotte Burgess, married first to Nathan Hammond and second to Vachel Hammond.

d. Ruth Burgess, married the Reverend John Wood.

e. Sarah Ann Dorsey Burgess, married in Frederick County by license dated February 3, 1827 to Reverend Thomas Green.

f. Juliana Burgess, married to Michael Lark.

g. William P. Burgess, married in Frederick County by license dated April 29, 1816 to Lydia C. Plummer.

h. John H. Burgess, married to Margaret Hyatt.

i. Washington Burgess, born c.1779; married twice.

12. Elizabeth Griffith, born December 16, 1768, died September 13, 1770

13. Ruth Griffith, born c.1770, of whom more following.

Ruth Griffith
1770-

This daughter of Henry Griffith (1720) and his second wife, Ruth Hammond, was born c.1770. She was married to Joab Waters, son of John Waters and his first wife, Precious, born February 4, 1776, probably in Prince George's County, although some records report Anne Arundel County. Under his father's will, he received the dwelling plantation with 150 acres of land, at the death or remarriage of his mother, located in Frederick County, where he finally settled.

In the will of his father, this child is clearly listed as Joab Waters, although in *Ancestral Colonial Families*, by Luther W. Welsh, published in 1928, on page 123, the author there assigns the name Joel Waters to this individual, without indicating the source of the information. He then lists one of the grandsons as Joab Waters Hyatt, and parenthetically observes "doubtless Joel Waters for his mother's father." *History of Frederick County, Maryland*, Volume II, by T. J. C. Williams and Folger McKinsey, Volume II, page 1461 refers to the marriage of Joel Waters and Ruth Griffith, which is perhaps the source of Luther W. Welsh. Scharf's *History of Western Maryland*, on page 375, reports that in 1788, Joab Waters patented four tracts of land totaling 401 acres in Frederick County; that in 1804, Joab Waters was a member of the House of Delegates from the county (page 479); that in 1803, Joab Waters was appointed to the Levy Court (page 481); and that Joab Waters was a member of Hiram Lodge of the Masonic Order (page 545). Finally, this child is named Joab in the will of his father, probated in Frederick County May 26, 1777. We conclude that Joab Waters is the proper name, and that Welsh was in error, as were Williams and McKinsey.

Joab and Ruth had seven children, and he was married secondly in Kentucky, June 14, 1812 to Mary Ann Elizabeth Caldwell, daughter of David Caldwell and Rosannah Logan, and by whom he had eight more children. He finally settled in St. Genevieve County, Territory of Missouri, where he was a delegate to the first State Constitutional Convention, and a Magistrate of Perry County until his death on August 15, 1831. The county seat of Perry County is

Perryville, located south of St. Louis, near the border of Illinois. Joab Waters left a will in Perry County, Missouri, dated January 18, 1830 and probated there September 13, 1831. He left very little to the seven named children of his first marriage, the principal inheritance being a debt owed him by his son Henry G. Waters, in the amount of three thousand dollars. Joab directed that his executor collect that debt and distribute it equally between the children of his first marriage. His daughter Jane Philips received a house and lot in New Market, Frederick County; and his daughter Miranda Hyatt received his interest in some land on Bennett Creek. He apparently had accumulated a valuable estate in Missouri, all of which he left to "my loving companion Polly Ann Elizabeth Caldwell, now known as Polly Ann Elizabeth Waters." She was his second wife, and was named Executrix, and upon her death, the property was to be distributed equally to "her children by me." The property consisted of 2,000 acres of land that he owned jointly with Joseph Horlich; and the farm on which he then lived; and also the 640 acres at the lower end of the (?) Bottom; as also the 100 acres he bought from a Sheriff's sale in Perry County; as also the tract of 300 acres bought of Rowland Boyd; all the negroes, stock, farm implements and personal property. As mentioned earlier, Joab and his second wife reportedly had eight children, but they were not named in his will. The seven children born to Ruth Griffith were:

1.   Annie Waters, born July 6, 1789; married May 24, 1805 to Thomas Burgee, Jr., born c.1780, died March 15, 1852. On November 16, 1812, he was appointed cornet in Captain John Cook's Troop of Horse, 2nd Regiment of the 1st Cavalry Division. (Webster defines a cornet as the standard-bearer in a troop of British cavalry). He was appointed Lieutenant of the same company on December 22, 1812. Head of household in the 1850 census of the New Market District, Frederick County, they had children still at home and there were reportedly a number of others. In *The Burgee Families*, by Bruce Burgee Geibel, June 15, 2000, it is reported that Annie Waters was born December 13, 1779 and died April 25, 1852, which appears to perhaps be the dates that are associated with her husband Thomas Burgee, Jr. instead. That report lists a number of the children:

a. Joab Waters Burgee, born August 25, 1806, went west to Missouri in 1826, joining his grandfather, and died December 12, 1881 in Perry County, Missouri. Married there May 24, 1832 to Elizabeth Burns, born there April 4, 1816, died February 11, 1876 in Perry County, daughter of James Burns and Nancy Tucker. Children, all born in Perry County, Missouri:

(1) Susan A. Burgee, born August 14, 1833, died July 17, 1856.

(2) James Burgee, born September 19, 1833, and died March 28, 1897. Married November 10, 1858 to Susan A. Clark, and second to Emily C. Brown.

(3) Ellen Jane Burgee, born December 17, 1834, died September 23, 1866. Married September 14, 1849 to Andrew Broadus Hogard.

(4) Nancy A. Burgee, born June 26, 1837, died October 24, 1837.

(5) Thomas A. Burgee, born April 26, 1839, died August 16, 1841

(6) Henry B. Burgee, born October 6, 1841, died January 2, 1862

(7) Letitia Ann Burgee, born August 18, 1844, and died December 15, 1929. Married April 28, 1863 to Thomas B. Sanders.

(8) Thomas Burgee, born August 15, 1847, died May 24, 1914. Married May 10, 1870 to Theresa Moore, and secondly to Mary Antoinette Prost.

(9) Joab Waters Burgee, Jr., born January 16, 1850, died June 12, 1875. Married October 9, 1872 to Catherine Hogard.

(10) Elizabeth Burgee, born October 28, 1852, married November 5, 1872 to Zachary Taylor McKenzie.

(11) Emily Burgee, born December 17, 1854, died August 20, 1936. Married April 17, 1875 to John Basil Moore.

(12) Mary America Burgee, born July 9, 1857, died March 12, 1898. Married December 13, 1877 to Peter C. Cissell.

b. Thomas H. Burgee, born March 18, 1808

c. Grafton Lewis Burgee, born c.1810

d. Elizabeth Ruth Burgee, born January 25, 1817

e. Mary Ann Burgee, born April 4, 1819

f. Emily Burgee, born September 10, 1821

g. Eliza Ann Burgee, born January 19, 1825

h. Clayton Burgee, born December 30, 1830

2. Eleanor Waters, born c.1804, died c.1860; married twice. She was first married December 9, 1812 to Miel Burgee, by whom she had three children in the Urbana District. He was a son of Thomas Burgee, Sr. and his wife Ellen (surname not known). Miel served as cornet in the 2nd Regiment of the 1st Cavalry Division, War of 1812, after the promotion of his brother Thomas Burgee, Jr. from that position to First Lieutenant in the same company. They marched through Hyattstown, and participated in the battle of Bladensburg under Major John Cook. Eleanor was married second in Frederick County by license dated September 11, 1827 to Ephraim Davis, born c.1793 near Ijamsville, Frederick County, died c.1858, who had also been previously married September 30, 1820 to Anne Anderson; one child died at birth. He was head of household in the 1850 census of the New Market District, Frederick County, with Eleanor and three children still at home. According to her father's will, she was married a third time to Gilbert, with no children reported. The children of Eleanor, from her three marriages, included:

a. Miel Burgee, Jr., born about November 14, 1818 in Urbana District of Frederick County and died January 11, 1903. Cemetery records report that he died on that date, but was then 79 years and 25 days of age, or born c.1824. He and his wife Clara were buried at Pleasant Grove Methodist Church near Browningsville Road. Married twice; first in Frederick County by license dated February 1, 1844 to Eleanor M. Linthicum, born c.1823, a daughter of Frederick Linthicum (1774), and his second wife Elizabeth McElfresh (1776). Miel and Eleanor had ten children, only three reaching maturity. Miel was married second by license dated September 8, 1860 to Clara

Elizabeth Lawson, born c.1843 and died July 20, 1888, daughter of John H. Lawson and Letha Ann Layton. In the 1850 census of the New Market District, he was listed with his wife, there called Ellen, and five children. There were others. Miel inherited part of the tract called *William and Elizabeth* from his father, and acquired other lands from Charles Worthington of Ijamsville known as part of *Resurvey on Daniel's Small Tract*. Miel was said to have been the father of twenty-one children from his two marriages, including these:

(1) Ann Rebecca Burgee, born c.1844, died c.1928. Married to Eli Price and lived in Washington.

(2) Elizabeth Burgee, born c.1846; died young, single.

(3) Frederick Lewis Burgee, born December 19, 1847; apparently the same of that name and birth year who died December 17, 1878; buried at Pleasant Grove. His wife was Margaret A. Lawson, born August 17, 1850, died July 15, 1917, buried in the Lawson family cemetery near Browningsville; daughter of James U. Lawson. They lived on the old Lawson farm near Price's Distillery, and had at least one son:

(a) John W. Burgee, born c.1877, died February 16, 1878; buried with his father.

(4) Miel Eldridge Burgee, born c.1848, died 1920, buried at Prospect Cemetery, Mt. Airy, with his wife and two children. She was Sadie Ida Davis, born 1853, died 1932, daughter of Richard Davis (1828) and Annie C. Williams (1830). They lived in or near the town of Mt. Airy, in New Market District of Frederick County, and had children. The Burgee families are well discussed in *The Burgee Families, Descendants of Thomas and Eleanor Burgee of Frederick, Maryland*, by Bruce Burgee Geibel, June, 2000, of 2010 Longwood Drive, Woodstock, Georgia, to which the reader is referred. A copy is lodged in the library of the Montgomery County Historical Society in Rockville. We will here report only the brief outline of this line of the family:

(a) Valira O. Burgee, born June, 1875; married December 12, 1894 to George Washington Runkles, born 1859 in Frederick County, son of Basil Runkles (1809) and Mary Ellen Mentzer (1834) his second wife. Apparently no children.

(b) Effa Ann Burgee, born March 27, 1879, died August 11, 1912. Married November 28, 1900 at the Moravian Church to Emory Manasseh Wagner, born c.1873, and lived in New Market. At least two children.

(c) Ray Safford Burgee, born May 11, 1882, died August 17, 1885.

(d) Margaret Burgee, born June 3, 1885, died June, 1982; married to John Molesworth and had at least a child.

(e) Howard Edward Burgee, born June 27, 1889 on Plane #4, Frederick County, died c.1951. Married July 12, 1910 Cora Todd Spurrier, born October 25, 1889, died October 25, 1971, daughter of George W. Spurrier (1859) of Woodville. Eight children.

(f) Mary Eva Burgee, born February 27, 1890 and died young.

(5) Lydia O. Burgee, born c.1850, died c.1860

(6) McKendree Riley Burgee, born c.1862, infant death.

(7) Amon Burgee, Sr., born c.1865, died c.1945. Married to Mayme Engleman of Union Bridge.

(8) Leathe Ellen Burgee, born c.1866, died c.1916, not married.

(9) Henry Burgee, born c.1868, died young.

(10) Guy Burgee, born c.1870, died young.

(11) William Keefer Burgee, born c.1872, died c.1933. Married at the parsonage in Kemptown June 15, 1896 to Sadie Estelle Davis, born 1877, died 1965, daughter of Samuel Byron Davis (1846) and Rebecca M. Ebert (1850). Geibel reports Sadie's birth as July 20, 1850, which is obviously incorrect.

(12) Ossie Delilah Burgee, born c.1875. Married Charles H. Linthicum of Fountain Mills in New Market area.
(13) Eli McSherry Burgee, born c.1878, died c.1936. Married Nettie Jane Day of Kemptown.
(14) Worthington Burgee, an infant death in 1880; buried with his parents.
(15) Gabriel Lewis Burgee, born c.1881, died c.1935. He was married twice: first to Annie Charlotte Murphy and second to Carrie M. Burdette.
(16) Clara Elizabeth Burgee, died September 1, 1888 at the age of six months; buried with her parents.

b.   Eli Thomas Burgee, who was a jockey, and died young.
c.   Elizabeth Ellen Burgee, born c.1822, died December 7, 1860. Married in Frederick County under license dated November 5, 1842 to Richard Browning, born c.1816 in Frederick County, and died there May 15, 1893. He was a son of Jeremiah Browning (1775) and his second wife, Drusilla (1800), and is buried at Kemptown Methodist Church, with his wife and two children. The family appears in the 1850 census for the New Market District of Frederick County, Maryland. There, Richard was said to have been born c.1820 and Elizabeth, c.1824. There were four children in the household. In the 1880 census for Kemptown, in Frederick County, Richard is living alone with three servants. This is believed to be the same individual whose will was dated December 24, 1887 and probated in May, 1893; filed in liber JKW 1 at folio 28 in the will records of Frederick County, Maryland. Lavinia (Lavinia Winona) Browning, daughter of Richard, was found living in the household of Jeremiah Thomas Browning during the 1850 census, being his niece. In his will, Richard does not name a wife, who had predeceased him, but does name a son and two daughters (his only surviving children), with their husband's names. His other children had predeceased their father. Their descendants are discussed in *Our Maryland Heritage, Book Twelve, Browning Families*, page 93, which please see.

d. Joab Waters Browning Davis, born September 27, 1834, died c.1912; buried at Kemptown. In 1855, he moved to Baltimore, but returned to Urbana District and for about fifteen years rented farms in the area, subsequently purchasing his own property. Married July 28, 1855 to Elvira W. Kindley, born March 4, 1839, died June 27, 1890, buried at Providence Cemetery at Kemptown, daughter of George F. Kindley (1806) and Hepsibah Etchison (1809) of Montgomery County. Six children:
   (1) Vernon Davis, born c.1854, lived at Denver, Colorado, where he was engaged in the real estate business. Married to Miss Kilgore, the daughter of Judge Kilgore of Muncie, Indiana.
   (2) Hepsibah E. Davis, born April 17, 1858, died July 7, 1942; buried at Providence Cemetery, Kemptown. Married to Henry Etchison of Frederick, who died before the taking of the 1900 census.
   (3) William K. Davis, born 1861, died 1938; buried at Kemptown Methodist Cemetery with his wife. Married Mary E. Linthicum, born 1867, died 1954, the daughter of John Warren Linthicum (1834) and Sarah Amanda Hendry. At least two children, both baptized April 20, 1901, Methodist Church South, Montgomery Circuit:
        (a) George Warren Gordon Davis.
        (b) Verna Louise Davis.
   (4) Joab Waters Browning Davis, Jr., born c.1865
   (5) George F. Davis, born 1867, died March 29, 1879; buried at Providence Cemetery, Kemptown, with parents.
   (6) Edith Davis, born 1869, died 1888, married to Richard Estep of Baltimore.
e. James Milton Davis, born c.1834, married October 26, 1857 to Lavinia Wolfe, born February 20, 1840, died August 6, 1926, daughter of George Wolfe (1806) and Mary Davis (1806). James Milton Davis was a blacksmith, and they first lived in Mt. Airy, then at Fountain Mills, both in Frederick County, and removed to Goshen,

in Montgomery County, where he died March 9, 1892, and is buried at Kemptown Methodist Church. Children:

(1) William Waters Davis, born c.1858

(2) Mary Eunice Davis, born 1867; married about 1882 to William Lee Dutrow, born 1861 in Adamstown, Maryland, died 1941, son of John W. Dutrow (1830) of Buckeystown and Mary Ellen Spaulding (1836). Two children, born at Adamstown:

    (a) Bertha Lucretia Dutrow, born June 5, 1883

    (b) William Milton Dutrow, born c.1885. Married April 19, 1905 to Mamie Purdum, born January 29, 1886, daughter of James Henning Purdum (1847) and his second wife Sarah Edith Lewis (1856). Children:

        1. Raymond Dutrow.

        2. Robert Dutrow.

        3. Grace Dutrow.

(3) Samuel Elbert Davis, born April 27, 1870, died March 18, 1956. Married to Beulah V., born June 17, 1878, died January 28, 1953. Both are buried at Mt. Olivet Cemetery in Frederick.

f. Annie Ellen Davis, born September 27, 1845, died October 22, 1908. Perhaps married to Thomas W. O'Bryan, born November 22, 1844. Buried at Mt. Olivet Cemetery, Frederick.

3. Henry Griffith Waters, born in Frederick County and married there by license dated November 15, 1811 to Elizabeth Gibson, born c.1795, and died January 26, 1831. After a few weeks, he was married secondly to Jane F. Foreman. No family has been reported, and no will was found in Frederick.

4. Jane Waters, married to John Oliver Philips.

5. Miranda Waters, born December 18, 1801; married December 31, 1818 to Eli Hyatt, Jr., born March 28, 1798 and died February 14, 1850; son of Eli Hyatt and Mary Warfield. For the numerous descendants of this couple, beyond those listed here, the reader is referred to *Nehemiah Moxley, His Clagettsville Sons and Their Descendants*, a major, detailed study by Allie May Moxley Buxton, 1989, BookCrafters. Miranda Hyatt of

the proper age was listed as head of household in the 1850 census of Frederick County for the New Market District and then a widow. There were four children in the household, presumably hers. There were a total of eleven:

a. Martha Ellen Hyatt, born November 19, 1819, died January 27, 1892. Married John Mussetter, born February 24, 1801 at Oakdean in Frederick County, son of Christopher Mussetter and Ruth Ijams.

b. Miel Hyatt, born c.1821, died c.1843

c. Henry M. Hyatt, born May 25, 1824, died February 20, 1881. Married c.1847 to Rhoda Walker.

d. Susannah Hyatt, born March 5, 1826, died March 4, 1889. Married to William Wolfe of Bartholows.

e. Joab Waters Hyatt, born March 3, 1828, died April 8, 1828.

f. William H. Hyatt, born March 18, 1829, died September 4, 1831.

g. Thomas A. Hyatt, born February 23, 1831, died March 11, 1912. Married Elcinda Moxley.

h. John Israel Hyatt, born c.1835; married Cordelia Poole.

i. Eli Hyatt, III, born June 4, 1837, of whom more.

j. Alverda Virginia Hyatt, born August 25, 1840, died March 5, 1919. Married Benjamin Murphy and had children in Gaithersburg.

k. Emily Janet Hyatt, born March 14, 1843, died August 23, 1854

6. Joab Waters, Jr., apparently the same married in Frederick County October 15, 1855 to Margaret V. Rowe, born c.1829 at Emmitsburg.

7. John Waters.

William Griffith
died 1699
The Immigrant
Chapter 2
*

Orlando Griffith
1688
*

Henry Griffith
1720
Chapter 4
*

Henry Griffith, Jr.
1744
*

Henry Griffith
1767
Chapter 5
*

*   *   *   *   *   *   *   *   *
*
*   * Sarah Griffith 1790
*
*   * Henry Griffith, Jr. 1793
*
*   * Amelia Dorsey Griffith 1795
*
*   * Ann R. Griffith 1797
*
*   * Eleanor Ann Griffith 1799
*
*   * Allen Griffith 1801
*
*   * Romulus Riggs Griffith 1803
*
*   * Elisha Riggs Griffith 1805
*
*   * Uriah Griffith 1808
*
*   * Ulysses Griffith 1810

58

CHAPTER 5

Henry Griffith
1767-1837

This son of Henry Griffith (1744) and Sarah Warfield (1746) was born December 31, 1767, and died October 27, 1837 in Montgomery County. Henry Griffith left a will in Montgomery County, dated June 5, 1832, probated November 15, 1837, recorded in liber V at folio 125; rerecorded in liber VMB 4 at page 83. He left to his wife part of the tract called *Retirement*, containing about 300 acres, and adjoining the tracts called *Tusculum* and *Samuel's Chance*, and the Hawlings River. She was also to receive several slaves, live-stock, personal property, meat and grain necessary for her needs. Three of the sons; Henry, Elisha and Ulysses; jointly received the Shop Lot of about three acres. Married c.1790 to Mary Riggs, born August 14, 1768, died January 21, 1846, daughter of Samuel Riggs (1740) and Amelia Dorsey (1749). As Polly Griffith, Mary left a will in Montgomery County, dated March 5, 184_, probated March 3, 1846, recorded in liber Z at folio 383; rerecorded in liber VMB 4 at page 408. She left bequests to three grandchildren; two children of her daughter Amelia Dorsey Griffith Macgill; and Henry, son of her son Ulysses Griffith. She also left to her daughter Sarah her large Bible, and to daughters Sarah Griffith and Ellen Ann Owings, bank stock in Union Bank of Georgetown. Children:

1. Sarah Griffith, born December 12, 1790, died October 25, 1850. Under his will, her father left her the farm then occupied by Richard Harding, called *Snowden's Purchase*, and also part of *Addition*, the whole containing about 30 acres; as well as one negro man. Should Sarah die without issue, the legacy was to go to Henry's granddaughter Marion Griffith.
2. Henry Griffith, Jr., born September 22, 1793, of whom more as Child 2.
3. Amelia Dorsey Griffith, born October 18, 1795. Married in St. Bartholomew's Episcopal Parish March 25, 1819 to Basil Macgill and had descendants in Ohio and elsewhere. Under her father's will, two of her children were named:

a. Robert Henry Macgill, who received the plantation on which William Fisher then lived, containing 25 acres.
   b. Marion Macgill, received a negro slave and furniture.
4. Ann R. Griffith, born September 3, 1797, an infant death.
5. Eleanor Ann Griffith, born November 17, 1799. Married September 5, 1822 to Basil Owings, born c.1798, and had as many as eleven children, whose descendants lived in various areas of Maryland. Under her father's will, she received the land in Anne Arundel County, containing about 170 acres of *Warfield's Range*. Also under her father's will, one of her children received the sum of fifty dollars:
   a. Richard Henry Owings.
6. Allen Griffith, born May 7, 1801, died April 18, 1875. Under his father's will, he received $300 in stock of the Union Bank of Georgetown. Married May 27, 1833 to Mary A. Stansbury and had children:
   a. William H. Griffith.
   b. George H. Griffith, a doctor, died single in California.
   c. Ellen Griffith, married P. Bantz.
   d. Claudena Griffith, married F. W. Keyes of Mississippi.
7. Romulus Riggs Griffith, born June 5, 1803, died July 5, 1872 at Gettysburg Springs, Pennsylvania. Under his father's will, he received $300 in stock of the Union Bank of Georgetown. Married first June 26, 1827 at Cincinnati, Ohio to Rachel Howard Meriweather, born March 5, 1805 in Anne Arundel County, Maryland, died February 4, 1842, and had as many as nine children, and numerous descendants in Ohio, Virginia, New York and elsewhere. He was married twice more, once in Ohio and once in Baltimore, without further issue. In the family folder file at the Montgomery County Historical Society library in Rockville, we found a print from the *Griffith Family Register*, which contains the descendants of this family. It is reported there as having been located at the West Virginia University Library, in Morgantown, West Virginia. The library lists the item as having been a "Gift of O. D. Lambert, 1958, Ms. 1074." We will not repeat any of that document here, confining our report primarily to Montgomery and Frederick Counties, Maryland. At least part of that *Griffith Fam-*

ily Register appeared in the *Maryland Genealogical Society Bulletin*, Volume 18, No. 3, Summer, 1977, including words of caution as to its use.

8. Elisha Riggs Griffith, born June 21, 1805, of whom more as Child 8.
9. Uriah Griffith, born July 5, 1808, buried July 18, 1824, St. Bartholomew's Episcopal Church.
10. Ulysses Griffith, born September 28, 1810, of whom more as Child 10.

CHILD 2

Henry Griffith, Jr.
1793-1836

This son of Henry Griffith (1767) and Mary Riggs (1768) was born September 22, 1793 and died May 13, 1836 (records of St. Bartholomew's Episcopal Church). Under his father's will, Henry received the plantation on which he then lived, containing about 210 acres of land. Henry, Jr. also left a will in Montgomery County, dated April 30, 1836, probated May 24, 1836 and recorded in liber U at folio 321; rerecorded in liber VMB 4 at page 40. He left to his wife Matilda a parcel of land (described in the will) for her lifetime or until remarriage, and in either case then to his two daughters Lucretia and Amelia. To his son Uriah Henry Griffith, he left the family plantation, his negro man Isaac, and his shot gun and accoutrements thereto. The two daughters also received the tract called *Retirement*, containing about 200 acres, and each received one slave. Married first on September 7, 1824 to Lucretia Ober, born January 18, 1806, died February 1, 1829, daughter of Robert Ober and Catherine Tenney. After her death, Henry Griffith married secondly to her sister, Matilda Ober, born March 14, 1812, died October 3, 1839, and had a child. The Ober sisters were descendants of Dr. Samuel Tenney, who joined the Continental Army on the day of the Battle of Bunker Hill and served as surgeon, later serving as Representative to Congress from 1800 to 1807. The children included:
1. Uriah Henry Griffith, born July 25, 1825, of whom more.

2. Albin Griffith, born August 12, 1828, an infant death
3. Lucretia O. Griffith, born October 3, 1830. Married June 3, 1853 to Howard Heald, born April 21, 1861, died March 16, 1883, and had descendants in Baltimore and elsewhere.
4. Amelia D. Griffith, mentioned in her father's will.

Uriah Henry Griffith
1825-1896

This son of Henry Griffith (1793) and his first wife, Lucretia Ober (1806), was born July 20, 1825 in Montgomery County and died January 3, 1896 at Laytonsville, where he was a member of the firm of U. H. Griffith and Son, livestock dealers. Married November 24, 1846 to Henrietta E. Wilcoxen, born December 8, 1821 at Buck Lodge, died January 9, 1905 at Laytonsville, daughter of Horatio Wilcoxen and Ann Gaither. Head of household in the 1850 census of the Cracklin District of Montgomery County, Uriah was listed with his wife Henrietta E. and their first two children. Living with them was Sarah Griffith, born c.1790, his aunt. Also in the household was Francis Dixon, born c.1831, a black laborer. Uriah was also listed as owning five slaves. During the preceding twelve months, he was listed with 140 acres of improved land and 70 acres unimproved, with $3,000 valuation. He owned 4 horses, 4 milch cows, 7 other cattle, 11 sheep and 38 swine. In the previous year, he had produced 275 bushels of wheat, 650 bushels of Indian corn, 199 bushels of oats, 1,800 pounds of tobacco, 25 pounds of wool, 1 bushel of peas and beans, 10 bushels of Irish potatoes, 250 pounds of butter, 8 tons of hay, and 1 bushel of clover seed. Head of household in the 1860 census of the First District, for the Laytonsville Post Office, Uriah owned $4,000 in real estate and $6,100 in personal property. His wife Henrietta was there, with four children. In the 1870 census of the First District, Uriah H. Griffith was listed as a Revenue Assessor, with $6,000 in real estate and $1,000 in personal property, with his wife Henrietta and five children. Uriah H. Griffith was head of household in the 1880 census of the county for the Cracklin District, with his wife Henrietta E. and five children at home. She was found in the 1900 census of the county for the First District, living in a household headed by her son

Henry, single, with her daughter Matilda also in the household. Henrietta was listed as a widow, married for 53 years, and the mother of ten children, six of them then surviving.

Uriah H. Griffith left a will in Montgomery County, dated June 12, 1888, probated January 7, 1896, and recorded in liber GCD 2 at folio 302. He left to his wife all of his real estate and personalty, for her lifetime. At her death, that property was to be divided between four of his children: Uriah H. W. Griffith; Henry H. Griffith; Thomas C. Griffith; and Matilda O. Griffith. He then specified that there were two additional daughters: Annie L. England, wife of John G. England; and Henrietta G. Christopher, wife of James C. Christopher. Finally, he mentions that he has for some time been in partnership with his son Uriah H. W. Griffith in the business of buying and selling stock and cattle, and that he is leaving that business to Uriah, separate and apart from any other relationship with his general estate. The children included:

1.   Ann L. Griffith, born September 29, 1847. Married April 23, 1867 to John George England, Jr., born c.1847, the son of John George England (1809), an attorney, and Emily Howard (1814), who lived in the Fourth District of Montgomery County. Head of household in the 1870 census of the Fourth District, John George England, Jr. was listed as a merchant, with $4,000 in personal property, apparently in the town of Rockville. His wife Annie L. was listed, with their first child. There is some question as to the proper name of John G. England, Sr. and Jr. The 1860 census of the Fourth District clearly lists the father as George England, apparently using his middle name. In *Genealogy of the Griffith Family*, by R. R. Griffith of Baltimore, in 1892, he states that the proper name was Major John Glisan England, which may be correct. That source also states that the wife of Major England was Emily Howard, daughter of Thomas W. Howard and Elizabeth Ridgely Crabb. John G. England was head of household in the 1900 census of the county for Rockville Town, with his wife Annie. They had been married for thirty-three years, and she had been the mother of fifteen children, thirteen of them surviving, and twelve then at home. They had children:

a. Howard G. England, born January 16, 1869, a minister, in 1940 living in Columbia, South Carolina.
b. Henrietta W. England, born July 29, 1871, died October 11, 1940 at her home in Laytonsville. Married June 7, 1906 at Christ Episcopal Church, Rockville to Ulysses Griffith, born January 29, 1871, died June 6, 1954; buried at Goshen Methodist with his wife; son of Ulysses Griffith, Jr. (1843). They had children:
   (1) Ann England Griffith, born August 8, 1909; married to Young, and mentioned in the obituary of her brother.
   (2) Ulysses Griffith, IV, born January 8, 1908 at Laytonsville on the ancestral farm, which he later operated, and died September 24, 1978; buried there in the local cemetery. Married April 7, 1947 at Scranton, Pennsylvania to Marion Margaret Taylor, born there c.1915, and died September 26, 1977. She was a daughter of George Rodney Taylor of Scranton, and a school teacher at Gaithersburg Elementary School at the time of her marriage. Ulysses, known as Lit, was Chief Clerk of the District Court in Rockville, a former member of the House of Delegates, and former chairman of the Upper Montgomery County Planning Commission, and numerous other civic and political positions. Two children:
      (a) Jane Ann Griffith, born c.1952. In her early twenties, Jane Ann spent a year and a half in Swaziland, Africa as a Youth Development Programmer. She was also selected by the Maryland 4-H clubs to represent Maryland in Greece for several months. Married February 28, 1981 at Woodfield to Richard O. Evans, son of Mrs. LaRue B. Evans of Benton, Pennsylvania.
      (b) Ulysses Griffith, V, born c.1954
c. Emily H. England, born September 13, 1872; at home in 1900, listed as a clerk in the census bureau. Married to Greenlee.

d. Edward W. England, born June 15, 1874; at home in 1900, listed as a deputy clerk in the court house.
e. Elizabeth G. England, born October 25, 1875; a teacher
f. Thomas England, born March 22, 1877
g. Anne L. England, born September 10, 1878
h. Elsie M. England, born May 21, 1880
i. Lillian C. England, born January 31, 1882
j. John A. England, born December 25, 1883
k. Matilda O. England, born August 19, 1885
l. Mabel England, born February 23, 1887, died 1891
m. Carrie Crabb England, born September 13, 1888
n. Harrison L. England.
o. Maude England.

2. Albert O. Griffith, born c.1849, died July, 1850
3. Ursula Griffith, died March, 1853
4. Henrietta Griffith, born August 14, 1853. She is possibly the same individual listed as Nettie C. Griffith, of the proper age, found in the 1870 census of Montgomery County for the Fifth District, attending school in the household of Francis Miller (1830), a lawyer, and his wife Caroline H. Miller (1832), a school teacher. Married at Emanuel Church on October 18, 1876 to James C. Christopher, born August 3, 1846. Reportedly lived in Baltimore.
5. Mary W. Griffith, born c.1860 according to the 1860 census, died October 3, 1882 at the home of her father (*Sentinel* obit).
6. Uriah H. W. Griffith, born November 21, 1857, died February 17, 1918 of pneumonia at his home in Laytonsville, leaving his wife and children (*Sentinel* obituary); the oldest child still at home in 1870. Buried at the Laytonsville Cemetery. Head of household in the 1900 census of the county for the First District, listed as Uriah W. Griffith of the proper age. Married in the county at Goshen Methodist Church by license dated November 12, 1895 to Laura Eleanor Waters, born March 13, 1860 (or 1862), died July 22, 1950 at her home in Laytonsville, daughter of Zachariah Maccubbin Waters (1832) and Sarah Virginia Magruder. He was head of household in the 1900 census of the First District, with his wife Laura and two children. He was listed as a cattle dealer and they had then

been married four years, having had two children, both living. Also in the household was Elizabeth Magruder, born May, 1833, an aunt. The children included:

    a.   Elizabeth Waters Griffith, born October 7, 1897 and died August 10, 1949 at her home in Laytonsville, single. Buried at Laytonsville Cemetery.

    b.   Henrietta Wilcoxen Griffith, born June, 1899; married William Pitt Sherman.

    c.   Virginia M. Griffith, born c.1901, died September 16, 1976 at Holy Cross Hospital, Montgomery County, single; buried at Laytonsville.

7.   Henry Hicks Griffith, born January 15, 1862, died August 28, 1951 at the ancestral family home in Laytonsville. Head of household in the 1900 census of Montgomery County for the First District, single. His mother Henrietta was living with him, and his sister Matilda O. was also in the household, single. His mother was listed as a widow, married for 53 years, and the mother of ten children, six of them then surviving. In his obituary, there was the statement that he was the sixth lineal descendant of Henry Griffith, who formed the first Montgomery County Council in Rockville in 1774. An interesting statement, when one realizes that Montgomery County was not formed until 1776, and further, that the county did not have the Council form of government until well into the twentieth century. There is also the obituary of Alice Riggs Bartlett Griffith, born January 2, 1875, who died February 2, 1964 at Passa Grille Beach, Florida, and is reported to have been the wife of the late Henry Hicks Griffith; and sister of Miss Vashti R. Bartlett of Laytonsville. Buried in Rockville Cemetery with her husband. The *Sentinel* reported the marriage on November 11, 1920 at Ascension Chapel in Gaithersburg between Henry H. Griffith of Laytonsville and Alice Riggs Bartlett of the vicinity of Gaithersburg. The two Bartlett girls were daughters of George W. B. Bartlett (1850) and Amanda S. Griffith (1842); Alice born c.1877 and Vashti born c.1875. Henry and Alice were both buried at the Union Cemetery in Rockville.

8.   Matilda Ober Griffith, born January 25, 1864, died January 3, 1907; buried at Laytonsville with her parents. She left a will in

Montgomery County dated March 1, 1906, probated March 26, 1907 and recorded in liber HCA 4 at folio 385, leaving her entire estate to her brother Henry Hicks Griffith (above).

9. Thomas Cranmer Griffith, born April 14, 1866, died June 1, 1924 at his home in Laytonsville; buried at Laytonsville Cemetery. Married November 22, 1898 at St. Bartholomew's Church in Laytonsville to his cousin, Louisa Hood Griffith, born c.1874, died November 27, 1922 at her home at Laytonsville, leaving her husband and three children; buried at Laytonsville (*Sentinel* obituary), daughter of William H. Griffith (1847) and Sarah Ann Griffith (1850). Children were:

    a. Matilda O. Griffith, married to William Hodges and lived at Ellicott City, Maryland. This is perhaps Matilda Ober Griffith, born February 11, 1900, according to records of St. Bartholomew's Episcopal Church. She, and the other two children, were all mentioned in the will of their maternal grandfather, William H. Griffith.

    b. Louisa Hood Griffith, born July 3, 1902, of whom more.

    c. Thomas Cranmer Griffith, Jr., born May 28, 1906, died August 4, 1934; buried at Laytonsville with his parents.

Louisa Hood Griffith
1902-1976

This daughter of Thomas Cranmer Griffith (1866) and Louisa Hood Griffith (1874), was born July 3, 1902, and died at her home in Laytonsville, April 22, 1976. Married February 14, 1924 at St. Bartholomew's Episcopal Church in Laytonsville to Washington Waters White, Jr., born September 2, 1903 at Buck Lodge, grew up in Washington, and died March 27, 1984. He was active in financial circles, for many years associated with Peoples Life Insurance Co.; chairman of Citizens Building and Loan Association, and member of the Board of Gaithersburg National Bank (later Suburban Trust). He was a charter member and former President of the Laytonsville Lions Club (elected to the club's Hall of Fame in 1978), and a church vestryman. During the 1950s, he was Mayor of the Town of Laytonsville. Children, all baptized at St. Bartholomew's Church in Laytonsville:

1. Louisa Hood Griffith White, born March 2, 1925, baptized October 18, 1925. Married December 11, 1948 Robert Darrington Riggs, born c.1918, died November 11, 1974, the son of Douglas and Chloe Riggs. They had children:
   a. Louisa W. Riggs, married Eldon Krebs; two children:
      (1) Kami Krebs.
      (2) Ty Krebs.
   b. Robert B. Riggs, married Yvonne Mediary and had three children:
      (1) Jason Riggs.
      (2) Aaron Riggs.
      (3) Lindsay Riggs.
2. Dorothy Virginia White, born July 26, 1927 and baptized August 30, 1931. Married to James Tessier. Children:
   a. James Tessier.
   b. Thomas Tessier, married Tootie Williams, and had two children:
      (1) Katie Tessier.
      (2) Tyler Tessier.
   c. Laura Tessier.
3. Washington Waters White, born March 1, 1929, baptized August 30, 1931. Married on March 27, 1954 at Gaithersburg to Kay Harding, born February 6, 1934 at Washington, D. C., the daughter of George Warren Harding (1904) and Cathryn Marguerite Sagrario (1908). They had children, the first born in Montgomery County; the second in Washington, D. C.; and the last four in Leesburg, Virginia:
   a. Washington Waters White, born November 8, 1954. Married February 5, 1977 to Michele Cuseo, daughter of Michael Angelo Cuseo, Jr. and Donna Irene Thompson.
   b. George Warren White, born May 25, 1956. Married May 23, 1981 to Susan Lynne Janney.
   c. John Michael White, born September 12, 1957. Married September 12, 1981 to Kimberly Dee Burdette.
   d. William Wynkoop White, born February 14, 1959
   e. Tracy Marguerite White, born April 13, 1961. Married Michael Watson.
   f. Nancy Elizabeth White, born May 29, 1963.

4. Charles Thomas White, born March 13, 1933, baptized October 21, 1934. Married August 27, 1955 to Barbara Jeanette Harding, born November 9, 1933, daughter of Brawner Zachariah Harding and Marie Frances Briggs of Gaithersburg, Montgomery County, Maryland. Charles has been the Mayor of Laytonsville for a number of years, following in the footsteps of his illustrious father. Children, born there:
   a. Carol Marie White, born June 4, 1958. Married June 17, 1989 to Michael Kamp. A daughter:
      (1) Jenna Marie Kamp, born January 30, 1992
   b. Deborah Griffith White, born March 22, 1960. Married July 20, 1985 to Barry Bennett, and had children:
      (1) Bradley Wayne Bennett, born October 2, 1989
      (2) Cory Thomas Bennett, born March 21, 1994
      (3) Dylan White Bennett, born March 18, 1996
   c. Julia Briggs White, born May 21, 1962.
   d. Mary Louisa White, born May 14, 1966. Married December 15, 1989 to Kevin Helmick, and had a son:
      (1) Kyle Wayne Helmick, born January 5, 1994

CHILD 8

Elisha Riggs Griffith
1805-1885

This son of Henry Griffith (1767) and Mary Riggs (1768) was born June 21, 1805 at the family farm of *Woodland*, died October 19, 1885. Under the will of his father, he received the plantation on which he was then living, being about 260 acres of *Retirement*. Married first April 29, 1829 to Martha J. Ober, born November 18, 1809, died May 2, 1833, daughter of Robert Ober and Catherine Tenney, and had two children. He was married second October 9, 1834 to Elizabeth Gaither, born May 18, 1805 near Unity, daughter of Frederick Gaither and Jane Gartrell, and had six more children. Elizabeth's obituary in the *Sentinel* reports that she died October 25, 1902 at the home of her daughter, at the age of 98 years, and was buried in the family cemetery. He lived his life in Montgomery County, in the Cracklin District, placing him in the Laytonsville vicinity. Head of household in the 1850 census of the County for the First District, he was a farmer, with $3,600 in real estate, and five slaves. His wife Elizabeth was listed, with six children. In the 1850 agricultural census, Elisha had 200 acres of improved land and 100 acres unimproved, valued at $3,600 in total. He owned 5 horses, 6 milch cows, 2 working oxen, 6 other cattle, 12 sheep and 35 swine. In the past year, he had produced 300 bushels of wheat, 30 bushels of rye, 500 bushels of Indian corn, 200 bushels of oats, 2,000 pounds of tobacco, 50 pounds of wool, 100 bushels of Irish potatoes, 550 pounds of butter, 9 tons of hay, and 10 bushels of clover seed. Head of household in the 1860 census of the First District, Laytonsville Post Office, he had his wife and four children at home. Elisha was listed in both the 1870 and 1880 census of the First District as a retired farmer, in 1870 owning $4,000 in real estate and $6,500 in personal property. Living alone with his wife, they had one domestic servant in the household.

Elisha R. Griffith left a will in Montgomery County, probated October 27, 1885 and recorded in liber RWC 15 at folio 48. He leaves to his wife Elizabeth, for her lifetime, the home plantation, being part of *Retirement* and part of *Addition to Brooke Grove*, described in the will, containing 102 acres and 10 perches of land, plus about eight acres attached to the dwelling house. She also received for life, all the household furniture and some government bonds at 4% interest. At her death, that bequest was to descend to their daughter Mary C. Carroll. Daughter Maria G. Warfield was to receive government bonds also, valued at $3,000. To his son, Charles H. Griffith, he left that part of the plantation and buildings which Charles then occupied, being part of *Retirement*, also described by metes and bounds, containing 203 and 1/2 acres, more or less. His children were:

1. Mary Catherine Griffith, born February 14, 1830, died February 9, 1889. Married in Montgomery County December 25, 1856 to Thomas W. Carroll, and had children:
   a. Thomas W. Carroll, Jr.
   b. Howard H. Carroll, died September 6, 1891
2. Henry Clay Griffith, born September 11, 1831; died at the age of twenty-four years. Not in the 1850 census.

3. Martha Jane Griffith, born December 23, 1836, died September 7, 1866. Married November 8, 1865 in Montgomery County to Fletcher Magruder; no children.
4. Maria Gaither Griffith, born May 28, 1838. Married in Montgomery County at St. Bartholomew's Episcopal Church June 7, 1860 to Israel Griffith Warfield, born February 17, 1832, and died February 27, 1907 at Laytonsville in Montgomery County, having moved there at about the age of six with his parents; buried with his wife at the Laytonsville Cemetery. He was the son of Robert Warfield of Levin and Sarah Griffith. The descendants of Maria and Israel are discussed in detail under the name of their father in the chapter devoted to the descendants of Samuel Griffith (1752), which please see.
5. Charles Harrison Griffith, born January 28, 1840, died March 15, 1917 at his home near Laytonsville (*Sentinel* obituary). At home in 1860, he was identified as the farm manager. He was Judge of the Montgomery County Orphans Court and was married November 24, 1864 to Hester Boone Dorsey, born December 6, 1843, died December 24, 1915 at Laytonsville, daughter of Stephen Boone Dorsey of Roxbury, Howard County. Charles Harrison Griffith was the third generation owner of the farm known as *Woodland*, comprising more than three hundred acres near Laytonsville, where he made his home. He was head of household in the 1870 census of the county for the First District, with $1,000 in personal property. His wife Hester was there, with their first two children. He was listed as Charles Griffith, head of household in the 1880 census of the county for the Cracklin District, with Hester and seven children. Living with them were two black servants, and James M. Griffith, born c.1840, his widowed cousin, not yet identified in a family. Charles H. was next head of household in the 1900 census of the county for the First District, which his wife Hester, and five children. They had been married for thirty-six years and she had been the mother of eleven children, eight then surviving. They had children:
   a. Sarah E. Griffith, born September 5, 1865, died August 15, 1866

b. Margaret Boone Griffith, born March 2, 1867; married August 10, 1885 at Aberton to Edward B. Kimble of Laytonsville. He was head of household in the 1900 census of the county for the Village of Laytonsville, born c.1863, with his wife Margaret of the proper age, and three children. The surname was spelled Kimball, which could be correct. The children were:
    (1) Carey B. Kimball, a son, born December, 1886
    (2) Hester M. Kimball, born May, 1890
    (3) Bessie C. Kimball, born September, 1893
c. Washington Griffith, born August 26, 1868, died July 7, 1869
d. Frank Griffith, born December 18, 1869, died November 12, 1903 at his home in Roxbury Mills; buried at Laytonsville. Married November 9, 1893 at Hawlings Episcopal Church to Alverda Griffith, born c.1876, died December 28, 1946, buried with her husband; daughter of William H. Griffith (1847) and Sarah Ann Griffith (1850). The *Sentinel* announced that they would live in Howard County. At least these children:
    (1) Mary Louise Griffith, born October 13, 1896
    (2) William Franklin Griffith, born January 27, 1899 and died January 17, 1978; buried at Monocacy Cemetery at Beallsville, with his wife and other family members. Married to Alice Rebecca Darby, born March 29, 1900, and died October 4, 1995, daughter of Remus R. Darby and Clara Fowler. They had one son:
        (a) William Robert Griffith, born March 26, 1931 in Frederick, died January 3, 1985, was buried at Monocacy. His obituary appeared in the *Gaithersburg Gazette*. At the time of his death, he lived in Clarksburg, survived by his mother, his wife, Mary Lowe Griffith, one son and two daughters:
            1. John F. Griffith, of Poolesville.
            2. Shirley L. Griffith, married to Williams.
            3. Mary Jean Griffith, married to Nickens.

(3) Charles Harrison Griffith, born July 23, 1903

e. Lillian C. Griffith, born July 2, 1871, died May 1, 1956. Married February 10, 1904 to William Thompson Warfield, born December 26, 1866, died December 20, 1945 at Woodfield, Maryland, son of John Thomas Warfield (1835) and Rachel Virginia Dorsey (1845). William Thompson Warfield left a will dated February 6, 1942, probated January 15, 1946 and filed in liber OWR 14 at folio 223, will records of Montgomery County, Maryland, naming his wife and daughter:

(1) Mary Cornelia Warfield, born October 27, 1905, died October 20, 1972, single. Buried Goshen Cemetery, in Montgomery County.

f. Mary Carroll Griffith, born September 17, 1872, died August 8, 1952; married June 14, 1900 to Victor M. Pressman, and mentioned in the obituary of her mother.

g. Greenberry Gaither Griffith, born April 15, 1874, died November 22, 1961 at Montgomery General Hospital; buried at Goshen Cemetery. He was married twice; first on March 19, 1900 at the Darnestown Presbyterian Church to Elizabeth Rebecca Tschiffely, daughter of Wilson B. Tschiffely. An obituary in the *Sentinel* reports that Elizabeth Tschiffely died March 15, 1905 at the age of twenty-five years (born August 9, 1881; buried at Darnestown Presbyterian), daughter of Wilson B. Tschiffely, and wife of Greenberry Griffith, leaving her husband and one child, not named. Greenberry was married second at Neelsville Presbyterian Church, Montgomery County, November 4, 1908 to Cornelia Isabelle Warfield, born 1877, died April 18, 1969 at Montgomery General, daughter of John Thomas Warfield (1835) and Rachel Virginia Dorsey (1845), and had two sons:

(1) Vernon Tschiffely Griffith, born March 26, 1903, died August 8, 1973 at St. Petersburg Beach, Florida; buried Goshen Cemetery, Montgomery County, Maryland. The *Sentinel* announced that he would marry June 30, 1934 to Ada Mallonee of Woodlawn, Maryland. She was born c.1901, died April 14,

1974 at St. Petersburg, and was buried with her
husband at Goshen. No children reported.

(2) Wiley Gaither Griffith, born June 11, 1914 at Lay-
tonsville. Married November 9, 1940 to Carrie Wil-
liams Allnutt, born October 25, 1919, daughter of
Edwin Ruthvin Allnutt, Jr. (1892) and Carrie
Wheeler Williams (1895). Two children, born at
Frederick, Maryland:

    (a) Marilyn Ann Griffith, born January 11, 1947.
Married June 12, 1971 to Michael Lloyd Newman, born 1945.

    (b) Barbara Jean Griffith, born January 20, 1951.

h.   Charles H. Griffith, born May 21, 1876, died July 28,
1958 at his home in Goshen, north of Gaithersburg, a retired carpenter; buried Laytonsville Cemetery. Records of
St. Bartholomew's Episcopal Church, and of Laytonsville
Cemetery, report his birth date as March 21, 1877. Married March 10, 1904 in the Darnestown Presbyterian
Church to Vandalia Tschiffely, daughter of Wilson B.
Tschiffely. She was granted a divorce about February 4,
1921, and awarded custody of their only child (*Sentinel*
notice). He was married second to Margaret Benson, her
second marriage, and his obituary mentions his one son
and three step-children: Leroy Benson, Eugene Benson,
and Mrs. Helen Esworthy. Margaret was born September
30, 1884, and died August 26, 1971 at Suburban Hospital; buried at Neelsville. The one son was:

(1) Wilson Dorsey Griffith, born c.1905

i.   Jonathan Worthington Griffith, born September 23, 1879,
and of whom more following.

j.   Dorsey Griffith, born December 25, 1880, died October
26, 1942. Married September 14, 1911 to Rachel Bell
Higgins, born July 19, 1887, died August 29, 1960 at
Doctors' Hospital, daughter of Joseph C. Higgins (1862),
all of Laytonsville. Buried in the cemetery there; no mention of children in obituary. He left a will in Montgomery
County dated April 19, 1932, probated December 1,
1942 and recorded in liber JWN 2 at folio 1, in which he

left his entire estate to his wife Rachel B. Griffith. At the time, his home address was listed at 9116 New Hampshire Avenue, NW, Washington, D. C.

   k.   Daniel Henry G. Griffith, born September 26, 1883, baptized St. Bartholomew's Episcopal Church February 2, 1885 as a son of this family; buried February 28, 1886

6.   Washington Griffith, born September 14, 1842, died October 27, 1864. In the 1860 census, he was living with his parents, and identified as a clerk. It was not very common, but he was also listed in the 1860 census in the household of George W. Mobley (1820), a merchant, probably his place of work.

7.   Clarence Griffith, born June 6, 1843, died September 16, 1846

8.   Elizabeth G. Griffith, born September 27, 1847, died July 31, 1863

Jonathan Worthington Griffith
1879-1956

This son of Charles Harrison Griffith (1840) and Hester Boone Dorsey (1843), was born September 23, 1879 in Laytonsville and died February 8, 1956; buried at St. Rose Catholic Church at Cloppers, Montgomery County. The only record in which we found the first name of Jonathan was birth and baptismal record of St. Rose of Lima Catholic Church at Cloppers, which listed the dates incorrectly as 1899 rather than 1879. Apparently commonly called Worthington Griffith. Married at the home of the bride November 12, 1907 to Lena Gertrude Gloyd, born March 5, 1880, died October 21, 1964, buried with her husband; daughter of Jacob Alexander Gloyd (1833) and his second wife, Ann Eliza Clements (1849) of Middlebrook. Four children:

1.   John Worthington Griffith, born October 14, 1908 at Laytonsville, died of a heart attack at his home June 7, 1967 at Gaithersburg, in Montgomery County, Maryland. Known as Jack to his many friends, he was active in civic affairs, serving as President of the local Lions Club and later as Deputy District Governor, Lions International. Elected to the Gaithersburg City Council in 1954, he became Mayor in 1966, serving in that capacity until his death. In honor of his many accom-

plishments and years of community service, the City of Gaithersburg and the Chamber of Commerce have established the John W. Griffith Summer Internship Award, presented each year to an outstanding student of Gaithersburg High School. Married November 15, 1929 at Grand Rapids, Michigan, to Jane Alice Clements, born February 7, 1910 at Detroit, daughter of Jouette Henry Clements (1883) of Shenandoah, Virginia, and Marguerite Alice Niles (1890) of Troy, Michigan. Two children:

a. Suzanne Clements Griffith, born December 7, 1938 and married first to Michael Dennis Flynn, born September 23, 1936; one child. She married second to Ralph Worthington Offutt, Jr., born July 29, 1937 and had two more children. He had been previously married also and had one child, adopted by the second marriage. Children:

(1) Lisa Kay Flynn, born May 31, 1958, and adopted by Suzanne's second husband.

(2) Pamela Elaine Offutt, born October 17, 1857; adopted by Suzanne.

(3) Jeffrey Worthington Offutt, born August 16, 1962

(4) Drew Griffith Offutt, born May 9, 1969

b. John Worthington Griffith, Jr., born May 30, 1943 and married to Mary Grace Broschart, born December 7, 1950. One child:

(1) John Worthington Griffith, III: February 23, 1972

2. Harrison Alexander Gloyd Griffith, born March 29, 1910, died January 29, 1975 at Suburban Hospital, Bethesda. Buried at St. Rose Catholic Church at Clopper. At the time of his death, they were living on DeSellum Avenue in Gaithersburg. Married to Catherine Cole Sappington of Libertytown, Maryland, born October 8, 1911. They had children:

a. Harrison Gloyd Griffith, born December 16, 1938 and became a priest, named Father Sydney.

b. Robert Cole Griffith, born May 2, 1944. Married Pamela Schettler and had children, including:

(1) Hilary Catherine Griffith, born February 1, 1975

   c. Michael Joseph Griffith, born May 7, 1945. Married first to Karayn Weichold and had a child. Married second to Jo Pfeiffer and had a child:

     (1) Sean Michael Griffith, born July 24, 1965, died September 15, 1865.

     (2) Mindy Lynn Griffith, born February 27, 1968

   d. Julia Marie Griffith, born June 19, 1947, and had a child:

     (1) Ian Harrison McNeil, born May 16, 1976

   e. Barbara Ann Griffith, born October 19, 1955

3. Dorsey Clements Griffith, born November 21, 1914, died February 6, 1953; buried at Mt. Olivet in Frederick. Married first to Marguerite Barr, divorced and married second May 13, 1939 in Winchester, Virginia, to Helen Maye Sadtler, born May 10, 1922, at Kemptown, daughter of Allan Philip Sadtler (1892) and Lorena Maye King (1900). Divorced after having two children, and Dorsey was married third to Katherine Beall. Children included at least:

   a. James Dorsey Griffith, born February 7, 1940, died January 16, 2000 at his son's home in Knoxville, Maryland. His birth name was Neal Leon Griffith, changed when he was adopted by his uncle and aunt, Douglas Augustine Griffith and Mary Opal Wiggins. The obituary of James D. "Rooster" Griffith rather clearly demonstrates that we are here dealing with the same individual. However, it reports his mother as being Ellen May Horman of Gaithersburg, and his wife as Hazel E. Griffith, to whom he was married to fifteen years; and a brother, Jerry A. Horman. His obituary reports that he was survived by seven children, and that two more predeceased their father. He was apparently first married to Cynthia Ann Voight, and had children:

     (1) Cynthia Lynn Griffith, born April 19, 1960; married to Codwell, and lived in Caton, North Carolina.

     (2) James Douglas Griffith, born March 30, 1961

     (3) Michael Dorsey Griffith, born August 7, 1962

     (4) William Earl Griffith, born July 29, 1963

     (5) Joseph Milligan Worthington Griffith, born September 12, 1964; reportedly lived in Wisconsin.

      (6) Abraham F. Brown, Sr., of Dover, Pennsylvania, perhaps a stepson from his second marriage.

      (7) Melvin E. Brown, Jr. of Dover, Pennsylvania, perhaps another stepson.

      (8) Kathy Steck, predeceased her father.

  b. Joyce Jean Griffith, born January 21, 1942, and married February 1, 1959 to Paul Xavier Reid, Jr., born July 3, 1940; they had two children. Married second Halbert Davidson, and had four children:

      (1) Anthony Eugene Reid, born September 13, 1959. Married Kimberly Weber and had children:

          (a) Lisa Reid, born March 30, 1981

          (b) Jacquelyn Reid, born May 2, 1982

      (2) Paul Xavier Reid, III, born February 7, 1963

      (3) Timothy Davidson, born January 19, 1965; married to Shelley Burkett.

      (4) Salina Marie Davidson, born October 12, 1966

      (5) Ronald Davidson, born December 5, 1968

      (6) Lorena Mae Davidson, born July 16, 1970

  c. Carol Ann Griffith; apparently had a child:

      (1) Ethna Lena Griffith.

4. Douglas Augustine Griffith, born December 11, 1918, died October 29, 1982 in Clyde, North Carolina. Married to Mary Opal Wiggins of Robinsville, North Carolina, born June 23, 1918. No children.

CHILD 10

Ulysses Griffith
1810-1869

This son of Henry Griffith (1767) and Mary Riggs (1768) was born September 28, 1810 and died January 7, 1869. Under his father's will, at the death or remarriage of his mother, Ulysses was to receive her part of the home plantation called *Retirement*, as well as negro slaves, livestock, farm equipment, crops and other personalty. Married April 19, 1838 in Montgomery County to Julia Riggs, born March 30, 1811, died April 13, 1886 in Baltimore at the home of her daughter, Mrs. George W. B. Bartlett; daughter of Reuben Riggs (1775) and Mary Thomas. Ulysses was head of household in the 1850 census of the county for the First District, with $3,800 in real estate, and the owner of fourteen slaves. His wife Julia was listed, with six of their children. In the agricultural census of 1850, he owned 200 acres of improved land and 114 acres unimproved, valued at $3,800 in total. He owned 7 horses, 12 milch cows, 2 working oxen, 4 other cattle, 17 sheep and 45 swine. In the previous year, he had produced 200 bushels of wheat, 750 bushels of Indian corn, 450 bushels of oats, 4,500 pounds of tobacco, 70 pounds of wool, 5 bushels of peas and beans, 200 bushels of Irish potatoes, 500 pounds of butter and 25 tons of hay. Ulysses was next found as head of household in the 1860 census of the First District, Laytonsville Post Office, listed near or adjacent to a group of five Griffith households. He then owned $24,000 in real estate and $24,000 in personal property, quite well-to-do for the time. His wife Julia was there, with seven of their children. Julia was found as head of household in the 1870 census of the county for the First District, perhaps widowed. She then had $6,600 in real estate, and $1,000 in personal property. Three of her children were still living at home, and there were four black domestic servants or laborers. Julia Griffith left a will in Montgomery County dated February 15, 1883, probated May 4, 1886, recorded in liber RWC 15 at folio 75, in which she named her children, with various bequests, generally relatively small amounts in cash (by today's standards), and personal items of furniture, silver and the like. She then notes that the cash bequests are nearly all then in the form of railroad bonds which the Executor is directed to sell. No mention was made of real estate, slaves, or farm items. The children were:

1. Henry Griffith, born April 4, 1839, of whom more.
2. Virginia Griffith, born November 3, 1840, died August 10, 1864
3. Amanda S. Griffith, born June 4, 1842, at home in 1870. Married November 26, 1872 to George W. B. Bartlett. Reportedly lived in Baltimore and had at least four children. In the 1900 census, however, he and Amanda were living in the household of her brother Harry, with two of their children. In that report, George Bartlett was listed as born April, 1850 and

Amanda as born June, 1849, seven years later than her apparent actual birth date. They were reported as married for thirty-five years and she had been the mother of four children, all living, and two then living with them. They were:

a. Vashti R. Bartlett, a daughter, born April, 1875

b. Alice Riggs Bartlett, born January 2, 1875, died February 2, 1964 at Passa Grille Beach, Florida. Buried in Rockville Cemetery with her husband. Married on November 11, 1920 at Ascension Chapel in Gaithersburg to Henry Hicks Griffith of Laytonsville, born January 15, 1862, died August 28, 1951, son of Uriah W. Griffith (1825) and Henrietta E. Wilcoxen (1821). No children.

4. Ulysses Griffith, Jr., born August 1, 1843, died April 28, 1929; buried at Goshen Methodist Cemetery. Married in the county June 17, 1868 to M. Blanche Linthicum, born October 10, 1847, died December 27, 1925 at her home near Laytonsville; daughter of Lloyd Linthicum. She was buried at Goshen Cemetery with her husband. They were living in their own household in the 1870 census of Montgomery County for the First District, next door to the household of his mother. He then owned $3,800 in real estate and $1,000 in personal property. He was listed as the head of household in the 1880 census of the county for the Cracklin District, but his wife was there interpreted from the microfilm as Mary A. of the proper age. Marriage records listed her as M. Blanche as we reported above, which may have been Mary Blanche, and we could have read her middle initial incorrectly from the census. Her obituary reports her name as Blanche M. Griffith. There is no evidence of a second marriage. The couple next appeared in the 1900 census of the county for the First District, with her name listed as Blanche. They had then been married for thirty-two years, and she had been the mother of two children, both living, with the son still at home. Ulysses Griffith left a will in Montgomery County dated May 20, 1924, probated May 28, 1929 and recorded in liber PEW 14 at folio 219. He left to his grandson Ulysses Griffith, IV his watch, and a cash bequest. The will names Margaret Linthicum, sister of his wife; Nettie E. Griffith, wife of his son Ulysses Griffith, Jr.; Annie E.

Griffith, daughter of his son Ulysses Griffith, Jr.; his son-in-law Humphrey D. Wolfe; and wife Blanche, who received all interest in the home farm. Children:

a. Ulysses Griffith, born January 29, 1871, died June 6, 1954; buried at Goshen Methodist with his wife. Married June 7, 1906 at Christ Episcopal Church in Rockville to Henrietta W. England, born July 29, 1871, died October 9, 1940 at her home in Laytonsville, daughter of John George England, Jr. (1847) and Ann L. Griffith (1849), and was the father of at least two children:

(1) Ann England Griffith, born August 8, 1909; married to Young, and mentioned in the obituary of her brother.

(2) Ulysses Griffith, IV, born January 8, 1908 at Laytonsville on the ancestral farm, which he later operated, and died September 24, 1978; buried there in the local cemetery. Married April 7, 1947 at Scranton, Pennsylvania to Marion Margaret Taylor, born there c.1915, and died September 26, 1977. She was a daughter of George Rodney Taylor of Scranton, and a school teacher at Gaithersburg Elementary School at the time of her marriage. Ulysses, known as Lit, was Chief Clerk of the District Court in Rockville, a former member of the House of Delegates, and former chairman of the Upper Montgomery County Planning Commission, and numerous other civic and political positions. They had two children:

(a) Jane Ann Griffith, born c.1952. In her early twenties, Jane Ann spent a year and a half in Swaziland, Africa as a Youth Development Programmer. She was also selected by the Maryland 4-H clubs to represent Maryland in Greece for several months. Married February 28, 1981 at Woodfield to Richard O. Evans, son of Mrs. LaRue B. Evans of Benton, Pennsylvania.

(b) Ulysses Griffith, V, born c.1954

b. Margaret Jones Griffith, born May 12, 1874. Married at the Goshen Methodist Church in November, 1899 to Humphrey Dorsey Wolfe of Howard County. He was then the member elect to the House of Delegates from Howard.

5. Julian Griffith, born June 10, 1846, died January 3, 1929 at his home near Darnestown. By the will of his brother Henry Griffith (liber HCA 22, folio 435, Montgomery County), Julian inherited all the tract of land called *Julian's Chance*. Married in the county May 5, 1870 to Mary Virginia Harper, born c.1848, died August 21, 1923 at her home near Darnestown, daughter of Richard Harper (1816), a wheelwright of Darnestown, and Rebecca Mackall (1821). Julian was head of household in the 1870 census of the county for the Fourth District, listed as a merchant, with $3,500 in real estate and $4,000 in personal property. His wife was there listed as Jennie, and there were no children yet born to their marriage. He was next head of household in the 1880 census of the county for the Sixth District, with his wife and five children. Julian was next head of household in the 1900 census of the county for the Sixth District, with his wife Mary, and four children. They had been married thirty years, and Mary had been the mother of eight children, all of them surviving. Children were:

a. Virginia Griffith, born March 21, 1871; baptized December 12, 1880 at Darnestown Presbyterian Church. Died February 24, 1950 at Potomac. She left a will in Montgomery County dated January 7, 1924, probated March 8, 1950 and recorded in liber WCC 18 at folio 107, in which she left all her estate to her brother Clyde, in trust, for the benefit of her father Julian, and then to pass on to Clyde at their father's death. Also mentioned was a niece Virginia Griffith of Chicago, and a sister Ethel Griffith Mullikin (sic) of Baltimore.

b. Julian Griffith, Jr., born May 20, 1873, died December 27, 1946, buried at Darnestown Cemetery. Listed as a school teacher in the 1900 census of the county for the Fifth District, living in the household of James G. Boss (1844).

c. H. Roland Griffith, born August 19, 1873, daughter. Not mentioned in the obituary of the father. Baptized December 12, 1880 at Darnestown Presbyterian Church.

d. Ethel Griffith, born June 12, 1875; married to Harwood Mullican and lived in Baltimore as of 1923.

e. Ulysses Griffith, born June 19, 1876; in 1923 living in Philadelphia.

f. Clyde Griffith, born March 17, 1880, baptized December 12, 1880 at Darnestown Presbyterian Church, died July 18, 1957 at Suburban Hospital; buried at Darnestown. Married August 14, 1920 at Epworth Methodist Church to Myra Landella Etchison, born August 18, 1890, baptized at Grace United Methodist Church, Gaithersburg, died August 4, 1954; the daughter of Doctor Elias Henning Etchison (1856) and Charlotte A. Ward (1865) of Gaithersburg. Children:

   (1) Alice M. Griffith; in Frankfort, Germany at the time of her father's death. She died single March 4, 1983 at Tucson, Arizona, and is buried there.

   (2) Patricia Griffith, married Harry Biondi and had at least two children, including:

      (a) Stephen R. Biondi.

g. A. Wirtie Griffith, born May 12, 1881. In the 1900 census of the Sixth District, this child is listed at home, reported as Willie, a daughter. Not mentioned in the obituary of the father or the mother. She is probably Amanda Griffith, who was baptized November 4, 1894, and died July 25, 1923, according to records of Darnestown Presbyterian Church, and reported there as a daughter of this family. Cemetery records of the Darnestown Presbyterian Church report Amanda B. Griffith, born 1881, and died 1923 at Seneca, buried in the Julian Griffith plot, apparently this individual. Amanda Bartlett Griffith left a will in Montgomery County, probably this individual. It was dated April 8, 1916, probated September 19, 1923 and recorded in liber PEW 2 at folio 22, leaving the entire estate to her sister Virginia Griffith (see above).

h. Reginald Griffith, born June 3, 1883; in 1923 living in Chicago.

6. Mary Alice Griffith, born March 11, 1850, at home in 1870. Married December 19, 1876 to John S. Larcombe. Lived in District of Columbia.

7. William Riggs Griffith, born April 19, 1852, died December 1, 1921 of heart trouble at his home near Laytonsville. Buried at Rock Creek Cemetery in Washington. In his obituary, three married daughters are listed by the husbands' names: Mrs. H. K. Fleck of Baltimore; Mrs. William Riggs of Howard County; and Mrs. David Clark. Following, we have listed three daughters by their birth names, who apparently are the wives of these three listed spouses, but matches not yet determined. William R. was living at home in 1870, listed as a farmer, with $2,000 in real estate and $1,000 in personal property. Married May 2, 1872 in the county to Isabelle Griffith, born December 14, 1852, daughter of Richard H. Griffith, Jr. (1828) and Susan Barbour (1831). The *Sentinel* reported the celebration of her eightieth birthday in 1932, at the home of her son-in-law Harvey K. Fleck in Baltimore. The article noted that she had seven children, fifteen grandchildren and fifteen great grandchildren. Head of household in the 1880 census of the county for the Cracklin District, he was listed as Willie R. Griffith, with his wife Isabella and three children. Living with the family was Julia (Riggs) Griffith at the age of sixty-nine, mother of William R. Griffith. William R. was next found as head of household in the 1900 census of the county for the First District, with his wife Isabella and their three youngest children still at home. They had been married twenty-eight years, and Isabella had been the mother of seven children, with six surviving. Living with them was Richard H. Griffith, his father-in-law, and Frances C. Griffith (1852), listed as his mother-in-law. The latter couple, Richard and Frances, had then been married nine years, with no children, obviously a third marriage for Richard H. Griffith. William Riggs Griffith left a will in Montgomery County, dated December 10, 1896, probated January 10, 1922 and recorded in liber HCA 26 at folio 177. The first child following, who was

an infant death, is not mentioned; each of the other six children were listed to receive $25 each, with all the rest and residue of the estate to his wife Isabella Griffith. The children were:

a. William Vernon Griffith, born July 23, 1873, and died August 8, 1874

b. Lycurgus Matthew Griffith, born November 26, 1875, died February 19, 1951 at the home of his daughter in New Orleans. Buried at St. John's Cemetery in Olney. In the 1880 census, there was a child listed at the age of five years, but interpreted from the microfilm as Kirke M. Griffith. As Lycurgus M. Griffith he was head of household in the 1900 census of Montgomery County for the First District, with a wife reported there as Minnie R., born March, 1874. They had been married two years, with one child. The *Sentinel* reported that Lycurgus Matthew Griffith was married November 22, 1898 at St. Bartholomew's Church in Unity to Minnie W. Riggs, died January 25, 1964 in Covington, Louisiana, daughter of Elisha Riggs (1845). A family group sheet found in the family file at the library of the Montgomery County Historical Society lists her name as Milcah W. Riggs, which is also the way it was reported in the 1880 census of the Cracklin District, when she was a nine-year old listed with her parents. Cemetery records of St. John's Episcopal in Olney report her name as Milcah R., born c.1873, died c.1964; buried with her husband. It is evident from obituaries that they had other children:

(1) Olivia Meyers Griffith, born November, 1899. Married on August 9, 1924 at Christ Episcopal Church in Rockville, to Milburn Simpers Waters, born c.1899, and died November 7, 1981 at the Wilson Health Care Center in Gaithersburg. He was the son of Franklin Waters (1869) and Harriet Roberta Watkins (1872). Known to all his friends as "Booze" Waters, he was for many years employed by King Pontiac, Gaithersburg, and was buried at Neelsville Presbyterian Church cemetery.

(2) Lycurgus Matthew Griffith, Jr., born April 25, 1905, died December 24, 1983 at the Collingswood Nursing Home in Rockville; buried at Forest Oak Cemetery in Gaithersburg. His obituary listed his name as Lycurgus Matthew (Kirk) Griffith, reflecting the entry in the 1880 census, discussed above. Married June 29, 1929 at Epworth Methodist Church to Clarice Helen Kingsley, born November 25, 1906, and died June 26, 1993 at Collingswood; daughter of Harold Sherwood Kingsley and Carrie Crawford of Gaithersburg. They had a son:

(a) Lycurgus Matthew (Kirk) Griffith, III, married to Genevieve and had three children:
1. Matthew Griffith.
2. Paul Griffith.
3. Joanna Griffith, married to Allen.

(3) Marshall P. H. Griffith, mentioned in his father's obituary as living in Alexandria.

(4) Mildred Wayman Griffith, born May 15, 1901; married Evarts Wagg of Sykesville; lived at Silver Spring. Her birth record at St. Bartholomew's Episcopal Church reports that she was a daughter of Lycurgus M. Griffith and Milcah W. Griffith (not Minnie W.).

(5) Agnes Riggs Griffith, born July 11, 1907; married to Richard Barton, of Covington, Louisiana.

(6) Margaret Griffith, married to Judson Earle of Covington, Louisiana.

(7) William Riggs Griffith, born April 19, 1908, died May 25, 1962 at Key West, Florida. Married to Babette Everette and had children:
(a) Betsy R. Griffith.
(b) William R. Griffith.
(c) Henry H. Griffith.

c. Florence Anderson Griffith, born May 18, 1877; at home in 1880 census. Married May 12, 1897 at *Retirement* to David W. Clark December, 1875. He was head of household in the 1900 census of Montgomery County for the

First District, with Florence, married three years, and one child:

(1) Isabella Clark, born July, 1899

d. William Waters Griffith, born May 14, 1879 at the family home of *Retirement* at Laytonsville, died October 5, 1959 at the Simpson Nursing Home in Boyds; buried at Laytonsville with his wife. This may be the same as William Griffith, of the proper age, listed alone in his own household in the 1900 census of the county, First District, single, a salesman. Married December 5, 1912 at the home of the bride's parents to Jessie Higgins Magruder, born c.1888, died February 19, 1973, and was buried at the Laytonsville Cemetery; daughter of Robert P. Magruder of Grifton. He was a plumbing and heating contractor and active in the Redland Hunt. There were two daughters:

(1) Genevieve Magruder Griffith, born March 25, 1921. Married November 8, 1941 to Frederick Donald Cissel, born c.1915, of Silver Spring, son of Henry H. Cissel and Bertha Scaggs.

(2) Dorothy Isabelle Griffith, born January 12, 1924; married to Joyner.

e. Jeffrey Magruder Griffith, born November 14, 1881, died in June, 1947 at Retirement Farm. Married at Neelsville March 31, 1910 to Lillian Neel, daughter of James Neel. She was born c.1883 and died October 18, 1967 on the home farm at Laytonsville; buried at Neelsville with her husband. Her obituary mentions children, and their place of residence as of 1967:

(1) Kathryn Griffith, married to Doane of Baltimore.

(2) Isabella Griffith, married to Willett of the home farm

(3) Jeffrey Magruder Griffith, Jr., born July 13, 1913, died at home January 24, 1960; buried with parents.

f. Isabelle Griffith, born June 23, 1885

g. Susan Matilda Griffith, born December 29, 1888; married first to William H. Riggs and second to Gordon Hobbs and lived in Baltimore.

Henry Griffith
1839-1920

This son of Ulysses Griffith (1810) and Julia Riggs (1811), was born April 4, 1839, died November 24, 1920; buried at Goshen Cemetery. Married to Alverda Griffith, born August 9, 1848, the daughter of Lebbeus Griffith and Sarah Ann Wood. The obituary of Alverda appearing in the *Montgomery County Sentinel* states that she died November 15, 1915 near Laytonsville, and that she was then aged 78 years, which would place her birth as c.1837, which is eleven years earlier than her birth date reported from other sources. Cemetery records at Goshen Methodist Church report her birth as c.1848, which is probably correct. There is no question of her identity; the obituary reports the name of her husband and the married names of three surviving daughters. Head of household in the 1870 census of Montgomery County for the First District, he was listed there as Henry Griffith, which is probably more accurate. He then had $5,000 in real estate and $1,000 in personal property. His wife was listed as Verda, and they then had their first child at home. Living with them was Eliza A. Riggs, born c.1830, relationship not stated. Next found as head of household in the 1880 census of the Cracklin District, he was listed as Harry, his wife as Verda, and they had two daughters. Living with them was Eliza Riggs, reported as born c.1816, perhaps the same individual as found in 1870, but with a difference in age reporting. As Harry Griffith, he was next found as head of household in the 1900 census of the county for the First District, with his wife Alverda (there read as Alvertha), and one daughter, there listed as Verdie. Living with them was Harry's sister Amanda and her husband George W. Bartlett (1850), with two of their children.

Henry Griffith left a will in Montgomery County, dated August 7, 1907, probated December 7, 1920, and recorded in liber HCA 22 at folio 435. He begins the will by leaving the sum of $500 to each of his grandchildren, without naming them. He left to his brother Julian Griffith all of the tract called Julian's Chance, and to his wife Alverda a large sum of cash, and for her lifetime, the farm inherited from this father, supposed to contain about 320 acres. His will mentions an Equity Case in 1869 filed in liber EBP

6, at folio 92, which we have not examined. It apparently was what is known as a "friendly suit" within a family to settle his father's estate, and could contain some genealogical information. He names his own three children, who were:

1. Julia Riggs Griffith, born July 9, 1869, died January 1, 1920, buried near the town of Laytonsville at Goshen Methodist with her husband. Married at Goshen in Montgomery County December 10, 1890 to Nathan Smith White, born December 11, 1864, died January 31, 1907, the son of Richard Thomas White (1829) and Mary Elizabeth Waters (1830). Julia received a specific bequest of cash and a dozen silver desert spoons in her grandmother's will. Children:

   a. Harry Griffith White, born c.1892, baptized May 12, 1901 at Rockville Methodist, died 1948; buried at Laytonsville cemetery with his wife and a son. Married January 3, 1914 to Margaret Howard Riggs, born April 3, 1895, died October 27, 1978 at her home in Laytonsville, the daughter of L. Elgee Riggs and Anna (Riggs) Riggs. Children:

      (1) Alverda Griffith White, born December 11, 1914. Married January 2, 1937 to Richard William Wotthlie, born June 15, 1912, died March 17, 1971 and had five children:
         (a) Margaret Ann Wotthlie, born October 20, 1939
         (b) Patricia Ann Wotthlie: May 24, 1942
         (c) Mary Estelle Wotthlie: July 3, 1945
         (d) Judith Ann Wotthlie: July 27, 1948
         (e) Richard William Wotthlie, Jr.

      (2) Margaret Riggs White, born April 15, 1916 near Laytonsville. Married June 4, 1938 in Olney, to Douglas Howard Riggs, Jr., born July 31, 1913 in Brookeville, Maryland, died August 15, 1974 at Laytonsville. Three children:
         (a) Nancy Lee Riggs, born July 13, 1941; married October 21, 1961 to Robert Brawner Harding and had three children.
         (b) Douglas Howard Riggs, III, born May 8, 1944.
         (c) Linda Ann Riggs, born October 30, 1948.

(3) Harry Griffith White, Jr., born February 15, 1922 near Laytonsville, baptized December 3, 1922 at St. Bartholomew's Episcopal Church, died October 15, 1924; buried at Goshen Methodist Church.

(4) Richard Thomas White, born March 13, 1924, baptized October 22, 1939. Married June 5, 1948 to LaVerna Ray Miller, born August 13, 1925. Three children, born in Baltimore:

    (a) Karen Lorraine White: November 24, 1949
    (b) Barbara Jean White, born January 14, 1952
    (c) Diane Lee White, born December 29, 1953

(5) Mary Waters White, born January 16, 1926; married June 12, 1947 her cousin, Mansfield White Daniel, born June 13, 1918 in West Virginia, died March 20, 1994 at Asbury Methodist Home, in Gaithersburg, Montgomery County, Maryland; the son of William Aglionby Daniel (1878) and Elsie Lee White (1889). Three children.

(6) Anne Riggs White, born August 13, 1931, baptized October 22, 1939, St. Bartholomew's Episcopal Church. Married February 21, 1952 to Maurice Crittenden King, born February 21, 1922, son of Leslie Crittenden King (1896), and Bertha Marie Beall (1901), and had children:

    (a) Maurice Crittenden King, Jr., born November 27, 1957
    (b) Ann Lyn King, born August 8, 1959. Married to Steven Palmer, and had children: Amy Nichole Palmer, born January 4, 1986; and Stephen Joseph Palmer, born October 29, 1987
    (c) Jane Marie King, born June 14, 1963. Married to Bertali Rojas, born April 24, 1954. Child: Mauricio Rojas, born January 29, 1996

b. Nathan Smith White, Jr., born October 22, 1894. Married February 2, 1917 to Marguerite Welti, born July 14, 1898 Washington, D. C. and died May 18, 1986; daughter of Oswald Welti and Adelaide Cauldfield. Children:

(1) Nathan Smith White, III, born July 7, 1928. Married to Barbara Lee Adamson, born March 12, 1927, daughter of Leonidas Wells Adamson and Mabel Olivia Gaither, and had two children:
    (a) Nathan Smith White, IV, born April 7, 1955
    (b) Sharon Lee White, born August 9, 1956 and married to McFarland.
(2) John Welti White, born February 10, 1935. Married April 22, 1967 to Mary Ella Hill, born May 1, 1937, and had two children:
    (a) John Welti White, Jr., born May 29, 1969
    (b) Marguerite Louise White: October 11, 1971

c. Mary Waters White, born c.1896, died September 1, 1980 at Shady Grove Hospital, single. Lived in Gaithersburg, and was a retired Lieutenant Commander in the US Navy Nurses Corps. Buried at Goshen cemetery.

2. Sarah Maude Griffith, born July 14, 1872, died September 4, 1961. Married December 17, 1895 at the Goshen Methodist Church to Zadoc Magruder Cooke, born August 13, 1865, died March 28, 1944, son of Nathan Cooke (1829) and Harriet Ann Waters (1840). Head of household in the 1900 census of the county for the Ninth District, Zadoc and Sarah had been married for 4 years, and had one child. Living with them was his sister, Nannie Cook, born c.1868. The child was:

a. Alverda Griffith Cooke, born November 25, 1897

3. Alverda Griffith, born August 3, 1881; married to Balthis.

William Griffith
died 1699
The Immigrant
Chapter 2
*

*

Orlando Griffith
1688
*

*

Henry Griffith
1720
Chapter 4
*

*

Henry Griffith, Jr.
1744
*

*

Nicholas Griffith
1771
Chapter 6
*

*

*   *   *   *   *   *   *   *   *
*
*   * Sarah Ridgely Griffith 1792
*
*   * Nicholas Griffith, Jr. 1793
*
*   * Charles Henry Griffith 1796
*
*   * Mary Ann Griffith 1798
*
*   * Harriet Griffith 1800
*
*   * Nicholas Griffith, Jr. 1801
*
*   * Thomas G. Griffith 1803

CHAPTER 6

Nicholas Griffith
1771-1803

This son of Henry Griffith (1744) and Sarah Warfield (1746) was born November 10, 1771, and died August 5, 1803, the youngest son. Buried at *Edgehill Farm* near Laytonsville. Married December 16, 1791 to Anne Ridgely, born October 8, 1771, died March 26, 1861, daughter of Charles Greenberry Ridgely (1735) and Sarah Macgill (1737). Anne Ridgely Griffith was buried on *Edgehill Farm* near Laytonsville, and a note on the cemetery card at the Historical Society library in Rockville states that a relative says her name should be Nancy Anne Ridgely Griffith. Children:

1. Sarah Ridgely Griffith, born September 19, 1792, died March 31, 1866. Married in Montgomery County January 23, 1808 to Amos Brown of Philadelphia, died December 8, 1845. Sarah R. Brown appeared as head of household in the 1850 census of the First Election District of Montgomery County, a widow, with $6,000 in real estate. There were then six children still at home. Living with them was Anna Griffith, reported there as born c.1772, who would have been her widowed mother. In the 1850 census, Sarah R. Brown was listed as owning eight slaves. In the Agricultural Census of 1850, Sarah was listed as owning 240 acres of improved land and 93 acres unimproved at $6,000 value. She owned 6 horses, 7 milch cows, 2 working oxen, 1 other cattle, 12 sheep and 21 swine. In the previous twelve months, she had produced 150 bushels of wheat, 500 bushels of Indian corn, 400 bushels of oats, 40 pounds of wool, 1 bushel of peas and beans, 35 bushels of Irish potatoes, 450 pounds of butter, 10 tons of hay, 4 pounds of hops, and 35 pounds of beeswax and honey. Sarah and Amos Brown had children:

   a. William Brown, born April 17, 1809, died July 1, 1809
   b. Amos Brown, Jr., born June 17, 1810
   c. Annie Griffith Brown, born October 10, 1811, died April 24, 1892, single. At home in 1850.

d. William N. Brown, born January 5, 1814, died September 20, 1868. Married c.1838 to Elizabeth R. Walker and had four children.

e. Elizabeth R. Brown, born August 7, 1815, died January 15, 1881, single. At home in 1850.

f. Louisa M. Brown, born January 26, 1817, died February 24, 1857, single. At home in 1850.

g. Sarah R. Brown, born October 8, 1818, died February 23, 1839

h. Harriet A. Brown, born July 14, 1821, died August 26, 1833

i. Mary E. Brown, born May 7, 1823, died May 21, 1858, single. At home in 1850.

j. Henrietta Brown, born October 19, 1825, died August 13, 1833.

k. Amos P. Brown, born July 26, 1827, died November 27, 1887. Lived at Philadelphia.

l. Alice C. Brown, born May 15, 1829, died May 23, 1846

m. Lydia H. Brown, born July 7, 1831, died July 30, 1889. At home in 1850. Married January 17, 1856 to Washington Bowie Chichester, and had children. He was head of household in the 1860 census of the First District of Montgomery County, listed as born c.1828 in Virginia and owning $6,000 in real estate and $6,700 in personal property. Lydia was present, and they then had three children at home. He was next found as head of household in the 1870 census of the First District, with $8,000 in real estate and $2,000 in personal property. Lydia was still present, and there were then four children at home. Also listed in the household were six black individuals, domestic servants, farm laborer and children. In the 1880 census of the Eighth District, father and mother are present, with five children at home. There were also five black servants listed. There is an interesting listing first appearing there; the father of Lydia was noted as having been born in New Hampshire. The children of Lydia and Washington Bowie were:

     (1) Margaret B. Chichester, born c.1856. Married January, 1890 to Warrington Gillet Smith and lived at Baltimore.

     (2) Lydia Hanson Chichester, born c.1859

     (3) Harriet R. Chichester, born c.1859

     (4) Washington Bowie Chichester, Jr., born c.1868. Married in the county by license dated December 21, 1891 to Eliza M. Hallowell, born October, 1867. He was head of household in the 1900 census of the Eighth District, with his wife, and four children. They had been married eight years, and she had been the mother of five children, with four surviving and at home. In the household was one black servant. Children:

         (a) Robert H. Chichester, born December, 1893

         (b) Lydia Chichester, born July, 1894

         (c) Sarah Chichester, born September, 1895

         (d) Ridgely B. Chichester, born February, 1899

     (5) Mary R. Chichester.

  n. Ridgely Brown, born November 13, 1833, Lt. Col., 1st Maryland Cavalry, CSA; killed June 1, 1864 near Ashland, Virginia in a skirmish with Sheridan's Cavalry. At home in 1850, listed as a student.

2. Nicholas Griffith, Jr., born December 17, 1793, died August 5, 1794

3. Henrietta Griffith, born April 14, 1795, died March 7, 1864; married July 10, 1819 to William Penniman and lived at Baltimore.

4. Charles Henry Griffith, born December 20, 1796, died January 6, 1797

5. Mary Ann Griffith, born April 21, 1798; married March, 1821 to John Hathaway; no children.

6. Harriet Griffith, born May 17, 1800, died August 12, 1874, single. Buried at St. John's Episcopal Church cemetery, Olney. She left a will in Montgomery County, dated October 6, 1870, probated August 24, 1874, and recorded in liber RWC 6 at folio 67. Harriet left her entire estate for life to her niece Lydia Hanson Chichester, and at her death, to Lydia's children.

7. Nicholas Griffith, Jr., born November 9, 1801, second use of the name after the earlier infant death. Married twice and had descendants in Pittsburg, Pennsylvania.

8. Thomas G. Griffith, born September 15, 1803, died January 9, 1870. Married in Montgomery County November 1, 1825 to Elizabeth Griffith, born April 8, 1800, died April 3, 1860, daughter of Colonel Lyde Griffith and Anne (Poole) Dorsey. Thomas Griffith was head of household in the 1850 census of the First District, with $4,000 in real estate. His wife Elizabeth was listed, and they then had the five youngest children at home. Listed in the household were two black laborers. In the 1850 census, Thomas was listed as owning ten slaves. He then owned 185 acres of improved land and 200 acres unimproved, with $4,000 total value. He owned 6 horses, 7 milch cows, 2 working oxen, 7 other cattle, 23 sheep and 45 swine, the livestock valued at $1,100 total. In the previous year, he had produced 200 bushels of wheat, 1,125 bushels of Indian corn, 650 bushels of oats, 60 pounds of wool, 1 bushel of peas and beans, 75 bushels of Irish potatoes, 300 pounds of butter, and 12 tons of hay. He was next found as head of household in the 1860 census of the First District, Laytonsville Post Office, quite wealthy for the period. He was a farmer, and owned $15,000 in real estate and $17,700 in personal property. Living with him was his mother Ann (sic), then reported as eighty-eight years of age, and probably a widow. Also living with him was his sister Harriet, then sixty years old. Three of his children were also at home, but no wife, she having died about two months before the taking of the census. Our subject here is quite possibly the same Thomas Griffith who was listed in the 1867-1868 Slave Census of Montgomery County, as the owner of fifteen slaves, nine of them bearing the King surname. Thomas Griffith left a will in Montgomery County dated September 13, 1869, probated February 15, 1870 and recorded in liber JWS 1 at folio 317. To his sons Thomas and Franklin, he left the farm purchased from Samuel R. Gaither, containing 160 acres of *Bostick*. He left cash, US bonds, railroad bonds and personal notes to his daughter Mary Ann, and directed that the rest of the estate be divided between five

named children, apparently those surviving: Thomas, Mary Ann, David, Festus and Franklin. They had children:

a. William Penniman Griffith, born October 2, 1826, died December 26, 1846. Buried on *Edgehill Farm* near Laytonsville.

b. Nicholas R. Griffith, born October 10, 1828, died January 22, 1864. Buried on *Edgehill Farm* near Laytonsville. Married to Mary S. Jones, who died March 20, 1899 in Baltimore, no children. Her *Sentinel* obituary stated that she was a sister of the late Josiah W. and Gustavus Jones, and Mrs. Enoch Hutton. We found Nicholas R. Griffith as head of household in the 1860 census of Montgomery County for the First District, living alone with his wife. He was quite wealthy for the time period, with $38,000 in real estate and $70,000 in personal property.

c. Thomas G. Griffith, Jr., born April 29, 1831, died July 13, 1912 near Olney. At home in the 1860 census, listed as a farm manager. He was Captain, Co. A., 1st Maryland Cavalry, CSA. Married first in Montgomery County by license dated March 2, 1869 to Elizabeth Davis Singleton, born April 28, 1838, died April 10, 1876. Buried at St. John's Episcopal Church cemetery, Olney, she was reportedly the daughter of John Singleton and Anne Bowie. (The *Sentinel* obituary of Elizabeth Singleton states that she was the daughter of the late Thomas D. Singleton and Anne Bowie of Easton, Talbot County, Maryland; as does *Across the Years in Prince George's County*, by Effie Gwynn Bowie; which is probably correct). He was married second September 20, 1877 to Sarah J. Ball, born May 29, 1832 in Virginia, daughter of Thomas Ball (1794) and Ann Randolph McNeal. Thomas Griffith appeared as head of household in the 1870 census of the First District of Montgomery County, with his wife Elizabeth and their first child, then just four months old. Thomas was listed as a farmer, with $2,000 in real estate and $8,000 in personal property. In the 1880 census of the county for the Eighth District, Thomas and

Sarah were listed with four children. Living with them was Ginney W. Ball, born c.1855, a teacher, listed as sister-in-law. Thomas G. Griffith was head of household in the 1900 census of the county for the Eighth District, with his wife Sarah and four of his children. He and Sarah had been married for twenty-two years, and she had no children. Living with them was F. W. Ball, born July, 1834, single, female, a teacher, listed as sister-in-law. Children born to the first marriage only:

(1) Nicholas Ridgely Griffith, born February 18, 1870, died October 5, 1947 at Montgomery General. Records of St. John's Episcopal Church report that he was about 83 years of age at the time of death.

(2) William Dulley Griffith, according to census, born September 1, 1871, died March 19, 1935, buried at St. John's Episcopal in Olney; served in US Artillery 1898-1899. In the obituary of his father, this child is listed as William Dallas Griffith, which appears to be correct.

(3) Anne Singleton Griffith, born December 31, 1872, died June 16, 1918 of acute nephritis in Baltimore, single. She left a will in Montgomery County, dated June 13, 1918, probated July 16, 1918, and recorded in liber HCA 19 at folio 485. She left cash bequests to her two brothers, identified only by their initials as N. R. Griffith and W. D. Griffith; and all of her interest in the farm left by their father. To her sister, not named, but obviously Charlotte, she left all her interest in the farm left by their mother, and named her Executrix of the estate. She also named two cousins, Frances Spurrier and Catherine Spurrier, and the Vestry of St. John's Episcopal in Olney, for cemetery maintenance.

(4) Charlotte Elizabeth Griffith, born October 22, 1874, died April 29, 1967, buried at St. John's Episcopal Church, Olney. Married to William J. P. Farquhar.

d.   Edward Griffith, born June 2, 1833, died c.1857

e. Mary Ann Griffith, born March 8, 1835, died May 1, 1890; at home in the 1860 census. She was buried on *Edgehill Farm* near Laytonsville. Married June 6, 1871 to Richard H. Lansdale; no children. He was head of household in the 1880 census of Montgomery County for the Cracklin District, born c.1838. His wife Mary A. was keeping house and they had living with them Annie Griffith, born c.1873, listed as a niece, then in school. From her age, we would suggest that she was Anne Singleton Griffith, just above, daughter of Mary's brother Thomas Griffith, Jr.

f. David Griffith, born April 9, 1837, died January 28, 1914; buried at Rockville Cemetery. Private, Co. A, 1st Maryland Cavalry, CSA; enlisted from Redland, Montgomery County. Married May 29, 1867 to Anne S. Taylor, born January 10, 1836 in the District of Columbia. He was a Judge of the Orphans' Court of Montgomery County. In the 1860 census of the county, for the First District, he was living alone, two doors from the household of his father, listed as a farmer, with $400 in real estate. David was next found as head of household in the 1870 census of the county for the First District, with $3,000 in real estate and $2,000 in personal property. His wife Anna S. was present, born c.1837, and they then had two children. He was head of household in the 1880 census of the county for the Cracklin District, with his wife Anna S. and three children at home. Head of household in the 1900 census of Montgomery County for the First District, he was listed as a farmer, with his wife Ann and two of their children. Living with them were three black servants and Martha L. Taylor, born c.1837, a single sister-in-law. David and Ann had been married 33 years, and she had been the mother of three children, all living, with the two youngest still at home. An obituary in the *Sentinel* reported that Mrs. Anne Stone Griffith, aged 87, widow of Judge David Griffith, died May 23, 1923 at her home near Redland, and was buried in Rockville Cemetery. We assume that to be the same Anne S. Taylor reported as his bride (with both her given names). David Griffith left a will in Montgomery County dated January 2, 1908, probated February 3, 1914 and recorded in liber HCA 14 at folio 287. He there named his wife as Ann Stone Griffith, one son, and two daughters. They had children:

(1) Elizabeth Griffith, born April 9, 1868. Married in Montgomery County at Christ Episcopal Church in Rockville, March 1, 1894 to Walter W. Mobley, born February 23, 1869, son of William B. Mobley (1843) and Louisa Hood Griffith (1845). Walter was head of household in the 1900 census of the county for the Fourth District, he and Elizabeth had been married for six years, with three children:

    (a) Louise G. Mobley, born December, 1894

    (b) William B. Mobley, born May, 1896

    (c) Alice S. Mobley, born April, 1898

(2) Harriet Mackall Griffith, born June 11, 1869, died single February 8, 1962 at Suburban Hospital. Buried at Rockville Cemetery.

(3) Thomas David Griffith, born January 29, 1871 at Redland, Montgomery County, died June 8, 1959 in St. Petersburg, Florida, where he had been living in retirement; buried at Rockville Cemetery, Maryland. Married January 12, 1910 to Laura Worthington Bradley, formerly of Rockville, born c.1875, died August 14, 1954 in St. Petersburg; buried at Union Cemetery in Rockville. She was daughter of George G. Bradley of Potomac, Maryland. No children. She left a will in Montgomery County dated November 8, 1946 in which she mentioned her husband by name, but left three cash bequests to a niece and two nephews: Laura G. Bradley; Charles Bradley and George G. Bradley. A codicil dated October 27, 1950 noted that her husband was by then deceased.

g.   Festus Griffith, born July 12, 1838 at the family farm of *Edgehill Farm* near Laytonsville. Captain, Co. H, 8th Virginia Infantry, CSA. He participated in the battles of

Manassas, Ball's Bluff, Yorktown, Williamsburg, Seven Pines, and the siege of Richmond. Wounded in the hip at the second battle of Manassas, and captured in 1864 in the Valley of Virginia; exchanged that fall in Savannah, Georgia. He was a merchant in Baltimore until about 1870, when he went to Texas for the next four years, before returning to Maryland. Married June 28, 1871 to Avolina Riggs, born July 7, 1838, died January 25, 1892, daughter of Elisha Riggs (1810) and Avolina Warfield; no children. In the 1880 census of the county for the Eighth District, they were in the household of her parents, with no children.

h. Franklin Griffith, born October 29, 1840, died July 28, 1892 at his home near Brookeville; at home in the 1860 census. Buried on *Edgehill Farm*, near the town of Laytonsville. Lieutenant, Co. A, 1st Maryland Cavalry, CSA. Married Montgomery County by license dated January 5, 1869 to Katherine L. Riggs, born March 2, 1844, died of heart failure June 28, 1914 near Unity, daughter of Doctor Artemus Riggs and Amanda Warfield. Buried on the family estate called *Edgehill Farm* near Laytonsville. In the 1870 census of Montgomery County for the First District, he is listed as a farmer, with his real estate valued at $10,000 and $2,600 in personal property. At the time, they had living with them Georgina White, born c.1848, as a domestic servant, and Mary A. Griffith, born c.1837, perhaps a sister of Artemus. There are also four black servants and farm laborers living in the household. Franklin was head of household in the 1880 census of the county for the Cracklin District, with his wife, and their two children both at home. In that census, his wife Kate was reported as born in Ohio. They had children:

(1) Frances I. Griffith, born September 24, 1871. Married at the home of her mother near Unity January 26, 1898 to Doctor Henry G. Spurrier. In the 1900 census of the First District of Montgomery County, he was listed as head of household, but there entered

as Harry G. Spurrier, born c.1866. He and Frances had been married 2 years, and there was one child:

    (a) Catherine G. Spurrier, born August, 1899

(2) Artemus Riggs Griffith, born May 10, 1874, died 1938; buried in *Edgehill Farm* family cemetery near Laytonsville. Married in Montgomery County at St. Bartholomew's Episcopal Church at Unity by license dated October 24, 1898 to Hattie Maynard Colliflower, born November, 1876. He was head of household in the 1900 census of the county for the First District, with his wife. They had been married one year, and had one son. Living with them was his mother, Kate L. Riggs Griffith (1844), and also his grandmother Amanda (Warfield) Riggs, then listed at seventy-eight years of age. Their children were:

    (a) Frank Riggs Griffith, born August 18, 1899, died February 29, 1936; buried at Mt. Carmel.

    (b) Helen Lucretia Griffith, born May 11, 1901, died July 25, 1901; buried in the family cemetery on *Edgehill Farm* at Laytonsville.

William Griffith
died 1699
The Immigrant
Chapter 2
*

Orlando Griffith
1688
*

Henry Griffith
1720
Chapter 4
*

Samuel Griffith
1752
Chapter 7
*

*   *   *   *   *   *   *   *   *
*
*   * Lyde Griffith 1774
*
*   * Samuel B. Griffith 1780
*
*   * Walter Griffith 1781
*
*   * Alfred Griffith 1783
*
*   * Ruth H. Griffith 1784
*
*   * Mary Griffith 1785
*
*   * Richard H. Griffith 1787
*
*   * Henry G. Griffith 1788
*
*   * Horatio Griffith 1790
*
*   * Sarah Griffith 1792
*
*   * Philemon Griffith 1794
*
*   * Michael Berry Griffith 1796

CHAPTER 7

Samuel Griffith
1752-1833

This son of Henry Griffith (1720) and his second wife, Ruth Hammond, was born May 7, 1752, and died May 12, 1833, first child from the second marriage. As early as 1777, he owned a working plantation in the Upper Part of Newfoundland Hundred, and is buried at Laytonsville, in Montgomery County. Under the will of his father, he inherited the plantation on which he was living at the time of his father's death, supposed to contain 500 acres, and adjoining the tracts called *That's All* and *Damascus Plains*, next to the plantations left to his brothers Henry and Joshua.

Captain, 7th Co., 3rd Battalion Regulars, Continental Army. January 24, 1775, appointed to Frederick County Committee of Observation. Served in the Revolution at the Battle of Brandywine. His military service and the applications for pension, as well as some general family history, are all set forth in *Revolutionary Patriots of Montgomery County, Maryland 1776-1783*, by Henry C. Peden, Jr., which is recommended reading.

Samuel was married first to Rachel Warfield, born October 1, 1757, died December 28, 1775, daughter of John Warfield of John and Rachel Dorsey. Samuel was married second April 1, 1779 to Ruth Berry, died May 23, 1846, daughter of Richard Berry (1732) and Sarah Dorsey (1739) and had children. Under his father's will, he received the plantation upon which he was living, known as *That's All* and *Inman's Plains*. His descendants have spread all across the country. Samuel's second wife, Ruth, left a will in Montgomery County, dated 1845, probated June 16, 1846, recorded in liber Z at folio 439, rerecorded in liber VMB 4 at page 413. To her daughter Ruth H. Griffith, she left the lot where testator then lived, containing about 21 acres, plus another lot of 21 and 3/4 acres, and also the slaves, crops, animals and other personalty. To her daughter Sarah Lyons, she left $250. She then named several children, who were to receive ten dollars, divided between them: sons Alfred; Richard H.; Philemon; Horatio; Michael; Israel; Berry; heirs of

Henry B.; daughters Mary Cheney and Kitty Matthews. Son Jefferson and daughter Ruth H. received the negro man, Isaac. Known children included:

1. Lyde Griffith, born January 13, 1774, and of whom more as Child 1.
2. Samuel B. Griffith, born January 24, 1780, first child of the second marriage, died single. Not named in his mother's will.
3. Walter Griffith, born August 12, 1781 in Montgomery County, died in Neville, Ohio. A minister, he was married to Sarah Pigman, probably in Montgomery County. Not named in his mother's will.
4. Alfred Griffith, born March 16, 1783, died April 15, 1871 at Alexandria, Virginia, having served 65 years in the ministry, including as Chaplain of the Maryland Senate in 1825. He left a will in Montgomery County dated September 1, 1863, probated June 12, 1871 and recorded in liber JWS 1 at folio 377. His wife was apparently deceased, and he states that he is then living with his daughter Catherine S. Uhler (in Alexandria), to whom he bequeaths all his furniture and personal effects then in her home. After two personal bequests to her children, he directed that all the remainder of his estate be divided equally between his four named children (also noting their place of residence at the time of the will). He was married March 30, 1812 to Catherine E. Scholl, born c.1785, died June 15, 1859, and had at least four children:

    a. Lycurgus Edward Griffith, born January 19, 1813. He was a doctor, and moved to Texas. Married January 18, 1844 to Sarah J. Clark, born January 17, 1826, of Ohio, and had at least eight children.
    b. Catherine S. Griffith, born August 15, 1814. Married to Peter G. Uhler as noted in her father's will, lived in Alexandria, and had at least two children, both mentioned in the will:
        (1) Catharine Elizabeth Uhler, who received her grandfather's gold watch.
        (2) Alfred G. Uhler, who received his grandfather's gold watch key marked AG.
    c. Alfred Griffith, died c.1877, single, lived in Texas.

d. Samuel R. Griffith, born January 1, 1828; lived in the District of Columbia.

5. Ruth H. Griffith, born July 13, 1784, died September 11, 1863, single. She was listed as head of household in the 1850 census of the First District, next door to the household of her brother Richard H. Griffith. Living with her was Angelina Griffith, born c.1831 in Tennessee, not otherwise identified, and Ruth then owned eight slaves. In the agricultural census, she was listed with 30 acres of improved land, and 11 acres of unimproved land, valued at $400 in total. She owned 2 horses, 3 milch cows, 2 other cattle, 5 sheep and 10 swine. In the last year, she had produced 20 bushels of wheat, 130 bushels of Indian corn, 15 bushels of oats, 10 bushels of Irish potatoes, 50 pounds of butter, a ton of hay, and 20 pounds of beeswax and honey. Ruth H. Griffith was next found as head of household in the 1860 census of the First District of the county, with $1,500 in real estate and $6,000 in personal property. Living with her was F. M. Price, born c.1834, with $3,000 in real estate and $1,000 in personal property. They were living next door to the household of Ninian Easton, born c.1810, and in his household, we found Eliza B. Griffith, born c.1802. She owned $2,000 in personal property, and was probably related in some way to Ruth H. Griffith. We suggest that she may have been the widow of Lyde Griffith, Ruth's older brother. Ruth H. Griffith left a will in Montgomery County, dated August 8, 1863, probated September 15, 1863 and recorded in liber JWS 1 at folio 145. To her niece Columbia A. Griffith (1828), daughter of her brother Jefferson, she left all her real estate and buildings where she then lived, lying on both sides of the public road from Unity to Damascus, and containing about 41 acres, as well as her negro boy Henry. After making a number of bequests to a niece and nephews (primarily slaves), she left the residue of her estate to Columbia and Kitty Mathews (who was her sister Catherine).

6. Mary Griffith, born December 30, 1785; apparently the daughter Mary Cheney mentioned in her mother's will.

7. Richard H. Griffith, born March 26, 1787, and of whom more as Child 7.

8. Henry G. Griffith, born November 16, 1788; deceased with issue prior to 1845, when his mother wrote her will.
9. Horatio Griffith, born June 9, 1790, and of whom more as Child 9.
10. Sarah Griffith, born April 28, 1792, and of whom more as Child 10.
11. Philemon Griffith, born March 22, 1794, and of whom more as Child 11.
12. Michael Berry Griffith, born February 26, 1796 in Montgomery County, Maryland, died in Texas. Married in Montgomery County August 28, 1823 to Lydia Ridgely Crabb, born there June 24, 1799, died March 20, 1864 in Texas, daughter of General Jeremiah Crabb and Elizabeth Griffith. The family moved to Terrell, Texas about 1839, having first had children in Montgomery County. Descendants of the family born in Texas are not followed here. The children were:
    a. Jeremiah Crabb Griffith, born April 30, 1825
    b. A. Elizabeth Griffith, born May 23, 1827
    c. John Summerfield Griffith, born June 17, 1829. Lt. Colonel commanding, 6th Texas Cavalry, CSA, appointed Brigadier General of State troops by Governor Murrah in March, 1864.
    d. Joseph H. B. Griffith, born August 20, 1831
    e. Ruth Matilda Griffith, born August 20, 1835
    f. Amanda J. Griffith, born August 20, 1838, died May 7, 1852.
13. Catherine Griffith, born August 28, 1797, mentioned in the will of her sister Ruth H. Griffith to receive a negro woman Ann. Married April 7, 1818 to James B. Mathews, born November 2, 1791 and had fourteen children. Lived in Howard County, and had children, including:
    a. Leanna Mathews, born January 16, 1821. Married September 1, 1846 to Milton Welsh, born April 6, 1816, died January 6, 1853. Children included:
        (1) Elizabeth Welsh, born 1847, died 1853
        (2) Kate M. Welsh, born 1852, died 1853
    b. Israel Griffith Mathews, mentioned in the will of his aunt Ruth H. Griffith, to receive a negro boy Jefferson.

c.   Ruth Mathews, mentioned in the will of her aunt Ruth H. Griffith, to receive a negro girl Fanny.

d.   Kate, or perhaps Catherine, Mathews; mentioned in the will of her aunt Ruth H. Griffith, to receive a sorrel colt.

14. Israel Griffith, born August 17, 1799, died January 19, 1875 at his home in Baltimore, a retired dry goods merchant. Married in Frederick County September 28, 1824 to Sarah Ann Griffith, born March 23, 1803, died April 22, 1877, daughter of Colonel Philemon Griffith (1756) and Eleanor Jacob (1762). Children, and apparently lived at Baltimore:

a.   Charles Henry Griffith, born December 21, 1825

b.   Mary Eleanor Griffith, born July 8, 1828

c.   Frances Ann Griffith, born July 28, 1830, died August 31, 1863.

d.   Alverda Griffith, born August 7, 1832

e.   Israel Griffith, Jr., born September 16, 1835, a twin, died August 9, 1863, single

f.   Sarah Ann Griffith, born September 16, 1835, a twin. Married to Joseph H. Ruddach, first Lieutenant of the Chesapeake Riflemen, Co. F, during the Mexican War.

g.   George Griffith, born February 8, 1838, an infant death.

h.   George Griffith, second use of the name, born October 24, 1839, an infant death.

i.   Emma Griffith, born October 2, 1842

j.   David Israel Griffith, born October 26, 1844

15. Jefferson Griffith, born March 16, 1801, died November 28, 1880. Married in Montgomery County by license dated November 14, 1827 to Cordelia R. Magruder, born c.1804, died February 7, 1882. He was head of household in the 1850 census of the First District, owning one slave, and $1,500 in real estate, listed with his wife and nine children. In the agricultural census of 1850, he was reported as owning 100 acres of improved land and 206 acres unimproved, valued at $1,500 total. He owned 3 horses, 3 milch cows, 1 other cattle, and 20 swine. In the previous year, he had produced 100 bushels of wheat, 250 bushels of Indian corn, 100 bushels of oats, 45 bushels of Irish potatoes, 40 bushels of buckwheat, 100 pounds of butter and 3 tons of hay. The children were:

a. Columbia A. Griffith, born November 19, 1828. This is perhaps the same as Columbia Griffith found in the 1860 census of the First District, there reported as born c.1830, living with Mary A. Layton, born c.1808, who was listed as head of the two-person household.

b. Samuel Griffith, born July 4, 1832, a twin; married and lived in Sumner County, Kansas.

c. Eliza V. Griffith, born July 4, 1832, a twin; married and lived in Kansas.

d. Leonidas Magruder Griffith, born May 8, 1835, died April 14, 1906. Reportedly lived in Pennsylvania. Married to Ruth Elizabeth Gaither Warfield, born December 3, 1836 in Anne Arundel County, died April 24, 1910. She was a daughter of John Davidge Warfield (1799) and Corilla Elizabeth Hobbs (1806). Children:

    (1) Mary Warfield Griffith, born January 16, 1861, died July 23, 1861.

    (2) Florence May Griffith, born May 31, 1862. Married November 20, 1888 to Ephraim Butzer, of Tuscarora, New York.

    (3) John Jefferson Griffith, born May 21, 1865, died July 25, 1903. Married December 29, 1897 to Mildred Messenger; no children.

    (4) Cordelia Elizabeth Griffith, born January 4, 1867. Married June 25, 1891 to George Ellsworth Miller of Amos, West Virginia. Two children.

    (5) Rosalie Griffith, born May 11, 1869, died April 20, 1902. Married June 24, 1895 to Dr. Charles Thatcher Waggoner and had two children.

    (6) Columbia Magruder Griffith, born August 24, 1870, died June 16, 1931. Married January 24, 1893 to William T. Knickerbocker and second November 3, 1898 Rolland McCaslin. Apparently there were no children.

    (7) Leonidas Magruder Griffith, Jr., born August 6, 1876. Married first Flora Golden and second March 10, 1926 to Amelia Lee Johnson.

e. Ruth Griffith, born November 10, 1836, an infant death.

f. Anna Maria Griffith, born August 1, 1838; married and lived in Indiana.

g. Ruth Berry Griffith, born October 29, 1840, a twin, died October 17, 1869

h. Susannah M. Griffith, born October 29, 1840, a twin, died January 6, 1852

i. Robert Emory Griffith, born July 17, 1843; married and lived in Missouri.

j. Jefferson Griffith, Jr., born July 23, 1846

16. Berry J. Griffith, born June 21, 1804; married and had descendants in Illinois, Texas and California.

CHILD 1

Lyde Griffith
1774-1839

This son of Samuel Griffith (1752) and his first wife, Rachel Warfield (1757), was born January 13, 1774 in an area that became part of Montgomery County when it was formed in 1776, and died June 28, 1839. He was a Colonel, married first to Anne (Poole) Dorsey, born August 6, 1773, died January 9, 1808, and had at least four children. He was married second to Amelia Wayman, died December, 1823, daughter of John Wayman and Ann Warfield and had four more children. Lyde Griffith left a will in Montgomery County, dated June 1, 1836, probated July 2, 1839, recorded in liber W at folio 212; rerecorded in liber VMB 4 at page 146. To his eldest son Henry, he left the plantation on which he lived, being about 200 acres of *Griffith's Burgh*. He then made specific bequests to three more sons as noted following, and a bequest to his three daughters: Elizabeth, wife of Thomas Griffith; Milcah, wife of Samuel Riggs; and Louisa Griffith, single. The three girls were to receive the farms where Ruth Griffith lived, being the widow of Samuel Griffith, consisting of 80 acres, 360 acres, and attached woodlots, totaling 478 acres in all. Lyde then mentioned his "unfortunate" daughter Rachel, who had apparently not married well, or was perhaps divorced. In any case, she was given a symbolic one dollar as her full share of the estate. Further in the will, however, 160 acres of land and nine negroes, together with one thousand dollars in cash, was bequeathed to son Lyde, in trust, for the benefit of his sister Rachel. The will also provided that as Louise, Charles and Walter should marry, each was to receive horses, cows, hogs, sheep and other necessities of life. All of the children were:

1. Henry Griffith, born February 9, 1797. Married in Montgomery County by license dated May 27, 1823 to Eliza V. Magruder; no children. He was found as head of household in the 1850 census of Montgomery County, First District, living alone with his wife, Eliza V., there reported as born c.1805. He then owned four slaves, and in the agricultural census, was reported with 100 acres of improved land and 210 acres unimproved, valued at $2,000 in total. He owned 5 horses, 6 milch cows, 1 other cattle, 14 sheep and 13 swine. In the previous year, he had produced 200 bushels of wheat, 375 bushels of Indian corn, 100 bushels of oats, 3,300 pounds of tobacco, 30 pounds of wool, 1 bushel of peas and beans, 50 bushels of Irish Potatoes, 300 pounds of butter, 10 tons of hay, and 5 bushels of clover seed. Henry left a will dated January 2, 1851 in Montgomery County, probated September 8, 1857. He left his entire estate in trust to "*my mother-in-law and esteemed friend Thomas Griffith*" in trust to the benefit of his wife Eliza V. Griffith during her lifetime or widowhood, and should she remarry, she would then take her one third of the estate. (One suspects that the intent was brother-in-law rather than mother-in-law, in that the Executor of the estate was described as esteemed friend and brother-in-law Thomas Griffith). At her death or remarriage, the estate was to pass to his sister Elizabeth Griffith, wife of Thomas Griffith (see next). A special bequest was made to his nephew Lyde Griffith, son of brother Walter Griffith, who received a gold watch, chain and seals. Eliza V. Griffith left a will in Montgomery County dated May 21, 1863, probated September 22, 1863 and recorded in liber JWS 1 at folio 147. She named two of her sisters to receive small cash legacies, and some personal property: Ellen V. (Magruder) Warfield, and Cordelia R. (Magruder) Griffith. She also named six nieces, each to receive small bequests.

2. Elizabeth Griffith, born April 8, 1800, of whom more.
3. Rachel Warfield Griffith, born January 21, 1802, died April 1, 1861. Married April 27, 1819 Lemuel Griffith, born April 22, 1795, the son of Colonel Philemon Griffith (1756) and Eleanor Jacob (1762). Their descendants are discussed in Chapter 8, which see.
4. Lyde Griffith, Jr., born March 15, 1804, died February 16, 1882 at his home near Damascus, single (*Sentinel* obituary titled him Colonel). Under his father's will, he received the 250 acre plantation on which he was then living. Buried on *Edgehill Farm* near Laytonsville. Head of household in the 1850 census of Montgomery County for the Second District, he had $3,000 in real estate, and owner of seven slaves. Living with him was John Sheckells, born c.1814, a laborer. In the agricultural census of 1850, Lyde owned 150 acres of improved land and 450 acres unimproved, valued at $3,000 in total. He owned 7 horses, 4 milch cows, 4 working oxen, 4 other cattle, 20 sheep and 45 swine. In the previous year, he had produced 200 bushels of wheat, 300 bushels of Indian corn, 400 bushels of oats, 250 pounds of tobacco, 140 pounds of wool, 5 bushels of peas and beans, 30 bushels of Irish potatoes, 130 pounds of butter, 20 tons of hay and 2 bushels of clover seed. He is probably the same as Lyde Griffith found as head of household in the 1860 census of the Second District, with $4,000 in real estate and $11,200 in personal property, apparently still single. However, he is there reported as born c.1810, somewhat different from other reports, but still within reason. There were three white, and one black, laborers listed with him. In the 1867-1868 Slave Census of the county, Lyde was shown as owning thirteen slaves, primarily of the Snowden, Orem and Frazier families. Lyde Griffith was next head of household in the 1870 census of the Second District, Damascus Post Office, with $10,000 in real estate and $15,648 in personal property. He was apparently single, with John Griffith living with him, born c.1828. There were nine black individuals listed in the household, six of them from the Orem or Orum family, formerly listed among his slaves. Lyde A. Griffith was listed as head of household in the 1880 census of the

113

county for the Clarksburg District, but is the same individual here under study. He had living with him Filmore W. Poole, born c.1852 and apparently his wife, Maggie L. Poole, born c.1857, listed as a grand niece. They then had an infant child, Sebastian Poole, born c.1879. Also in the household was George G. Watkins, born c.1856, listed as a grand nephew, and a farm laborer. Maggie (or Margaret) and George G. (or George Greenberry) Watkins were probably children of William Watkins (1817) and Ann Griffith (1820). Lyde Griffith left a will in Montgomery County, dated January 21, 1874, probated March 14, 1882, and recorded in liber RWC 6 at folio 286 in the will records of the county. Being single, his heirs were to have equal shares in his entire estate, which would have been substantial, and were named as being: Thomas Griffith, David Griffith, Festus Griffith, Frank Griffith and Mary Ann Lansdale; and Lyde Griffith, Henry A. Griffith, David Griffith, Columbus Griffith, and Mary Eleanor Plummer; sons and daughters of my sisters Elizabeth Griffith and Rachel W. Griffith, deceased. They are both listed here above as children 2 and 3 in this tabulation of the family.

5. Charles W. Griffith, born January 4, 1810, and died c.1870, single. In the 1860 census of Montgomery County for the First District, living as a farmhand in the household of William Thompson of R (1812). Under his father's will of 1839, he was to receive the 263 acre farm on which Walter Applebee lived, and 137 acres of *Griffith's Burgh*, to include the land on the river.

6. Milcah Wayman Griffith, born December 12, 1812, and of whom more.

7. Louisa Hood Griffith, born October 4, 1815, died December 21, 1844, single.

8. John Samuel Griffith, born c.1818, buried April 30, 1821; St. Bartholomew's Episcopal Church. This child is shown in church records as a son of Lyde Griffith, and the Colonel is the only one of that name in the proper time period to have been the father. He is not, of course, mentioned in the will of his father, having been an infant death.

9. Walter Griffith, born April 4, 1820, of whom more.

Elizabeth Griffith
1800-1860

This daughter of Colonel Lyde Griffith (1774) and his first wife Anne Poole Dorsey (1773) was born April 8, 1800, and died April 3, 1860. Married November 1, 1825 to Thomas G. Griffith, born September 15, 1803, died January 9, 1870, the youngest son of Nicholas Griffith (1771) and Anne Ridgely (1771). Thomas Griffith was head of household in the 1850 census of the First District, with $4,000 in real estate. His wife Elizabeth was listed, and they then had the five youngest children at home. Listed in the household were two black laborers. In the 1850 census, Thomas was listed as owning ten slaves. He then owned 185 acres of improved land and 200 acres unimproved, with $4,000 total value. He owned 6 horses, 7 milch cows, 2 working oxen, 7 other cattle, 23 sheep and 45 swine, the livestock valued at $1,100 total. In the previous year, he had produced 200 bushels of wheat, 1,125 bushels of Indian corn, 650 bushels of oats, 60 pounds of wool, 1 bushel of peas and beans, 75 bushels of Irish potatoes, 300 pounds of butter, and 12 tons of hay. He was next found as head of household in the 1860 census of the First District, Laytonsville Post Office, quite wealthy for the period. He was a farmer, and owned $15,000 in real estate and $17,700 in personal property. Living with him was his mother Ann (sic), then reported as eighty-eight years of age, and probably a widow. Also living with him was his sister Harriet, then sixty years old. Three of his children were also at home, but no wife, she having died about two months before the taking of the census. Our subject here is quite possibly the same Thomas Griffith who was listed in the 1867-1868 Slave Census of Montgomery County, as the owner of fifteen slaves, nine of them bearing the King surname.

Thomas Griffith left a will in Montgomery County dated September 13, 1869, probated February 15, 1870 and recorded in liber JWS 1 at folio 317. To his sons Thomas and Franklin, he left the farm purchased from Samuel R. Gaither, containing 160 acres of *Bostick*. He left cash, US bonds, railroad bonds and personal notes to his daughter Mary Ann, and directed that the rest of the estate be divided between five named children, apparently those surviving: Thomas, Mary Ann, David, Festus and Franklin. Children:

1. William Penniman Griffith, born October 2, 1826, died December 26, 1846. Buried on *Edgehill Farm* near Laytonsville.
2. Nicholas R. Griffith, born October 10, 1828, died January 22, 1864. Buried on *Edgehill Farm* near Laytonsville. Married to Mary S. Jones, who died March 20, 1899 in Baltimore, no children. Her *Sentinel* obituary stated that she was a sister of the late Josiah W. and Gustavus Jones, and Mrs. Enoch Hutton. We found Nicholas R. Griffith as head of household in the 1860 census of Montgomery County for the First District, living alone with his wife. He was quite wealthy for the time period, with $38,000 in real estate and $70,000 in personal property.
3. Thomas G. Griffith, Jr., born April 29, 1831, died July 13, 1912 near Olney. At home in the 1860 census, listed as a farm manager. He was Captain, Co. A., 1st Maryland Cavalry, CSA. Married first in Montgomery County by license dated March 2, 1869 to Elizabeth Davis Singleton, born April 9, 1838, died April 10, 1876, reportedly the daughter of John Singleton and Anne Bowie. (The *Sentinel* obituary of Elizabeth Singleton states that she was the daughter of the late Thomas D. Singleton of Easton, Talbot County, Maryland). He was married second September 20, 1877 to Sarah J. Ball, born May 29, 1832 in Virginia, daughter of Thomas Ball (1794) and Ann Randolph McNeal. Thomas appeared as head of household in the 1870 census of the First District of Montgomery County, with his wife Elizabeth and their first child, then just four months old. Thomas was listed as a farmer, with $2,000 in real estate and $8,000 in personal property. In the 1880 census of the county for the Eighth District, Thomas and Sarah were listed with four children. Living with them was Ginney W. Ball, born c.1855, a teacher, listed as sister-in-law. Thomas G. Griffith was head of household in the 1900 census of the county for the Eighth District, with his wife Sarah and four of his children. He and Sarah had been married for twenty-two years, and she had no children. Living with them

was F. W. Ball, born July, 1834, single, female, a teacher, listed as sister-in-law. Children born to the first marriage only:

a. Nicholas Ridgely Griffith, born February 18, 1870, died October 5, 1947 at Montgomery General. Records of St. John's Episcopal Church report that he was about 83 years of age at the time of death.

b. William Dulley Griffith, according to census, born September 1, 1871, died March 19, 1935, buried at St. John's Episcopal in Olney; served in US Artillery 1898-1899. In the obituary of his father, this child is listed as William Dallas Griffith, which appears to be correct.

c. Anne Singleton Griffith, born December 31, 1872, died June 16, 1918 of acute nephritis in Baltimore, single.

d. Charlotte Elizabeth Griffith, born October 22, 1874, died April 29, 1967, buried at St. John's Episcopal Church, Olney. Married to William J. P. Farquhar.

4. Edward Griffith, born June 2, 1833, died c.1857

5. Mary Ann Griffith, born March 8, 1835, died May 1, 1890; at home in the 1860 census. She was buried on *Edgehill Farm* near Laytonsville. Married June 6, 1871 to Richard H. Lansdale; no children. He was head of household in the 1880 census of Montgomery County for the Cracklin District, born c.1838. His wife Mary A. was keeping house and they had living with them Annie Griffith, born c.1873, listed as a niece, then in school. From her age, we would suggest that she was Anne Singleton Griffith, just above, daughter of Mary's brother Thomas Griffith, Jr.

6. David Griffith, born April 9, 1837, died January 28, 1914; buried at Rockville Cemetery. Private, Co. A, 1st Maryland Cavalry, CSA; enlisted from Redland, Montgomery County. Married May 29, 1867 to Anne S. Taylor, born January 10, 1836 in the District of Columbia. He was a Judge of the Orphans' Court of Montgomery County. In the 1860 census of the county, for the First District, he was living alone, two doors from the household of his father, listed as a farmer, with $400 in real estate. David was next found as head of household in the 1870 census of the county for the First District, with $3,000 in real estate and $2,000 in personal property. His

wife Anna S. was present, born c.1837, and they then had two children. He was head of household in the 1880 census of the county for the Cracklin District, with his wife Anna S. and three children at home. Head of household in the 1900 census of Montgomery County for the First District, he as listed as a farmer, with his wife Ann and two of their children. Living with them were three black servants and Martha L. Taylor, born c.1837, a single sister-in-law. David and Ann had been married 33 years, and she had been the mother of three children, all living, with the two youngest still at home. An obituary in the *Sentinel* reported that Mrs. Anne Stone Griffith, aged 87, widow of Judge David Griffith, died May 23, 1923 at her home near Redland, and was buried in Rockville Cemetery. We assume that to be the same Anne S. Taylor reported as his bride (with both her given names). They had children:

a. Elizabeth Griffith, born April 9, 1868. Married in Montgomery County at Christ Episcopal Church in Rockville, March 1, 1894 to Walter W. Mobley, born February 23, 1869, son of William B. Mobley (1843) and Louisa Hood Griffith (1845). Walter was head of household in the 1900 census of the county for the Fourth District, he and Elizabeth had been married six years, with three children:

     (1) Louise G. Mobley, born December, 1894
     (2) William B. Mobley, born May, 1896
     (3) Alice S. Mobley, born April, 1898

b. Harriet Mackall Griffith, born June 11, 1869, died single February 8, 1962 at Suburban Hospital. Buried at Rockville Cemetery.

c. Thomas David Griffith, born January 29, 1871 at Redland, Montgomery County, died June 8, 1959 in St. Petersburg, Florida, where he had been living in retirement; buried at Rockville Cemetery, Maryland. Married January 12, 1910 to Laura Worthington Bradley, formerly of Rockville, born c.1875, died August 14, 1954 in St. Petersburg; buried at Union Cemetery in Rockville. She was daughter of George G. Bradley of Potomac, Maryland. No children.

7. Festus Griffith, born July 12, 1838 at the family farm of *Edgehill Farm* near Laytonsville. Captain, Co. H, 8th Virginia Infantry, CSA. He participated in the battles of Manassas, Ball's Bluff, Yorktown, Williamsburg, Seven Pines, and the siege of Richmond. Wounded in the hip at the second battle of Manassas, and captured in 1864 in the Valley of Virginia; exchanged that fall in Savannah, Georgia. He was a merchant in Baltimore until about 1870, when he went to Texas for the next four years, before returning to Maryland. Married June 28, 1871 to Avolina Riggs, born July 7, 1838, died January 25, 1892, daughter of Elisha Riggs (1810) and Avolina Warfield; no children. In the 1880 census of the county for the Eighth District, they were in the household of her parents, with no children.

8. Franklin Griffith, born October 29, 1840, died July 28, 1892 at his home near Brookeville; at home in the 1860 census. Buried on *Edgehill Farm*, near the town of Laytonsville. Lieutenant, Co. A, 1st Maryland Cavalry, CSA. Married Montgomery County by license dated January 5, 1869 to Katherine L. Riggs, born March 2, 1844, died of heart failure June 28, 1914 near Unity, daughter of Doctor Artemus Riggs and Amanda Warfield; and had children. Buried on the family farm called *Edgehill Farm* near Laytonsville. In the 1870 census, he is listed as a farmer, with his real estate valued at $10,000 and $2,600 in personal property. At the time, they have living with them Georgina White, born c.1848, as a domestic servant, and Mary Griffith, born c.1837, perhaps a sister of Artemus. There are also four black servants and farm laborers living in the household. Franklin was head of household in the 1880 census of the county for the Cracklin District, with his wife, and their two children both at home. In that census, his wife Kate was reported born in Ohio. Children were:

a. Frances I. Griffith, born September 24, 1871. Married at the home of her mother near Unity January 26, 1898 to Doctor Henry G. Spurrier. In the 1900 census of the First District of Montgomery County, he was listed as head of household, but there entered as Harry G. Spurrier, born c.1866. He and Frances had been married 2 years, and there was one child:

(1) Catherine G. Spurrier, born August, 1899

b. Artemus Riggs Griffith, born May 10, 1874. Married in Montgomery County at St. Bartholomew's Episcopal Church at Unity by license dated October 24, 1898 to Hattie M. Colliflower, born November, 1876. He was head of household in the 1900 census of the county for the First District, with his wife. They had been married one year, and had one son. Living with them was his mother, Kate L. Riggs Griffith (1844), and also his grandmother Amanda (Warfield) Riggs, then seventy-eight years of age. There were other children:

(1) Frank Riggs Griffith, born August 18, 1899, died February 29, 1936; buried at Mt. Carmel.

(2) Helen Lucretia Griffith, born May 11, 1901, died July 25, 1901; buried in the family cemetery on *Edgehill Farm* at Laytonsville.

Milcah Wayman Griffith
1812-1874

This daughter of Colonel Lyde Griffith (1774) and his second wife Amelia Wayman, was born December 12, 1812 and died February 19, 1874 at *Oakley*, in Montgomery County. Married December 3, 1833 to Samuel Riggs, born April 24, 1813, son of Reuben Riggs (1775) and Mary Thomas. Samuel was head of household in the 1850 census of the First District of Montgomery County, a farmer, with $3,500 in real estate. His wife Milcah was there, and they then had six children at home. He was listed as the owner of thirteen slaves. In the 1850 Agricultural census, he was listed as owning 175 acres of improved land and 125 acres unimproved, with a $3,500 valuation. He owned 5 horses, 6 milch cows, 2 working oxen, 7 other cattle, 18 sheep and 48 swine. During the previous year he produced 400 bushels of wheat, 500 bushels of Indian corn, 400 bushels of oats, 3,500 pounds of tobacco, 50 pounds of wool, 3 bushels of peas and beans, 60 bushels of Irish potatoes, 600 pounds of butter, 15 tons of hay, 9 bushels of clover seed, and 10 pounds of hops. Samuel Riggs of R was next head of household in the 1860 census of the First District, with Milcah and seven of their children. He had continued to prosper, now owning $9,500 in real estate and $29,100 in personal property, probably largely in the value of slaves. In the 1867-1868 Slave Census of the County, he was listed as owning thirteen slaves, ranging in age from thirteen to forty-eight years, all named, primarily from the Letcher and King families. In the 1870 census of the First District of Montgomery County, Samuel Riggs of R owned $16,000 in real estate and $10,000 in personal property. He and Milcah had three of their children at home; Samuel, Leta (apparently meant for Louisa), and Mary E. Riggs. They had a number of children, including:

1. Amelia Riggs, born September 4, 1834, died January 3, 1862. Married December 19, 1860 to William H. Myers, born March 26, 1831, and had children. They were not found in the 1870 census of Montgomery County. The children were:
    a. Olivia Riggs Myers, born January 3, 1862
    b. William H. Myers, Jr., an infant death
    c. Milcah Amelia Myers, an infant death
2. William H. Riggs, born April 26, 1836; not at home in 1860
3. Gilbert Riggs, born April 17, 1838, an infant death.
4. Reuben Riggs, born November 29, 1839. Married January 29, 1868 to Martha H. Canby, born c.1845, and had children. Her parents were Thomas Canby, born c.1795 in Pennsylvania and Deborah Duvall, born c.1807 in Maryland. Reuben was head of household in the 1870 census of Montgomery County for the First District, with his wife and their first child. He was next head of household in the 1880 census of the Cracklin District, with Martha and four children. An obituary appeared in the June 14, 1895 Sentinel, reporting that Martha Hughes Riggs, wife of Reuben Riggs, died in her 51st year, June 6, 1895, at her home, leaving a husband, and three sons: Samuel, Benjamin and William, and a daughter, Lulie Riggs. Her parents and five of her siblings were also named, and she was buried at Olney. Reuben Riggs of the proper age was next found as head of household in the 1900 census of the First District. However, he was there listed with a wife S. Emma Riggs, born April, 1845, apparently a second marriage. They

had been married for three years, with no children born to the union. Living with them was Somerset V. Jones (1834), single, listed as a brother; and Priscilla J. Jones, (1824), also single, listed as a sister-in-law. Childen:

a. Samuel Riggs, born August 15, 1869
b. Benjamin C. Riggs, born August 3, 1871
c. Lula Riggs, born January 29, 1874; in the 1880 census this child is listed as Sallie Riggs.
d. William C. Riggs, born October 7, 1876

5. Samuel Riggs, Jr., born April 9, 1843. Married in Montgomery County by license dated May 15, 1876 to Laura H. Neel, born c.1850, who had been previously married. Her maiden name was apparently Laura Virginia Howard. He was head of household in the 1880 census of the Cracklin District, with Laura and one child born to their marriage, and one stepchild, Thomas Neel, born c.1872. Living in the household was his father, Samuel Riggs, then 67 years of age. The children were:

a. Samuel H. Riggs, III, born c.1879. Married 1904 to Mary Darrington Christopher.
b. Laurie Howard Riggs.
c. Douglass Howard Riggs.

6. Elisha Riggs, born April 22, 1845. Married in Montgomery County by license dated February 23, 1869 to Margaret V. Howard, born c.1849, died June 25, 1878. He was head of household in the 1870 census of the First District, with $1,000 in real estate, one household removed from that of his parents. He had his wife Margaret and their first child. Living with him were two black laborers. In the 1860 census of the First District, there was a household headed by Anna Howard, born c.1828, who may be the mother of Margaret. There was a Margaret Howard of the proper age living with Anna, one of four children, three of whom, including Margaret, were reported there as born in North Carolina. Elisha was married second June, 1879 to Elizabeth D. Ridgely, born September, 1850. He was found as head of household in the 1880 census of the county for the Cracklin District, with his second wife, Elizabeth, and four children at home, all from his first marriage. Elisha was apparently married a third time. He was

head of household in the 1900 census of the First District, listed with a wife Annie E. Riggs, born August, 1860, and five children at home. They were reported as having been married for six years, and she had been the mother of five children, all five surviving. However, it seems that she must have been married before also, and that her five children were from that earlier marriage; there are no children listed of an age to have been born to Elisha and Annie within the six-year term of their marriage. Elisha and Margaret had four children, and there were five more from his second marriage:

a. Annie H. Riggs, born March 5, 1870
b. Milcha W. Riggs, born March 19, 1873
c. Eliza H. Riggs, born January 12, 1875
d. William H. Riggs, born February 2, 1876
e. Elisha Riggs, born August, 1881, died September 7, 1883
f. Leta W. Riggs, born March, 1884
g. Marguerite D. Riggs, born June, 1886
h. Georgia R. Riggs, born c.1888
i. Elizabeth R. Riggs, born November, 1891

7. Emanueleta Riggs, born January 18, 1850. Married December 17, 1874 to Charles J. Wood, born November 3, 1843 and had children. The family was not found in census records of the county of 1880 and 1900 (the 1890 census was destroyed). The children were:

a. Willie E. Wood, born September 26, 1875, infant death.
b. Charles J. Wood, Jr., born May 17, 1877
c. Arthur B. Wood, born December 10, 1881
d. Wayman A. Wood, born August 28, 1883
e. Edward M. Wood, born August 24, 1887
f. Leta Riggs Wood, born March 26, 1890

8. Louisa Griffith Riggs, born February 28, 1852, died April 27, 1863

9. Mary Elizabeth Riggs, born July 9, 1854. Married June 9, 1877 William E. Wood, born August 3, 1827 and had a son:

a. Samuel Riggs Wood, born December 5, 1878

Walter Griffith
1823-1864

This son of Colonel Lyde Griffith (1774) and his second wife Amelia Wayman was born April 4, 1823 and died May 25, 1864. Under the will of his father, Walter received 300 acres of *Griffith's Burgh*, subject to a life estate in the property reserved to his sister Louisa. He was married November 22, 1841 to Mary W. Riggs, born October 30, 1819, died September 1, 1898 in Laytonsville at the home of her son-in-law, William B. Mobley. She was the daughter of Reuben Riggs (1775) and Mary Thomas, and was buried in the family cemetery on her son's farm. Head of household in the 1850 census of the county for the First District, Walter was a farmer, with $5,000 in real estate, and eight slaves. His wife Mary W. was listed, and there were four children. Living with them was Charles W. Griffith, born c.1810, brother of Walter. In the 1850 agricultural census, Walter had 175 acres of improved land and 125 acres unimproved, valued at $3,000 in total. He owned 5 horses, 6 milch cows, 9 other cattle, 20 sheep and 38 swine. In the last year, he had produced 150 bushels of wheat, 625 bushels of Indian corn, 300 bushels of oats, 2,500 pounds of tobacco, 50 pounds of wool, 200 bushels of Irish potatoes, 600 pounds of butter and 12 tons of hay. In the 1867-1868 Slave Census of the county, Mary W. Griffith (probably this individual) was listed as the owner of ten slaves, principally of the Campbell and Jackson families. In the 1860 census of the First District of the county, we interpreted the microfilm to read Walton Griffith as head of household, which is obviously intended for Walter. He then had $8,000 in real estate and $10,900 in personal property. His wife Mary was there, and they then had four children at home. Mary was found as head of household in the 1870 census of the First District of Montgomery County, owning $6,000 in real estate and $2,000 in personal property. Living with her was Charles Griffith, single, brother of her deceased husband. There were also William H. Griffith, one of her sons, with his wife Sarah, and their infant first daughter. Children:

1. Lyde Griffith, born 1842, died April 29, 1864. Buried in the family cemetery on the Warfield farm in Montgomery County.

2. Louisa Hood Griffith, born March 23, 1845, died November 14, 1907. Married April 30, 1869 to William B. Mobley, born February 28, 1843, died March 6, 1920, and had children. They are buried at Laytonsville Cemetery. He was head of household in the 1870 census of Montgomery County for the First District, a merchant, with $2,500 in real estate and $4,000 in personal property. Louisa was present, and they then had their first child at home. We did not find the couple in any later census of Montgomery County. The children were:

    a. Walter W. Mobley, born February 23, 1869. Married in Montgomery County at Christ Episcopal Church in Rockville, March 1, 1894 to Elizabeth Griffith, born April 9, 1868, the daughter of Judge David Griffith (1837) and his wife Anne S. Taylor (1836) of Rockville. Head of household in the 1900 census of the county for the Fourth District, he and Elizabeth had been married for six years, with three children:

        (1) Louise G. Mobley, born December, 1894
        (2) William B. Mobley, born May, 1896
        (3) Alice S. Mobley, born April, 1898

    b. Edith Griffith Mobley, born May 4, 1872.

    c. George W. Mobley, born October 5, 1879, died December 23, 1937; buried with his parents.

3. William H. Griffith, born 1847, died December 29, 1923 at his home near Etchison; buried at the Laytonsville cemetery. Married Sarah Ann Griffith, born October 14, 1850, died February 11, 1917 at her home near Etchison, the daughter of Lebbeus Griffith (1804) and his second wife, Sarah Ann Wood, born c.1851, and had children. In the 1870 census of the First District of Montgomery County, he and his wife Sarah, and their first child, were living with his widowed mother. William H. was head of household in the 1880 census of the county for the Cracklin District, with Sarah A., and five children. Head of household in the 1900 census of the First District (although we transcribed his name as William A. Griffith and he was there reported as born January, 1843), with his wife Sarah A. and two sons. They had been married thirty-one years and she had been the mother of seven children,

125

six surviving. Sarah Ann left a will in Montgomery County, dated February 23, 1907, probated April 17, 1917, and recorded in liber HCA 19, at folio 311. She mentions her husband William H. Griffith, and her children. William H. Griffith left a will in the county, dated July 19, 1923, probated January 8, 1924, and recorded in liber PEW 2 at folio 65. It was a lengthy and somewhat complicated will, naming numerous grandchildren and children, with specific bequests to various family members. The children were:

a. Mary W. Griffith, born c.1870. The *Sentinel* reported the marriage of Mamie W. Griffith at St. Bartholomew's Church in Montgomery County, on November 13, 1889 to Bradley Worthington and, in 1917, lived at Hagerstown, Maryland. Named in her mother's will to receive the organ, and some silver. At least one son, mentioned in the will of his grandfather:

    (1) William B. Worthington.

b. Lyde Griffith, born May 28, 1871, died July 28, 1915 at Etchison; buried at Laytonsville. Not named in his mother's will, but known to be a son. Referred to in his father's will of 1923 as being deceased, with a bequest to some of his children. His *Sentinel* obituary assigns him the name of N. Lyde Griffith, the only time we have seen evidence of a first name. Married in Gaithersburg, at Ascension Episcopal Church by license dated December 4, 1894 to Julia Morgan Snouffer, born July, 1875, died May 21, 1951, the daughter of G. Fenton Snouffer. He was head of household in the 1900 census of the county for the First District, with his wife Julia. They had been married for six years, and she had been the mother of two children, both surviving, but only one at home. Living with them was Henry (A.) Griffith, born August 29, 1825, single, listed as a cousin. Also in the 1900 census of the First District, we found the household of G. Fenton Snouffer (1838), and living with them was a young Griffith child, listed as a granddaughter. She is apparently the other child of the two known in this family:

(1) Mary Ann Griffith, born March 6, 1896, at home with her parents in 1900. Married to Hawkins and mentioned in her grandfather's will.

(2) Julia Louisa Griffith, born December 24, 1897; living with her maternal grandparents in 1900. Named in her grandfather's will as Louisa Griffith.

c. Louisa Hood Griffith, born c.1874, died November 27, 1922 of heart trouble and pneumonia; buried Laytonsville Cemetery. Named in her mother's will by her husband's name. Married to her cousin Thomas Cranmer Griffith, born April 14, 1866, died June 1, 1924 at his home in Laytonsville; buried at Laytonsville Cemetery, son of Uriah Henry Griffith (1825) and Henrietta E. Wilcoxen (1821). Children, listed under father's name, which see.

d. Alverda Griffith, born c.1876, died December 28, 1946, buried with her husband at Laytonsville Cemetery. Referred to as Verda Griffith in both her mother's and her father's wills. Married November 9, 1893 at Hawlings Episcopal Church to Frank Griffith, born December 18, 1869, died 1903, son of Judge Charles Harrison Griffith (1840) and Hester Boone Dorsey (1843). The *Sentinel* announced that they would live in Howard County. At least these children:

(1) Mary Louise Griffith, born October 13, 1896

(2) William Franklin Griffith: January 27, 1899

(3) Charles Harrison Griffith, born July 23, 1903

e. William L. Griffith, born c.1878, buried October 27, 1934 (records of St. Bartholomew's Church). Mentioned in his mother's will. Under the terms of his father's will, he inherited the 195 and 1/2 acres of the home farm remaining after the bequest to his brother Walter. Married December 3, 1903 at Rockville to Nellie M. Allnutt, born c.1879, daughter of William J. Allnutt of near Laytonsville. Her obituary in the *Gaithersburg Gazette* reported that she died November 5, 1971, wife of the late William L. Griffith, buried at Laytonsville. They had children, not necessarily in this order:

(1) Nellie Griffith, married to Hardell.

(2) Anna Griffith, married to Waters.

(3) Helen Griffith, married to Kramer.

(4) Sarah Jane Griffith, born 1905, died October 12, 1925; buried with her parents.

(5) Ruth H. Griffith, born 1921, died 1921; buried with her parents.

(6) Margaret Wood Griffith, born June 6, 1912, died November 16, 1976 at Montgomery General Hospital, single. Buried at Laytonsville.

(7) Mary Griffith, married to Collins.

f. Walter Griffith, born July 11, 1886; named in his mother's will. Under his father's will, he received part of the home farm, containing 179 and 1/4 acres of land, described in the deed. An obituary in the *Sentinel* reported the death of Walker Griffith (sic) on December 31, 1925 in a Washington hospital, son of the late William H. Griffith, leaving a wife, the former Nettie Griffith, and naming a brother and two sisters, which match the family here reported. Buried at Laytonsville Cemetery. In the will of William H. Griffith, he refers to a daughter-in-law, Mary Estelle Griffith, who is probably this individual by her proper name. They apparently had children, including:

(1) Nettie Estelle Griffith, married at Mt. Tabor Methodist Church in Etchison, Maryland, June 19, 1930, to Paul Winfred Burdette, born October 22, 1905, died July 24, 1977 in Bethesda, Maryland. He was a son of Millard Diehl Burdette (1885) and Ethyl Lansdale King (1886), and they had children:

(a) Jacolyn Burdette, born October 28, 1939. Married January, 1959 to Richard Conklin of Frederick. They had children:

1. Jean Michele Conklin: December 29, 1967

2. Richard Walter Conklin: March 12, 1961

(b) Paul Douglas Burdette, born July 11, 1944, and married August 23, 1969 to Jane Regina Long of Bowie, Maryland.

4. Mary E. Griffith, born c.1849

CHILD 7

Richard H. Griffith
1787-1864

This son of Samuel Griffith (1752) and his second wife, Ruth Berry, was born March 26, 1787 in Montgomery County, and died February 16, 1864. Married in the county by license dated February 25, 1813 to Mary Ann Magruder, born c.1794, died March 19, 1856, daughter of Doctor Jeffrey Magruder. Richard was head of household in the 1850 census of the First District of the county, with $12,000 in real estate, and nine slaves. His wife was listed, and apparently two children. Also living with them was Emily M. Bourne, born c.1819, a married daughter, with two small children. In the agricultural census of 1850, Richard H. Griffith was reported with 100 acres of improved land and 560 acres unimproved for $7,500 total value. He owned 7 horses, 5 milch cows, 2 working oxen, 7 other cattle, 23 sheep and 44 swine. In the previous twelve months, he produced 250 bushels of wheat, 850 bushels of Indian corn, 40 bushels of oats, 60 pounds of wool, 200 bushels of Irish potatoes, 50 bushels of buckwheat, 700 pounds of butter and 8 tons of hay. Richard H. Griffith was next found as head of household in the 1860 census of the First District, for the Laytonsville Post Office, a widower, with $10,000 in real estate and $2,300 in personal property. In that census, there were five Griffith households listed almost together, with only two intervening non-Griffith households. In 1860, four of Richard's children were still at home. Also listed with them was Gilbert Griffith, born c.1853, probably a grandchild.

Richard H. Griffith left a will in Montgomery County dated February 11, 1862, probated March 29, 1864 and recorded in liber JWS 1 at folio 158. He first mentioned that his son Richard H. Griffith, Jr. had already received his portion of the estate by deed of conveyance for lands known as the Patapsco Farm, which testator declared to be equal to one-ninth of the estate. The one-ninth portion allotted to his son Alfred B. Griffith was to be held in the hands of the Executors of the estate for the benefit of son Alfred, who was apparently of age, but not thrifty enough to suit his father.

The remaining seven-ninths was to be equally divided between the other seven children, all named. There were at least nine children, many of whom lived in Baltimore:

1. Susannah R. Griffith, born December 8, 1813. Married January 9, 1838 to William K. Merritt. No children.
2. Mary Ellen Griffith, born June 23, 1815; married to Emack.
3. Helen E. Griffith, born June 14, 1818; married to Groveman.
4. Emily M. Griffith, born March 16, 1819, married Bourne and had at least two children. In her father's will, we read this name as Bowen. The children were:
   a. Richard M. Bourne, born c.1847
   b. Mary A. Bourne, born c.1849
5. Alfred Bowie Griffith, born March 14, 1821, died July 8, 1862, single; buried at St. John's Episcopal Church, Olney.
6. Samuel Christopher Griffith, born December 18, 1823. In 1863 living in Baltimore City.
7. Richard H. Griffith, Jr., married first to Susan Barbour, born c.1831, died December 25, 1864, and had four children. He married second October, 1867 to Eliza (Palmer) Towers, and had six children. Eliza Palmer was born June 10, 1834, died July 5, 1879, and is buried at St. John's Episcopal at Olney. Richard H. Griffith was found as head of household in the 1870 census of the First District of Montgomery County, a farmer, reported there as born c.1828, owning $8,000 in real estate and $5,000 in personal property. His wife was listed as Eliza P. Griffith, born c.1834, died September 1, 1890 at her home near Unity, and was apparently his second wife. Living with them were two children, and from their ages, apparently one born to each of the marriages of Richard. He was next found as head of household in the 1880 census of Montgomery County, Cracklin District, with his wife Eliza P. and five children. Living with them was Rose V. Griffith, born c.1862, relationship not expressed, but perhaps the same of that name born January 29, 1861, and a daughter of David Porter Griffith (1835). Also living in the household was Mary E. Emack, born c.1820, identified as a widowed sister. Note above that we have included Mary E. Griffith as a sister, but there reported as born c.1815. The children were:

a.   Isabelle Griffith, born December 14, 1852. Married May 2, 1872 in the county to William Riggs Griffith, born April 19, 1852 of heart trouble at his home near Laytonsville. Buried at Rock Creek Cemetery in Washington, the son of Ulysses Griffith (1810) and Julia Riggs (1811). The *Sentinel* reported the celebration of her eightieth birthday in 1932, at the home of her son-in-law Harvey K. Fleck in Baltimore. The article noted that she had seven children, fifteen grandchildren and fifteen great grandchildren. Her husband died December 1, 1921 near Laytonsville, and in his obituary, three married daughters are listed by the husbands' names: Mrs. H. K. Fleck of Baltimore; Mrs. William Riggs of Howard County; and Mrs. David Clark. Following, we have listed three daughters by their birth names, who apparently are the wives of these three listed spouses, but matches not yet determined. William R. was living at home in 1870, listed as a farmer, with $2,000 in real estate and $1,000 in personal property. Head of household in the 1880 census of the county for the Cracklin District, he was listed as Willie R. Griffith, with his wife Isabella and three children. Living with the family was Julia (Riggs) Griffith at the age of sixty-nine, mother of William R. Griffith. William R. was next found as head of household in the 1900 census of the county for the First District, with his wife Isabella and their three youngest children still at home. They had been married twenty-eight years, and Isabella had been the mother of seven children, with six surviving. Living with them was Richard H. Griffith, his father-in-law, and Frances C. Griffith (1852), listed as his mother-in-law. The latter couple, Richard and Frances, had then been married nine years, with no children, obviously a third marriage for Richard H. Griffith. William Riggs Griffith left a will in Montgomery County, dated December 10, 1896, probated January 10, 1922 and recorded in liber HCA 26 at folio 177. The first child following, who was an infant death, is not mentioned; each of the other six children were listed to receive $25 each, with all the rest and residue of the estate to his wife Isabella Griffith. The children were:

(1) William Vernon Griffith, born July 23, 1873, and died August 8, 1874

(2) Lycurgus Matthew Griffith, born November 26, 1875, died February 19, 1951 at the home of his daughter in New Orleans. Buried at St. John's Cemetery in Olney. In the 1880 census, there was a child listed at the age of five years, but interpreted from the microfilm as Kirke M. Griffith. As Lycurgus M. Griffith he was head of household in the 1900 census of Montgomery County for the First District, with a wife Minnie R., born March, 1874. They had been married two years, with one child. The *Sentinel* reported that Lycurgus Matthew Griffith was married November 22, 1898 at St. Bartholomew's Church in Unity to Minnie W. Riggs, died January 25, 1964 in Covington, Louisiana, daughter of Elisha Riggs. A family group sheet found in the family file at the library of the Montgomery County Historical Society lists her name as Milcah W. Riggs, which is also the way it was reported in the 1880 census of the Cracklin District, when she was a nine-year old listed with her parents. Cemetery records of St. John's Episcopal in Olney report her name as Milcah R., born c.1873, died c.1964; buried with her husband. It is evident from obituaries that they had other children:

(a) Olivia Meyers Griffith, born November, 1899. Married on August 9, 1924 at Christ Episcopal Church in Rockville, to Milburn Simpers Waters, born c.1899, and died November 7, 1981 at the Wilson Health Care Center in Gaithersburg. He was the son of Franklin Waters (1869) and Harriet Roberta Watkins (1872). Known to all his friends as "Booze" Waters, he was for many years employed by King Pontiac,

Gaithersburg, and was buried at Neelsville Presbyterian Church cemetery.

(b) Lycurgus Matthew Griffith, Jr., April 25, 1905, died December 24, 1983 at the Collingswood Nursing Home in Rockville; buried at Forest Oak Cemetery in Gaithersburg. His obituary listed his name as Lycurgus Matthew (Kirk) Griffith, reflecting the entry in the 1880 census, discussed above. Married June 29, 1929 at Epworth Methodist Church to Clarice Helen Kingsley, born November 25, 1906, and died June 26, 1993 at Collingswood; daughter of Harold Sherwood Kingsley and Carrie Crawford of Gaithersburg. They had a son:

1. Lycurgus Matthew (Kirk) Griffith, III, married Genevieve and had three children:
   a. Matthew Griffith.
   b. Paul Griffith.
   c. Joanna Griffith, married to Allen.

(c) Marshall P. H. Griffith, mentioned in his father's obituary as living in Alexandria.

(d) Mildred Wayman Griffith, born May 15, 1901; married Evarts Wagg of Sykesville; lived at Silver Spring. Her birth record at St. Bartholomew's Episcopal Church reports that she was a daughter of Lycurgus M. Griffith and Milcah W. Griffith (not Minnie W.).

(e) Agnes Griffith, married to Richard Barton, of Covington, Louisiana.

(f) Margaret Griffith, married to Judson Earle of Covington, Louisiana.

(g) William Riggs Griffith, born April 19, 1908, died May 25, 1962 at Key West, Florida. Married to Babette Everette and had children:

1. Betsy R. Griffith.
2. William R. Griffith.
3. Henry H. Griffith.

(3) Florence Anderson Griffith, born May 18, 1877; married May 12, 1897 at *Retirement* to David W. Clark. He was head of household in the 1900 census of Montgomery County for the First District, with Florence, married three years, and one child:

(a) Isabella Clark, born July, 1899

(4) William Waters Griffith, born May 14, 1879 at the family home of *Retirement* at Laytonsville, died October 5, 1959 at the Simpson Nursing Home in Boyds; buried at Laytonsville with his wife. This may be the same as William Griffith, of the proper age, listed alone in his own household in the 1900 census of the county, First District, single, a salesman. Married December 5, 1912 at the home of the bride's parents to Jessie Higgins Magruder, born c.1888, died February 19, 1973, and was buried at the Laytonsville Cemetery; daughter of Robert P. Magruder of Grifton. He was a plumbing and heating contractor and active in the Redland Hunt. There were two daughters:

(a) Genevieve Magruder Griffith, born March 25, 1921. Married November 8, 1941 to Frederick Donald Cissel, born c.1915, of Silver Spring, son of Henry H. Cissel and Bertha Scaggs.

(b) Dorothy Isabelle Griffith, born January 12, 1924; married to Joyner.

(5) Jeffrey Magruder Griffith, born November 14, 1881, died in June, 1947 at Retirement Farm.. Married at Neelsville March 31, 1910 to Lillian Neel, daughter of James Neel. She was born c.1883, and died October 18, 1967 on the home retirement farm at Laytonsville; buried at Neelsville with her husband. Her obituary mentions children, and their place of residence as of 1967:

(a) Kathryn Griffith, married Doane of Baltimore.

(b) Isabella Griffith, married Willett.

(c) Jeffrey Magruder Griffith, Jr., born July 13, 1913; died at home January 24, 1960. Buried with his parents.

(6) Isabelle Griffith, born June 23, 1885

(7) Susan Matilda Griffith, born December 29, 1888; married first to William H. Riggs and second to Gordon Hobbs and lived in Baltimore.

b. Cleora P. Griffith, born c.1869. Married October 17, 1889 to J. H. Riggs Wolfe of Howard County.

c. Eliza B. Griffith, born c.1870

d. Ellen Cuyler Griffith, born c.1872; married November 28, 1888 to William L. Mathews of Howard County.

e. Maude Griffith, born c.1874

f. Priscilla Griffith, born c.1877

8. Jeffrey M. Griffith, born February, 1829

9. Angelina M. Griffith, born October, 1831; at home in 1850. By 1862, listed in her father's will as Angelina Falkner.

CHILD 9

Horatio Griffith
1790-1861

This son of Samuel Griffith (1752) and his second wife, Ruth Berry, was born June 9, 1790, and died c.1861. Married to Eliza Shepherd, born c.1793, died c.1833. He was head of household in the 1850 census of Montgomery County for the First District, with $1,700 in real estate, and one slave, living alone with his son Horatio. We note that Horatio apparently moved around a bit; he is here in Maryland, but it appears that at least his daughter Angelina was born in Tennessee. In the 1850 agricultural census, Horatio was listed as owning 46 acres of improved land and 300 acres unimproved, valued at $1,700 in total. He owned 3 horses, 1 milch cow, 10 sheep and 13 swine. In the previous year, he produced 20 bushels of wheat, 200 bushels of Indian corn, 40 bushels of oats, 25 bushels of buckwheat, 100 pounds of butter and 2 tons of hay. We next found Horatio living alone in the 1860 census of the First District, with $2,000 in real estate and $2,400 in personal property.

Horatio left a will in Montgomery County, dated July 16, 1861, probated November 5, 1861 and recorded in liber JWS 1 at folio 93. He there mentions his four children by name, and one granddaughter. After the specific bequests noted following, the residue was to be divided equally between the four children, who were:

1. Mary Griffith, born c.1826, died 1892, who received from her father the sum of one thousand dollars, and one negro woman named Charity. Married to George Whitman, and they had children:
   a. Anne M. Whitman. From her grandfather, she received a red and white spotted cow.
   b. Lizzie Whitman.
   c. Clara G. Whitman.

2. Lafayette F. Griffith, born c.1828 in Montgomery County, died November 23, 1902 at his home in Louisville, Kentucky, leaving his wife and five children. He was a veteran of the Mexican War (*Sentinel* obituary). He reportedly was married twice, and moved to Kentucky. However, he appeared as head of household in the 1880 census of Montgomery County, for the Fourth District, listed as a guano agent, and a widower, with four children at home, all listed as born in Maryland. He was not found in earlier census reports, nor in the 1900 census of the county. The *Sentinel* reported that Lafayette F. Griffith, formerly a resident of Montgomery County, but then a resident of Dallas, Texas, was married March 13, 1883 to Miss Ada L. Beard of Christianburg, Kentucky. The census microfilm was difficult to read, and the names of the children appeared to be:
   a. Lonie Griffith, a daughter, born c.1860
   b. Yourtie Griffith, a daughter, born c.1866
   c. Shepherd Griffith, a son, born c.1872
   d. Charity Griffith, a daughter, born c.1875

3. Angelina Griffith, born July 13, 1830; received from her father's will one negro woman named Fanny. The will further provided that her three siblings (Mary, Horatio and Lafayette) were to pay to Angelina annually, the sum of fifty dollars, during the lifetime of the negro woman, for her benefit, comfort and support. Angelina was married in Montgomery County by license dated January 5, 1852 to John Dorsey

Berry, born c.1824. He was head of household in the 1860 census of the county for the Fifth District, owning $2,730 in real estate and $1,200 in personal property, with his wife and two children. John was head of household in the 1870 census of the county for the Fifth District, with his wife Angeline and five children. However, Angelina was there reported as having been born in Tennessee. In the 1880 census of the county, for the Eighth District, the entire family is present, and Angelina is there again reported as born in Tennessee. There were six children:

a. Mary E. Berry, born September 27, 1854
b. Horatio G. Berry, born October 1, 1856
c. Charles L. Berry, born July 20, 1860
d. John Dorsey Berry, Jr., born May 21, 1864
e. Nena R. Berry, born June 25, 1867
f. Winifred E. Berry, a son, born April 7, 1873. Head of household in the 1900 census of the Ninth District of Montgomery County, his wife was Rosalie, born December, 1862. They had been married two years, and were as yet childless.

4. Horatio Griffith, Jr., born c.1832, married in Montgomery County on November 29, 1855 to Rebecca Hilleary Dorsey of Howard County and had children:
    a. Anne Eliza Griffith, born c.1858, died c.1944. Married November 30, 1880 to William Harvey Davis, born April 15, 1858, died c.1933, the son of Henry Shipley Davis (1808) and Drusilla Dade (1821). He has also been reported as William Henry Davis and they had ten children, including:
       (1) Horatio Griffith Davis, born September 4, 1881, died April 6, 1929.
       (2) Henry Dade Davis, born c.1883, married September, 1910 to Lelia England, born c.1887, died 1925. They had one daughter, and he was married second August 31, 1929 to Elsie I. Hall, by whom he had two more children:
           (a) Helen Louise Davis, born 1913, married to Major Howard Munford.

(b) Elsie Dade Davis, born December 9, 1930

(c) Elizabeth Ann Davis, born June 8, 1932

(3) Helen Ruth Davis, born c.1884, died c.1943. Married on March 4, 1908 to Walker Belt Townshend. One child:

    (a) William Grafton Townshend, born April 19, 1909. Married September 23, 1933 to Elizabeth Tapscott, born 1910. Children:

        1. Carolee Townshend, born 1941

        2. Helen Susan Townshend, born 1944

        3. Robert Grafton Townshend, born 1946

(4) Ann Maude Davis, born c.1886, married December 26, 1908 to James A. Hyatt, born c.1883, died c.1937, and had children:

    (a) Helen Griffith Hyatt, born July 27, 1910, married to Russell J. Jenkins, and had three children. She was married second to Charles Urick, Jr. Children:

        1. Russell J. Jenkins, Jr.; December 21, 1928

        2. Elizabeth Ann Jenkins; October 19, 1930

        3. Alan Wade Jenkins; April 6, 1934

        4. Edmund McDonald Urick, born November 9, 1943

    (b) James A. Hyatt, III, born 1912, married Elena Green, born 1914. One son:

        1. James Robert Hyatt: March 12, 1942.

(5) William Harvey Davis, Jr., born c.1888, married July 24, 1919 to Rose Magruder, born c.1892. One son:

    (a) William Harvey Davis, III: August 20, 1925

(6) Louis Dorsey Davis, born c.1889, died c.1945. Married January 19, 1911 to Mary Gartrell, born c.1889, and had children:

    (a) Anne Virginia Davis, born June 14, 1912. Married June 26, 1937 to Stuart MacIntosh Pindell, born c.1914 and had children:

        1. Stuart MacIntosh Pindell, Jr., born 1938

        2. Louis Spencer Pindell, born 1941

3. Eric Dorsey Pindell, born 1942
   (b) Louis Dorsey Davis, Jr., born January 30, 1915
   (c) Marion Dade Davis, born 1918, married February 7, 1942 to Charles Evans Williar, Jr., born 1917, and had children:
      1. Anna Mason Williar: October 5, 1944
      2. John Jay Williar, born August 21, 1947
(7) Joseph C. Davis, born October 19, 1892, died January 13, 1948.
(8) Alice Katherine Davis, born c.1895, married February 3, 1915 to Evan Aquilla Jones, born c.1892, died 1941, and had children:
   (a) Griffith Davis Jones, born August 9, 1916, married April 6, 1941 to Martha Lewis Randall, born 1919, and had children:
      1. Katherine Davis Jones; April 15, 1942
      2. Griffith David Jones, Jr., born October 11, 1943
      3. Louis Randall Jones; July 25, 1945
   (b) Evan Aquilla Jones, Jr., born April 25, 1918, married November 15, 1929 to Carolina (Lycett) Jones, and had two children. He married second Dorothy Lyon and had two children. The four were:
      1. Evan Aquilla Jones, 3rd: October 3, 1940
      2. Louise Davis Jones: July 14, 1942
      3. Joseph Davis Jones: July 31, 1949
      4. Lorraine Allen Jones: February 11, 1951
(9) Marion Virginia Davis, born October 31, 1897, died November 20, 1918.
(10) George Croxton Davis, born February 25, 1902, died January 23, 1923.
b. Helen Louise Griffith, married September 17, 1891 at Frederick, Maryland to John E. Gilson.
c. William B. Griffith.

CHILD 10

Sarah Griffith
1792-1859

This daughter of Samuel Griffith (1752) and his second wife, Ruth Berry, was born April 28, 1792 in Montgomery County, and died October 1, 1859. Married first February, 1831 to Robert Warfield, born March 4, 1790, died May 23, 1842, son of Levin Warfield (1753). They had two children. She was married second in 1845 to Benjamin Lyon, but had no children. Sarah Lyon appeared as head of household in the 1850 census of the First District, perhaps twice widowed, with her only surviving son, Israel G. Warfield. Her children were:

1. Israel Griffith Warfield, born February 17, 1832, and died February 27, 1907 at Laytonsville in Montgomery County, having moved there at about the age of six with his parents; buried with his wife at the Laytonsville Cemetery. Married at St. Bartholomew's Episcopal Church in Laytonsville by license dated June 5, 1860 to Maria Gaither Griffith, born May 28, 1838, daughter of Elisha Riggs Griffith (1805) and Elizabeth Gaither (1805). In the 1850 census of the Cracklin District of Montgomery County, Israel was found living with Sarah Lyon, born c.1794, and she was listed as head of household. In the 1860 census for Laytonsville District, Israel is listed as head of household, by his initials only, born c.1833, which appears to be the same individual. He there had a wife, Maria G., born c.1838. He was listed then as owning real estate valued at $2,500 and personal property valued at $2,000; not too bad for a young man, just twenty-seven years old, and recently married. By the census of 1870, Israel was found living in the Brighton area of Montgomery County, with his wife, and five children. In the 1880 census of the county for the Cracklin District, Israel was head of household, with his wife and six children. Head of household in the 1900 census for the county in the First District, Israel and Maria had her mother Elizabeth Griffith living with them at the age of ninety-five. She was a widow, having been married sixty-five years and

the mother of seven children, only two then surviving. Israel and Maria had been married for forty years, and she had been the mother of nine children, only five then surviving. The two oldest children were mentioned in the will of their maternal grandfather. The children were:

a. Robert Clarence Warfield, born June 15, 1861 at Laytonsville, died April 6, 1943 at Rockville. He was a dentist; married February 15, 1888 to Margaret Webb, daughter of Francis Ignatius Devereaux Webb (1833) and Mary T. Postley (1838) by whom he had five children before her death. He was married second in Philadelphia August 30, 1916 to Susan Natalie Dutrow, born August 14, 1872 in Ohio, and died August 25, 1963 at Potomac, Maryland, the daughter of Amos W. Dutrow and Sarah Howell. Robert was head of household in the 1900 census of the county for the Fourth District, Rockville Town, with his wife listed as Maggie, born November, 1861. He was listed as a dentist, and they had been married for thirteen years. She had been the mother of five children, with three surviving, and at home. Robert Clarence left a will dated March 8, 1943, probated April 20, 1943 and filed in liber JWN 2 at folio 113, will records of Montgomery County. He names his wife Susan, and his three surviving sons. The five children were:

(1) Robert Leroy Warfield, of Frederick, who founded a Ford auto dealership there in 1916. Born c.1889, died October 5, 1970 in a Palm Beach, Florida hospital. Before entering the auto business, he was an attorney in Rockville. Married Mabel Poole, and had two sons:

(a) John Clark Warfield, of Frederick.

(b) Robert Warfield.

(2) Helen Elizabeth Warfield, born December 18, 1889, died February 11, 1894.

(3) Clarence Griffith Warfield, an Admiral in the US Navy, Died June 28, 1982; married to Kathryn Knight and had a daughter:

(a) Kathryn D. Warfield, married O'Neill.

141

(4) Webb Warfield, died as an infant October 11, 1891; buried with parents.

(5) Gaither Postley Warfield, a minister, born February 13, 1896, died August 16, 1986 at his home in Rockville. He had been a Methodist Missionary in Poland, where he met and married his wife in 1928. She was Hania M. Drodiowski, born January 18, 1906 in Lvov, died March 16, 1995 in Rockville. In September, 1939, he was interned by the Russians and exchanged to the Germans; finally in 1942, being exchanged to American forces. He and his wife were co-authors of *Call Us to Witness*, an account of their experiences. One daughter:

    (a) Monica Warfield, born c.1937, probably in Poland, married to Kulp of Vermont.

b. Elisha Griffith Warfield, born May 15, 1863; married May 14, 1890 to Hattie S. Sargent and lived in Massachusetts.

c. Elizabeth Washington Warfield, born February 8, 1865, married July 15, 1890 at the Cedars, Laytonsville, to Francis Clarence Webb of Baltimore. *(Sentinel)*

d. Alfred G. Warfield, born November 14, 1867. He died September 2, 1877 at home near Laytonsville. The *Sentinel* obituary listed his name as Albert Griffith Warfield, with reference to his parents.

e. Israel Griffith Warfield, Jr., born November 18, 1869. Married at Ascension Chapel in Gaithersburg, by license dated November 3, 1897 to Mrs. Katie L. Church, born c.1869 in the District of Columbia. Her father had been born in Maine and her mother in Virginia. He was head of household in the 1900 census of the county, Ninth District, Town of Gaithersburg, with his wife Katie. They had been married two years, he was a dentist, and they had one child, surviving, but not at home.

f. Lena May Warfield, born May 7, 1872. Married October 26, 1898 at Laytonsville Methodist Church to Doctor Vernon Hilleary Dyson.

g. Martha J. Warfield, born July 25, 1874

h. Bertha Warfield, born March 21, 1876
i. Frederick G. Warfield, born June 15, 1879
2. Robert H. Warfield, born July, 1835, died 1846.

CHILD 11

Philemon Griffith
1794-1873

This son of Samuel Griffith (1752) and his second wife, Ruth Berry, was born March 22, 1794 in Montgomery County. He died October 8, 1873 and was buried in the family cemetery on Derwood Road in the county, north of Rockville. Married September 22, 1817 to Sarah Hammond Riggs, born September 19, 1797, died September 25, 1823, daughter of Thomas Riggs (1772) and Mary Hammond (1776), and had two children. Philemon was married second to Sarah Griffith Crabb, born January 27, 1793, died April 27, 1862 in Baltimore, daughter of General Jeremiah Crabb and Elizabeth Griffith, and had five children. Sarah is buried in the Griffith family cemetery on Derwood Road, Montgomery County. Philemon was head of household in the 1850 census of Montgomery County for the Rockville District. He then had $3,750 in real estate and his wife and three children were at home; Mortimer, Emeline and Philemon. He was head of household in the 1860 census of the Fourth District, Forest Oak Post Office, living alone with his wife Sarah, next door to the newly formed household of his son Philemon C. Griffith. The elderly Philemon was listed as a tobacco inspector, with $6,000 real estate and $5,600 in personal property.

It appears probable that Philemon was married a third time after the death of his second wife in 1862, although there is no record of children from that marriage. He left a will in Montgomery County dated December 28, 1866, probated October 14, 1873 and recorded in liber RWC 6 at folio 256. In the will, he leaves *"to my dearly beloved wife Ann Griffith, the dwelling house on Bare Street (numbered one hundred and forty-five) in the City of Baltimore, and in which I now reside, together with all the furniture therein contained."* In addition, he left to his wife Ann the sum of ten thousand dollars, explaining that the legacy is in lieu of the portion of his personal estate to which she would be entitled by law. The will then proceeds to describe legacies to other family members, mentioned following. The children of Philemon from his two marriages were:

1. Mary Riggs Griffith, born c.1819; married to Samuel C. Dorsey, born c.1816, and had children. Under her father's will, she received only five dollars, perhaps having been given more during his lifetime. Samuel was head of household in the 1850 census of the First District, with his wife and four children. He was next head of household in the 1860 census of the First District, for Damascus and Unity Post Office, owning $3,400 in real estate and $3,500 in personal property. His wife was at home, with six children. In the 1867-68 Slave Census of the county, he was listed as Samuel O. Dorsey, owner of six slaves, all members of the King family. He was head of household for the 1870 census of the First District, with $4,000 in real estate and $1,000 in personal property. His wife and daughters Caroline and Mary were still at home. Head of household in the 1880 census of the county for the Cracklin District, he was listed as Samuel O. Dorsey, with his wife, and son Samuel and daughter Mary still at home. Finally, he was listed as head of household in the 1900 census of the First District, a widower, married for sixty-four years. Living with him was his son Samuel and daughter Mary A. Dorsey. Also, there was Thomas Owens, born March, 1881, a grandson. Children were:

    1. Gustavus W. Dorsey, born c.1838. Married in the county by license dated November 26, 1866 to Margaret Owens, born c.1842. He was head of household in the 1870 census of the First District, with his wife, and four black servants. Head of household in the 1880 census of the Eighth District, he and his wife Margaret still did not appear to have children. Three other individuals were living with them, with ho relationships demonstrated. Finally, he was head of household in the 1900 census of the Eighth District, with his wife Margaret. They had been married for thirty-four years, but had no children. He lived at

Brookeville, Montgomery County, and was a Lt. Colonel, 1st Maryland Cavalry, CSA, in the Civil War.
b. Maria Dorsey, born c.1841; married to L. J. G. Owings and had children. Not found in Montgomery County census records. The children were:
(1) Willie Owings.
(2) Samuel Owings.
(3) Ruth Owings.
(4) Minnie Owings.
(5) Gillis Owings.
(6) Thomas Owings.
c. Samuel C. Dorsey, Jr., born c.1845; living alone in the 1870 census of the First District, single, two doors from the household of his father. He was then a farmer, with $2,500 in real estate and $800 in personal property.
d. Caroline Dorsey, born c.1849
e. Mary Dorsey, born c.1850
f. Sarah Dorsey, born c.1858
2. Thomas Riggs Griffith, born July 10, 1820, and died September 13, 1826.
3. Emeline Griffith, born December 10, 1829; infant death.
4. Mortimer Crabb Griffith, born July 8, 1831, died December 22, 1891; received one thousand dollars under his father's will. Married on November 15, 1859 to Mary Jane Cassell and had children. Head of household in the 1870 census of the Fourth District, we read his name as Mortimer E. Griffith, apparently incorrectly. He was a farmer, with $5,000 in real estate and $1,000 in personal property. His wife was there, with four children. Also living with him was his brother Philemon and his son Alfred. Mortimer was head of household in the 1880 census of the Fourth District of Montgomery County, with his wife Mary, and seven children. She was there reported as born c.1840. Children:
a. Philemon Griffith, born September 13, 1860. Under the will of his grandfather, he received a gold watch and five hundred dollars.
b. Mortimer Crabb Griffith, Jr., born October 8, 1863
c. Samuel C. Griffith, born April 17, 1867

d. Mary R. Griffith, born February 2, 1870
e. Alice Griffith, born November 13, 1873
f. Emory Griffith, born June 24, 1876; in the census of 1880, this child is listed as Emily, born c.1877, a female.
g. Sarah Griffith, born c.1879
5. Alfred Griffith, born July 10, 1832, a twin.
6. Emeline C. Griffith, born July 10, 1832, a twin; received one thousand dollars under her father's will. Married in Montgomery County (or Frederick County ?) by license dated July 27, 1858 to Walter A. Orme. They were not found in census records of Montgomery County.
7. Philemon Crabb Griffith, born c.1835, died July 18, 1885; buried in the family burying ground near Derwood, Montgomery County; received one thousand dollars under his father's will. His obituary in the *Sentinel* stated that he left a son and a daughter, and that his wife died "some years ago." Married June 6, 1857 to Elizabeth Anderson, born November 12, 1834, died May 25, 1868, daughter of Doctor John W. Anderson and Mira C. Magruder (married February 15, 1831). Head of household in the 1860 census for the Fourth District of Montgomery County, Forest Oak Post Office, with his wife Elizabeth, living next door to the household of his parents. In the 1870 census of the Fourth District, he was living in the household of his brother Mortimer, with a son Alfred. In the 1880 census of the county for the Fourth District, Philemon was living in the household of Chandler Keys (1805), with both his children with him. They were:
a. Alfred Charles Griffith, born May 27, 1864, died November 10, 1921 in Baltimore; buried Rockville Cemetery, apparently single. (*Sentinel* obituary). In birth records of Christ Episcopal Church in Rockville, the name of this child is reported as Alfred Crabb Griffith, probably correct.
b. Sarah Crabb Griffith, whose date of birth is questionable. Family file records in the library report February 22, 1868; records of Christ Episcopal Church in Rockville report February 27, 1865; tombstone reads February 14, 1866, died April 21, 1900. In the 1870 census of the

county for the Fourth District this child was living in the household of Thomas Anderson (1805), there listed as Sallie Griffith. In the 1880 census of the Fourth District, she was living with Julia Anderson (1841), keeping house, and William Anderson (1850), an engineer; both single. Sarah C. Griffith (probably this individual) was married in the county by license dated October 26, 1897 to Doctor Ernest T. Fearon of Washington. In the 1900 census of the county for Rockville Town, he was listed as born November, 1869 in Pennsylvania, a druggist, a widower, with a daughter, living in the household of Mitta B. Anderson (1850), establishing a relationship. The daughter was listed as a grand-niece:

(1) Julia A. Fearon, born August, 1898; married to Clyde Stout of Rockville.

William Griffith
died 1699
The Immigrant
Chapter 2
*

Orlando Griffith
1688
*

Henry Griffith
1720
Chapter 4
*

Philemon Griffith
1756
Chapter 8
*

*   *   *   *   *   *   *   *   *
*
*   * Jemima Griffith 1784
*
*   * Philemon Griffith, Jr. 1787
*
*   * Henry Griffith 1789
*
*   * Henry Griffith 1791
*
*   * Eleanor Griffith 1792
*
*   * Ruth Hammond Griffith 1794
*
*   * Lemuel Griffith 1795
*
*   * Agrippa Griffith 1796
*
*   * Almeda Griffith 1797
*
*   * Sarah Griffith 1799
*
*   * Sarah Ann Griffith 1803
*
*   * Mary Eleanor Griffith 1805

CHAPTER 8

Philemon Griffith
1756-1838

This son of Henry Griffith (1720) and his second wife, Ruth Hammond, was born August 29, 1756, and died April 29, 1838 in Frederick County, and was titled Colonel. Buried at Laytonsville Cemetery. As Captain of the Third Company of Rifles, he was taken prisoner at Fort Washington, and exchanged in 1776, when he was promoted to Major. He was named Colonel by the Governor of Maryland. He was married November 18, 1782 to Eleanor Jacob, born October 2, 1762, died April 15, 1838, buried with her husband; daughter of Mordecai Jacob and Jemima Isaac. Philemon left a will in Frederick County, dated December 30, 1837, probated May 3, 1838 and recorded in liber GME-2 at folio 309. It is quite lengthy, with numerous bequests to children and grandchildren, and its provisions will be discussed as we list the family. His wife Eleanor was to make her selection from the estate, not to exceed the amount of her legal dower. Philemon noted toward the end of the will, that having made gifts of negroes, money and other things to his children as they married and settled, he ratified each of those gifts. After all the bequests were satisfied, and the debts paid, all the residue of the estate was to be shared by two daughters; Ruth H. Warfield and Sarah Ann Griffith. The Executors were Charles D. Warfield and Lebbeus Griffith. The children included:

1. Jemima Griffith, born November 17, 1784, died August 26, 1799.
2. Philemon Griffith, Jr., born July 18, 1787, died August 25, 1827. married to Sarah Hammond Riggs, born September 19, 1797, the daughter of Thomas Riggs of Samuel.
3. Henry Griffith, born April 25, 1789, died February 8, 1790
4. Henry Griffith, born January 7, 1791, died June 5, 1791
5. Eleanor Griffith, born October 5, 1792, died June 20, 1793
6. Ruth Hammond Griffith, born February 27, 1794; married first to Caleb Dorsey and lived at *Glenwood*, in Howard County, and had children. Married second to Charles D. War-

field of *Bushy Park* and had at least two children. One of them born to her first marriage was:

a. John A. Dorsey, named as a grandson in the will of Philemon Griffith, to receive one hundred dollars. He also received a house and lot in the town of Lisbon, Anne Arundel County, where John Griffith then lived.

b. Charles D. Warfield, Jr., born to the second marriage.

c. Sallie Warfield, born to the second marriage, and married to Dr. Evan William Warfield.

7. Lemuel Griffith, born April 22, 1795, died April 10, 1846. He was a private in the War of 1812 under Captain Joseph Wood, from August 27 to October 13, 1814. Married April 27, 1819 to Rachel Warfield Griffith, born January 21, 1802, died April 1, 1861, daughter of Colonel Lyde Griffith (1774) and his first wife Anne (Poole) Dorsey (1773). The widowed Rachel appeared as head of household in the 1850 census of Frederick County, in New Market District with seven of their children still at home. She was there listed as owning $5,000 in real estate. In his father's will of 1837, four of the children of son Lemuel and his wife Rachel were specified: Philemon, Henry Sylvester, Lyde and Mary Eleanor. They were to divide equally all their grandfather's land on the northwest side of the road from New Market to Buckeystown by way of Zion Chapel; plus two negro men named Corbin and George; plus horses, cattle, hogs and all the crops of grain; and also the sixty shares of stock in the Peterboro Bank of Maryland. They had children:

a. Philemon Griffith, born April 15, 1820, a twin, and died July 26, 1858, single. US Navy, buried at New Market Methodist. Received one hundred dollars under his grandfather's will.

b. Ann Griffith, born April 15, 1820, a twin, of whom more.

c. Lyde Griffith, born April 29, 1823. Married to Louise Hammond and had children. She was born 1826, and died 1880; buried at Fairmount Cemetery, Libertytown. They had children, including:

(1) Mollie H. Griffith; perhaps the same of that name reported in the *Sentinel* as having obtained a mar-

riage license in Washington before May 2, 1890 to marry Joseph H. Clagett.

    (2)   Thomas H. Griffith.

    (3)   Rezin Griffith.

    (4)   Lyde Griffith.

    (5)   Jennie R. Griffith.

    (6)   Johnson Griffith.

d.   Henry A. Griffith, born August 29, 1825, listed as a farm laborer during the 1870 census of Montgomery County for the Second District, Damascus Post Office, living in the household of Ezekiel Moxley.

e.   Charles A. Griffith, born June 23, 1827, died 1863, leaving in will in Frederick County dated May 7, 1863, probated November 11, 1863, recorded in liber APK-1 at folio 328. It is a simple will, leaving his estate to be equally divided between the two children of his brother Mordecai (following), who was deceased, and naming Annie Mary Griffith as Executrix.

f.   Mordecai Griffith, born October 23, 1828. Married to Margaret B. Hammond, born c.1835, died February 21, 1857; buried at New Market Methodist and had children:

    (1)   Annie Mary Griffith.

    (2)   Brian C. Griffith.

g.   John A. Griffith, born February 5, 1830, killed 1883, and single. He left a will in Montgomery County, dated February 25, 1882, probated March 25, 1884 and recorded in liber RWC 6 at folio 364. He left to his cousin William H. Griffith all his interest in the estate of Colonel Lyde Griffith, deceased, as well as all property of any nature that might be due him, or become due him.

h.   Christopher Columbus Griffith, born May 28, 1832, died 1918, buried at Laytonsville, twin; married to Susannah Warfield. He is perhaps the same individual listed simply as Columbus Griffith, found in the 1860 census of the First District of Montgomery County, but there reported as born c.1835. He was listed as head of household, with Louisa Griffith, born c.1839, who was reported as owning $300 in personal property. At that time frame, relationships were not stated in the census, but the name Louisa does not correspond to his reported marriage. He is also perhaps the same individual listed as C. Columbus Griffith in the 1867-1868 Slave Census of Montgomery County, listed as owning two slaves. Columbus was next found as head of household in the 1870 census of the First District, apparently a widower, with Joseph Fisher living with him, a small child, born c.1864. In the 1880 census of the county for the Cracklin District, we found Columbus as head of household, with Henry Griffith listed with him as a brother. However, both were listed as single, and the ages reported were not quite the same as reported births for each of them. Columbus was there reported as being 45 years of age (born c.1835) and Henry as 50 years old (born c.1830), but they appear to be sons of this family.

 i. Mary Eleanor Griffith, born May 28, 1832, twin, married to Plummer.

8. Agrippa Griffith, born August 29, 1796

9. Almeda Griffith, born November 2, 1797, died January 4, 1798

10. Sarah Griffith, born August 12, 1799, died March 18, 1803

11. Sarah Ann Griffith, born March 23, 1803, died April 22, 1877. Married in Frederick County September 28, 1824 to Israel Griffith, born August 17, 1799, died January 19, 1875 at his home in Baltimore, a retired dry goods merchant, son of Captain Samuel Griffith (1752) and his second wife, Ruth Berry. They had ten children, and lived in Baltimore:

 a. Charles Henry Griffith, born December 21, 1825; received one hundred dollars under his grandfather's will.

 b. Mary Eleanor Griffith, born July 8, 1828

 c. Frances Ann Griffith, born July 28, 1830

 d. Alverda Griffith, born August 7, 1832

 e. Israel Griffith, Jr., born September 16, 1835, a twin, died August 9, 1863, single

 f. Sarah Ann Griffith, born September 16, 1835, a twin. Married to Joseph H. Ruddach, first Lieutenant of the Chesapeake Riflemen, Co. F, during the Mexican War.

g. George Griffith, born February 8, 1838, an infant death.
h. George Griffith, second use of the name, born October 24, 1839, an infant death.
i. Emma Griffith, born October 2, 1842
j. David Israel Griffith, born October 26, 1844
12. Mary Eleanor Griffith, born August 28, 1805, died June 30, 1835. Married January 27, 1829 in Frederick County as his first wife to Lebbeus Griffith, born February 11, 1804, son of Howard Griffith (1757) and Jemima Jacob (1759) and had three children, one of whom was deceased before 1882. They, and their descendants, are discussed under the name of their father, which please see. In the will of Mary Eleanor's father, he left to the two surviving children, to share equally, all the lands conveyed to him by Allen and Sarah Farquhar by deed dated June 5, 1811 called *Hickory Plains*, then occupied by Lebbeus Griffith, plus the sum of $1,500 and a negro boy and girl called Stephen and Dorcas. Briefly here, they were:
a. Philemon Howard Griffith, born May 7, 1830; received one hundred dollars under his grandfather's will.
b. Jemima Eleanor Griffith, born June 24, 1832
c. Festus Agrippa Griffith, born November 25, 1834. Listed in an old family Bible with the other two children here, and may have died young.

Ann Griffith
1820-1884

This daughter of Lemuel Griffith (1795), and Rachel Warfield Griffith (1802), was born April 15, 1820, a twin, died 1884. Married William Watkins, son of Gassaway Watkins (1772) and Arianna Norwood. William Watkins was head of household in the 1850 census for Clarksburg District, Montgomery County, Maryland, born c.1817, and had a wife, Ann Watkins, born c.1822 to 1826, and four children. Also in the household is Perry G. Watkins, born c.1826, his brother. In the 1870 census, Ann appears alone, with three of her children. They appear again in the 1860 census of Damascus District, with more of their family. Children:
1. Sarah Ann Watkins, born c.1842

2. William Henry Watkins, born c.1845
3. Mary E. Watkins, born c.1847. This is perhaps the same Mary E. Watkins born August 13, 1846, died June 8, 1911. Married December 18, 1865 in Montgomery County, Maryland, to Charles C. King, born September 18, 1846, and died February 12, 1920, son of John A. King (1808). Both are buried at Clarksburg United Methodist Church. At least one record reports their marriage as October 15, 1866. They appear in the 1870 census of Damascus, Montgomery County, with two children. Also in the household is George G. King, born c.1854, not otherwise identified. The 1880 census includes the family, with five children. Charles was next found as head of household in the 1900 census of the Ninth District of the county, with his wife Mary E. and three children at home. They were reported there as married 27 years, a bit off from marriage records, but the same couple. She had been the mother of seven children, all surviving. They were listed next door to the household of their oldest son. The children were:

a. Bradley T. King, born c.1867 and died 1959; married June 14, 1892 to Sarah Wilson Dowden, born May 31, 1867 and died 1948, daughter of Zachariah Dowden, III (1829) and Rebecca Miller (1831). Bradley and Sarah are buried at Salem United Methodist Church at Cedar Grove. Head of household in the 1900 census of the Ninth District, next door to his parents, he and Sallie had then been married eight years, and she had been the mother of two children, both surviving, and at home. They had children:

(1) Gladys R. King, born June, 1893
(2) Bertie Madeline King, born 1897; died 1983. Married May 26, 1937 William E. Crutchley, born 1868 and died 1942; no children were reported. He was apparently first married to Lydia M., born 1870 and died 1933, the mother of his children. The family is buried at Clarksburg Methodist Church cemetery.
(3) Wallace C. King, born 1903 at Cedar Grove, and died March 13, 1977. Buried with his parents.

b. Hannah M. King, or Annie M. King, born c.1869, and married December 12, 1894 John E. Harding.

c. Norris M. King, born c.1871. Married March 13, 1907 to Elizabeth Penner, both of them being of Montgomery County.

d. Florence G. King, born c.1875

e. Maggie M. King, born c.1877

f. Georgie E. King, female, born February, 1886

g. Algernon G. King, born March, 1888, known as Bud.

4. Lyde A. Watkins, a son, born c.1849. The 1880 census for Clarksburg District contains a family headed by Lyde Watkins, born c.1851 according to the census, listed as a laborer, who is probably this individual. His wife, Amanda E., was born c.1836, appreciably older than he was. They also appear in the 1900 census for Barnesville, with their youngest son. Five children:

a. Cora L. Watkins, born 1873

b. Richard Watkins, born 1875

c. Mary Watkins, born 1877

d. Theopholis, a son, born May, 1880.

e. Robert Watkins, born c.1882

5. Mordecai Watkins, born c.1851 to 1858. He is listed in the 1880 census of Damascus District, with his wife, Lavana W., born c.1855, and two children:

a. Lillie W. Watkins, born c.1874

b. Florida B. Watkins, born c.1877. Married on February 27, 1895 Vachel H. Davis.

6. Greenbury Watkins, born c.1853

7. Margaret S. Watkins, born c.1857

8. Philemon G. Watkins, born c.1859, according to census records. However, he is probably the same Philemon G. Watkins who was born March 4, 1862, died November 15, 1919. Married May 7, 1886 Amelia A. Kinder, born June 8, 1865, died February 28, 1936. In 1900 census of Laytonsville; no children listed. She married second Charles T. McClure. Buried at Montgomery Chapel, Claggettsville.

William Griffith
died 1699
The Immigrant
Chapter 2
*
*
Orlando Griffith
1688
*
*
Greenberry Griffith
1727
Chapter 9
*
*

*   *   *   *   *   *   *   *   *
*
*   * Hezekiah Griffith 1752 .... Chapter 10
*
*   * Lydia Griffith 1755
*
*   * Howard Griffith 1757 .... Chapter 11
*
*   * Caleb Griffith 1759
*
*   * Greenberry Griffith, Jr. 1761
*
*   * Ruth Griffith 1763
*
*   * Rachel Griffith 1766
*
*   * Catherine Greenberry Griffith 1769
*
*   * Mary Griffith 1771
*
*   * John Riggs Griffith 1773

CHAPTER 9

Greenberry Griffith
1727-1809

This son of Orlando Griffith (1688) and his wife Katherine Howard, was born December 31, 1727, died March 1, 1809, and inherited from his father the tracts called *Ward's Care* and *Howard's Luck*. Married January 20, 1752 in Christ Church, Queen Caroline Parish, Anne Arundel County, to Ruth Riggs of *Riggs Hills*. She was born October 28, 1730, and died October 18, 1779, daughter of John Riggs (1687) and Mary Davis (1702). Greenberry was one of the Committee of Observation, appointed January 24, 1775 in Frederick County. They had ten children:

1. Hezekiah Griffith, born November 25, 1752, of whom more in Chapter 10.
2. Lydia Griffith, born March 7, 1755; named in the will of her uncle Orlando Griffith. Married February 22, 1781 to Philip McElfresh and had six children, including:
   a. William McElfresh, born April 4, 1782. Perhaps the same married in Frederick County by license dated December 13,1802 to Sarah Linthicum.
   b. Caleb McElfresh, a twin, born September 18, 1784. Perhaps the same married in Frederick County by license dated March 4, 1808 to Elizabeth Owings Shipley.
   c. Rachel McElfresh, a twin, born September 18, 1784
   d. John McElfresh, born December 14, 1786
   e. Philip Greenberry McElfresh, born May 3, 1796
3. Howard Griffith, born June 18, 1757, and of whom more in Chapter 11.
4. Caleb Griffith, born April 11, 1759, died December 9, 1843. Married November 8, 1787 to Mary Richardson, born November 13, 1767, died December 11, 1835. On April 15, 1795, he was appointed an Ensign under Captain Jacob Waters, 13th Regiment, Maryland Militia. They had children:

a. Ann Griffith, born August 2, 1788; married April 23, 1806 to James L. Holmes, born February 28, 1785 and lived in Kentucky.

b. Thomas Griffith, born April 1, 1791; married twice, and lived in Kentucky.

c. Robert Griffith, born February 15, 1793, died September 21, 1837

d. Catherine Griffith, born February 7, 1795; married to George W. Barclay, and lived in Kentucky.

e. Ruth Griffith, born March 25, 1797; married January 24, 1822 to Raleigh D. Bryant, born August 24, 1829 and lived in Kentucky.

f. Greenberry Griffith, born September 18, 1802

g. Mary Griffith, born April 16, 1804; married February 20, 1834 in Davies County, Kentucky to William E. Young and had children.

h. Ridgely Griffith, born October 5, 1806; married April 11, 1849 to Emma Read and lived in Kentucky.

i. Emeline M. Griffith, born March 12, 1811; married September 9, 1844 to Reverend Hiram A. Hunter and lived at Louisville, Kentucky.

j. Sarah Ann Griffith, born June 13, 1815; married June 6, 1837 to Richard Holding and lived in Kentucky.

5. Greenberry Griffith, Jr., born July 28, 1761; reportedly married November 29, 1787 to Rebecca Gartrell and had children in Frederick County, Maryland. However, a biography of his grandson in *History of Frederick County, Maryland*, by T. J. C. Williams and Folger McKinsey, 1910, states that he was married to Lydia Guttrell. Greenberry left a will in Montgomery County, dated November 16, 1829, probated September 13, 1831 and recorded in liber S at folio 143; rerecorded in liber VMB 3 at page 461. He there specifically names his wife as Rebecca, leaving her the entire estate for life. At her death, the estate was to be divided between his surviving sons, William, Nacy and Greenberry, and his grandson John Griffith, including all the slaves with the exception of Lucy, who was to be freed upon the death of Rebecca. The negro man Hercules was to go to Greenberry's son Nacy, alone. Nacy was, of

course, Ignatius Griffith. He also left one sixth of his estate to the heirs of his deceased son Philip; and one sixth part to the heirs of his daughter Betsy G. Dorsey. The children included:

a. William Griffith, born November 17, 1788.
b. Ignatius Griffith, married Ruth McElfresh, daughter of Philip McElfresh, and of whom more.
c. Philip Griffith, born January 14, 1792, died before 1829; married to Sarah Pusey Stoner, born c.1802, and had children, including:
   (1) Eliza Hobbs Griffith, born c.1818
   (2) Ephraim Jackson Griffith, born January 16, 1820 on Beaver Dam Creek in Frederick County, Maryland. Married c.1842 to Elizabeth Rush, and had children:
      (a) Sarah Catherine Griffith, born April 29, 1843; married Stevens Moore.
      (b) Martha Eleanor Griffith, born December 24, 1844; married May 19, 1861 to Ranna Stevens Moore.
      (c) Thomas Asbury Griffith, born December 6, 1846; married Sabina McCandless.
      (d) John William Griffith, born January 16, 1848; married to Charlotte Borden.
      (e) James Admire Griffith, born March, 1857
      (f) Leania Subina Griffith, born March 12, 1859, died November 8, 1880; married September 7, 1876 to Thomas Bainbridge, born c.1783, died December 26, 1822
      (g) Robert Union Griffith, born March 18, 1861; married Margarita Angelina Vailliancourt.
   (3) Rebecca Griffith, born c.1822
d. Greenberry Griffith, born March 2, 1794
e. John Griffith, married Gaither.
f. Elizabeth Greenberry Griffith, born December 9, 1799; married Ezra Dorsey, and had at least one son. Members of this family moved to Jefferson County, Kentucky:
   (1) Owen Dorsey, born July 11, 1822

6. Ruth Griffith, born November 14, 1763; married July 18, 1786 to Jesse Plummer and had children in Maryland, perhaps in Frederick County:
   a. Greenberry Griffith Plummer; married Jane Millhouse.
   b. Ellen W. Plummer, married Caleb Fleming.
   c. Thomas Griffith Plummer, married Mary Ralston.
   d. Anna Plummer, died young.
   e. Ruth Plummer, married November 20, 1817 to Howard Griffith, Jr. (1774), son of Howard Griffith (1757) and Jemima Jacob (1759), and had ten children. Lived in Baltimore, and their children moved to various other locations, including Iowa and California.
   f. Lydia G. Plummer, married in Frederick County, Maryland by license dated May 29, 1816, William P. Burgess, son of John Burgess and Eleanor Griffith.
   g. Philip Plummer, married in Prince George's County by license dated May 6, 1823 to Ann Maria Waters, born January 2, 1804, daughter of Jacob Franklin Waters, born July 16, 1775. Later lived in Ohio.
   h. Jesse Baker Plummer, born July 21, 1803
   i. Sarah Plummer, married Stephen Hussey.
   j. Anna Plummer, married James H. Holmes.
7. Rachel Griffith, born April 9, 1766, died August 12, 1833; married March 27, 1788 to Edward Mobley. Four children:
   a. Chloe Mobley.
   b. Lydia Mobley.
   c. John Mobley.
   d. Mordecai Mobley.
8. Catherine Greenberry Griffith, born August 6, 1769, died June 11, 1816. Married October 29, 1793 in Anne Arundel County to Nathan Browning, Jr., born c.1767, died February 17, 1815 son of Nathan Browning (1728). He obtained from his mother the tract called *Moneysworth* and a lot in Clarksburg. On January 5, 1811, *Bartgis Republican Gazette* carried notice that Nathan Browning of Nathan would petition for relief from debts. The *Frederick-Town Herald* of September 7, 1811 carried a notice that Nathan Browning of Nathan of Montgomery County was an insolvent debtor. On June 11, 1814, the paper

reported that a public sale of certain properties of others would be held at Nathan Browning's tavern in Clarksburg. Local newspapers also advertised the sale of the tavern stand in Clarksburg for July 20, 1816, formerly occupied by Nathan Browning, probably this individual, soon after his death.

9. Mary Griffith, born December 25, 1771, died before April 22, 1859, single. Her obituary in the *Montgomery County Sentinel* of that date states that she died at the residence of William Benton, and that she was a sister of the late Howard Griffith. It further states that her father emigrated to Maryland from Wales "at an early period in our history" and that she was the last of a large family circle. According to other records of the family, it was her great grandfather who was the immigrant, not her father.

10. John Riggs Griffith, born December 10, 1773, of whom more following.

Ignatius Griffith
died c.1840

This son of Greenberry Griffith, Jr. (1761) was married to Ruth McElfresh, daughter of Philip McElfresh. Ruth was born November 25, 1789, died February 20, 1869, and is buried at the New Market Methodist Church. Nace reportedly died shortly before 1840 and after his death, his widow moved to New Market in Frederick County. Often known as Nace Griffith, he was Captain of a company of Home Militia about 1840, when he was engaged in a mercantile business at Clarksburg in Montgomery County. The widow Ruth was found as head of household in the 1850 census of Frederick County for New Market District, reportedly born c.1795 She then owned four slaves, and $1,400 in real estate. Four of her children were then at home. They had children:

1. Philip G. M. Griffith, born c.1820, probably at Clarksburg, died January 20, 1898; buried at Marvin Chapel Methodist Church, Mt. Airy. Married in Frederick County by license dated September 28, 1847 to Harriet Ann Thomas, born c.1827, died July 28, 1894; buried with her husband; daughter of Samuel Thomas of Buckeystown. Philip was first found as

head of household in the 1850 census of Montgomery County for the Second District. He was a farmer, born c.1820 in Maryland, owner of three slaves, with a wife Harriet, born c.1828, and one child. In the agricultural census of 1850, Philip owned 100 acres of improved land and 200 acres unimproved, for a value of $1,000 in total. He owned 2 horses, 2 milch cows, 2 working oxen, 2 other cattle, 4 sheep and 7 swine. In the previous year he had produced 30 bushels of wheat, 320 bushels of Indian corn, 65 bushels of oats, 14 pounds of wool, 20 bushels of Irish potatoes, 100 pounds of butter and 3 tons of hay. Head of household in the 1860 census of the Second District, he was listed as owning $2,500 in real estate and $4,600 in personal property. His wife Harriet A. was listed as born c.1831 and they then had three children. Harriet Ann Griffith left a will in Frederick County dated June 13, 1894, probated May 13, 1895, recorded in liber JKW-1 at folio 320, also signed by her husband. The will leaves all the property to daughter Ruth E. Griffith during her single life, and then to be sold and equally divided between daughters Ruth E. Griffith, Fannie M. Dorsey, and grandson Thomas P. Mullinix, Jr., son of deceased daughter Mary B. Mullinix. The children were:

a. Ruth E. Griffith, born c.1849; died November 3, 1916, single. Buried with her parents.
b. Fannie M. Griffith, born c.1851; married to Dorsey.
c. Mary B. Griffith, born c.1854, died November 2, 1884; buried at Mt. Airy Prospect Church with her husband. Married to Thomas Pratt Mullinix, born June 23, 1844, died December 18, 1903, and had at least one son:
    (1) Thomas Pratt Mullinix, Jr.

2. S. Rebecca Griffith, born c.1828; married Charles C. Smith.
3. Elizabeth Griffith, died at the age of three.
4. John McElfresh Griffith, born June 20, 1827 at Clarksburg, died May 1, 1908 on his home farm at McKaig, and is buried at Mt. Zion Church with his wife and three sons. Married June 5, 1856 to Rachel Ann Norris, born August 26, 1835 near Woodsboro in Frederick County, died February 10, 1911,

daughter of John Norris and Annie McElfresh. They had children, not necessarily in this birth order:

a. Ignatius L. Griffith, lived in Spokane, Washington. Married to a Miss Peters of Rich Hill, Missouri. There is an infant burial in the Fairview Cemetery (abandoned) at McKaig, believed to be a child of this couple:
   (1) Leroy Griffith, born c.1882, died February 22, 1882 and in cemetery records listed as a child of Nacy Griffith (Ignatius) and Clara G. Griffith.
b. Aurelea Griffith.
c. Annie Griffith, married to T. D. Gallagher of Washington, D. C. and had three children:
   (1) Airy Gallagher.
   (2) Lucy Gallagher.
   (3) Norris Gallagher.
d. Harry M. Griffith, born c.1868, died September 2, 1901 and buried with his parents.
e. Airy Griffith, married William J. Beasley.
f. Philip Griffith.
g. Charles Griffith, married to Edna Sundergill. Lived near Unionville, Maryland, and had at least one child:
   (1) John L. Griffith.
h. William Griffith, married Effie Julia Hood and had children. She was born c.1876, daughter of Ortho Hood, died December 23, 1977 at the age of 101 years; buried at the Prospect Cemetery, Woodville Road, Frederick County. The children were:
   (1) Lillian Griffith.
   (2) Roger Griffith.
   (3) Victor Griffith.
i. Victor B. Griffith, born c.1879, died August 26, 1898; buried with his parents.
j. Basil Norris Griffith, born September 18, 1874, died March 29, 1875.
5. Rachel Griffith, born c.1831; married to David G. Yingling of Baltimore.

John Riggs Griffith
1773-

This son of Greenberry Griffith (1727) and Ruth Riggs (1730) was born December 10, 1773 in Frederick County, Maryland, probably in an area that became Montgomery in 1776. *Early Families of Southern Maryland*, Volume 1, by Elise Greenup Jourdan, assigns this child as a son of Hezekiah Griffith (1752). It appears, however, that she is incorrect, and that the two are brothers. We note that Hezekiah Griffith was married November 14, 1775 to Catharine Warfield (1757), two years after the birth of John Riggs Griffith. He was married November 1, 1797 to Sarah Tracy, and had children:

1. Lydia Griffith, married R. W. Willett.
2. Catherine Griffith, married William W. Benton.
3. Mary Griffith, married Edward Jones.
4. Rebecca Griffith, married February 12, 1835 William Davis, son of Zachariah Davis and Elizabeth Hyatt, the daughter of Meshack Hyatt. Children:
   a Eldred Griffith Davis.
   b. Daughter Davis, married Dickerson.
   c. Daughter Davis, married Clarke.
5. Flavilla Griffith, born c.1814; married May 12, 1835 to John Etchison. We believe this to be John W. Etchison, found as head of household in the 1850 census for the First District of Montgomery County, born c.1808. Living just one dwelling removed from that of Perry G. Etchison (1809), following, he was perhaps a brother. No children listed in 1850. They next appeared in the 1860 census for the First District, still with no children. In the 1870 census, the couple was living next door to Perry G. Etchison; still no children. In the 1880 census, the elderly couple again appear, with Catherine Benton living with them, born c.1801, widowed, listed as a sister-in-law.
6. Ruth Elizabeth Griffith, born c.1814, and died January 31, 1899 at the home of her son-in-law, Horace Waters near Germantown; buried at Neelsville Presbyterian Church. Her obituary in the *Sentinel* states that she was the last of seven sisters, and was survived by four children. Married June 23,

1830 to Perry Etchison, son of Ephraim Etchison (1774). We believe this to be Perry G. Etchison, found as head of household in the 1850 census for the First District of Montgomery County, Perry was born c.1809, died February 17, 1895. He was a farmer, and tobacco inspector for a number of years. In the 1850 census, his surname appears as Etchinson, which is incorrect. In 1850, Perry owned one slave, and in 1850, there were six children at home. He next appeared as head of household in the 1860 census for the First District, with his wife listed as Elizabeth (her middle name) and six children. The family was listed in the 1870 census for the First District, with only Laura and Fannie still at home. Perry was listed as owning $2,500 in real estate and $1,000 in personal property. In the 1880 census of the Cracklin District, Perry G. and his wife Elizabeth still had three daughters at home, as well as two daughters-in-law. The children were:

a. Lysander Etchison, born c.1831. First found as head of household in the 1880 census of Clarksburg District, with a wife Corilla, born c.1844, and four children. Living with them was Mareen Duvall, listed as a retired farmer, with his wife Elizabeth A. Duvall. It is of some interest to note that *Mareen Duvall of Middle Plantation*, by Harry Wright Newman, on page 91, reports that Mareen Duvall, born 1814, was married November 2, 1845 to Elizabeth Simpson, born April 6, 1821 in Montgomery County, "but then the widow Etchison." If that is correct, then the Etchison that Elizabeth Simpson married could have been born slightly before 1821, and must have died quite soon after their marriage. We also found a marriage license in Frederick County dated May 20, 1843 between Robert Henry Etchison and Elizabeth Ann Simpson, which may well have been her first marriage. We have not yet identified Robert Henry Etchison in a family group, however. Finding Mareen Duvall and Elizabeth in the household of Lysander Etchison (1831) suggests that the first husband of Elizabeth may well have been an older brother of Lysander. We note, however, that Mareen Duvall was guardian of his brother Lewis Duvall's daughter, Catharine Simms Duvall, born c.1844. One might suspect that Catherine and Corilla may be the same individual, and that would perhaps explain the presence of Mareen Duvall in the household of Lysander, but we are not prepared to assume that here, absent further evidence. The children of Lysander and Corilla were:

(1) Francis B. Etchison, born c.1864; married in Frederick County October 15, 1889 to Florence C. Griffith, born May 8, 1861, died 1933, daughter of Lebbeus Griffith (1804); both buried at Forest Oak cemetery in Gaithersburg.

(2) Cora M. Etchison, born c.1867

(3) Grace Etchison, born January 5, 1869 at New Market, died April 8, 1946 at Boyds, married at Trinity Methodist Church in New Market, Frederick County December 24, 1889 to Clarence M. Griffith, born November 17, 1864, died April 8, 1924. Both are buried at Forest Oak in Gaithersburg. He was the son of Lebbeus Griffith, (1804). His *Sentinel* obituary states that he died as the result of a fall, leaving his widow and two daughters, although we have identified only one girl. The 1900 census of Montgomery County, for the Second District, carries a household headed by Clarence R. Griffith (sic), with a wife Grace and two children, which is apparently this family. However, Clarence R. is there listed as having been born November, 1855, ten years earlier than that reported above. The 1855 date does not appear to be accurate. The couple had been married ten years, and she had been the mother of three children, only two surviving. The obituary of their son Clarence Gorman reports that he was survived by a brother and two sisters, both of them identified only by their husband's names: Mrs. Alexandria C. Gawlis, and Mrs. Walter M. Royal, Jr. The obituary of their mother names the same two daughters, as well as the two surviving sons. Clarence M. Griffith left a will dated April 5, 1924, written at George-

166

town University Hospital, three days before his death. The will was probated May 20, 1924 and recorded in liber PEW 2 at folio 184, leaving his entire estate to his wife Grace, to do with as she pleases. The known children were:

(a) Gladys May Griffith, born May, 1891; referred to in the will of her uncle Seth W. Griffith as married to Alexander C. Gawlis.

(b) Elizabeth Etchison Griffith, who died at the age of 3 years, 3 months and 4 days.

(c) Clarence Gorman Griffith, born May 31, 1899 in Boyds, died February 28 1967 at his home on East Diamond Avenue in Gaithersburg. Married November 29, 1922 at Clarksburg to Addie Maria King, born May 8, 1893, and died April 30, 1962, daughter of James Edward King (1854) and Addie Cassandra Hurley (1859). Gorman Griffith was postmaster of Gaithersburg for a number of years. He and his wife are buried at Forest Oak in Gaithersburg. No children.

(d) Robert Leland Griffith. This may be the child referred to as Seth Robert Griffith in the will of his uncle Seth W. Griffith. He was born c.1908 and died August 5, 1970; buried at Glenwood Cemetery, Silver Spring, Maryland. His obituary reports that he was employed by the Civil Aeronautics Board, and died of cancer at Kensington Gardens Sanitarium. He was survived by his wife Margaret and two daughters. Also named were two surviving sisters. His children were:

1. Claire Ann Griffith, who married James Roupas.

2. Sarah Griffith, married Ronald G. Tipton.

(e) Mary Ann Griffith; referred to in the will of her uncle Seth W. Griffith; apparently married to Walter M. Royal, Jr.

167

  (4) Clarence H. Etchison, born c.1877

b. Sarah Roberta Etchison, born c.1833; not at home in 1860; married March 31, 1859 at *Brookfield*, Montgomery County, home of her father, to William Edgar Hammond of Anne Arundel County. There is a Roberta Hammond living at home with her parents in the 1880 census of Cracklin District, Montgomery County, widowed, with her two children. They are listed in the census as daughters-in-law but should apparently have been designated granddaughters:

  (1) Laura Hammond, born c.1861, teaching school.
  (2) Nettie Hammond, born c.1863

c. Mary Poultney J. Etchison, born c.1839, died c.1924. Married October 24, 1866 as his second wife to Horace Waters, born May 25, 1823, died November 16, 1902; buried at Neelsville Presbyterian Church. He was apparently first married January 24, 1850 to Mary J. Dorsey, by whom he had children, appearing in the 1850 and 1860 census, but not later with his second wife. He appears as head of household in the 1870 census for the Second District of Montgomery County, with his Mary P. J. and two children. Horace was quite wealthy for the time, owning $20,120 in real estate and $23,098 in personal property. Listed as a farmer, he had nine black individuals in his household, as domestic servants and farm laborers, and their small children. Horace and Mary were next found in the 1880 census, with five sons. In the 1900 census for the Second District, the couple had three sons at home, including one born after the 1880 census. The report states that they have been married for 33 years, and have had 6 children, 5 then living. The children of Horace and Mary Poultney J. Etchison were:

  (1) Perry E. Waters, born c.1868. Head of household in the 1900 census for the Second District, listed as a merchant in dry goods, with a wife Ella V., born c.1865, and four children. They have been married eleven years, and have had five children, four then living. Also listed in the household is a servant, and

eight boarders, listed as born in New York, England, Fiji, Maine, Texas, Maryland and Virginia. The children were:

(a) Harold G. Waters, born June, 1891

(b) Richard L. Waters, born March, 1893

(c) Mary A. Waters, born March, 1896

(d) Clinton C. Waters, born October, 1897

(2) Bowie F. Waters, born c.1869, listed as a lawyer in the 1900 census

(3) William A. Waters, born c.1872. Head of household in the 1900 census for the Second District, with wife Mary, born April, 1875, and one daughter. They have been married four years, and this is their only child thus far:

(a) Anna M. Waters, born August, 1898

(4) Clinton Carroll Waters, born July 20, 1875, died September 4, 1896; buried Neelsville Presbyterian.

(5) Julian B. Waters, born c.1879

(6) Eagh H. Waters, born c.1881

d. Laura Johnson Etchison, born January 4, 1844, died February 17, 1898, single, at the home of her brother-in-law, Horace Waters, near Germantown. Buried at Neelsville Presbyterian Church cemetery. Living at home in 1880.

e. Bowie Etchison, born c.1846

f. Frances Etchison, born c.1849, and died March 2, 1926, single. Living at home in 1880.

g. Frank Etchison, born c.1854

William Griffith
died 1699
The Immigrant
Chapter 2
*
*
Orlando Griffith
1688
*
*
Greenberry Griffith
1727
Chapter 9
*
*
Hezekiah Griffith
1752
Chapter 10
*
*

*   *   *   *   *   *   *   *   *
*
*   * Ann Griffith 1776
*
*   * Sarah Griffith 1778
*
*   * John Belford Griffith 1780
*
*   * Walter Griffith 1783
*
*   * Lydia Griffith 1785
*
*   * Roderick Griffith 1787
*
*   * Hezekiah Griffith, Jr. 1790
*
*   * Charles Greenberry Griffith 1792
*
*   * Jane Griffith 1794

170

CHAPTER 10

Hezekiah Griffith
1752-1825

This son of Greenberry Griffith (1727) and Ruth Riggs (1730) was born November 25, 1752, and died July 28, 1825. Married November 14, 1775 to Catharine Warfield, born April 7, 1757, died April 14, 1796, daughter of Azel Warfield and Sarah Griffith. Children:

1. Ann Griffith, born September 27, 1776; married to Jonas Clark and had children:
   a. Kitty Clark, born December 27, 1798
   b. Hezekiah Clark, born August 29, 1802; in the 1850 census of the Fifth District of Montgomery County, he was living in the household of James Smith (1822), listed as a farmer, marital status unknown.
   c. Sarah Clark, born July 25, 1804
   d. John Clark, born April 14, 1807
   e. Robert Clark, born November 24, 1809
   f. Mary Clark, born April 14, 1812
   g. Lydia Clark, born October 7, 1814
   h. Bazaleel Clark, born September 7, 1816
2. Sarah Griffith, born May 17, 1778, died July 10, 1839. Married c.1797 to Bazaleel Wells and had children. This family was not found in census records of Montgomery County, and is presumed to have moved out of the area. In any case, the children were:
   a. Catherine Wells, born April 17, 1798, died September, 1843. Married October 8, 1818 to John W. McDowell.
   b. Rebecca Wells, born October 11, 1799 Married November 10, 1822 to Philander Chase.
   c. James Ross Wells, born October 8, 1801, died October 23, 1846. Married April 17, 1834 to Ann Eliza Wilson, who died in 1868.
   d. Samuel D. Wells, born October 8, 1803, died December 13, 1849, single.

e. Alexander Wells, born September 16, 1805, died January 6, 1839, single.

f. Bazaleel Wells, Jr., born August 6, 1808

g. Hezekiah Griffith Wells, born January 16, 1811. Married to Achsah Strong.

h. Frank A. Wells, born September 4, 1813. Married to Jane Boggs.

i. Ann C. Wells, born August 28, 1815. Married the Reverend Ezra Kellogg.

j. Sarah Griffith Wells, born January 11, 1818, died August 24, 1866. Married the Reverend Dudley Chase.

k. Mary Wells, born February 12, 1822, died March 3, 1882.

3. John Belford Griffith, born December 28, 1780

4. Walter Griffith, born February 3, 1783

5. Lydia Griffith, born December 10, 1785, died c.1815; married George Fetter and had four children:

a. Daniel Fetter, born May 31, 1807

b. George Fetter, Jr., born October 6, 1809

c. Hezekiah Fetter, born November 1, 1811

d. Roderick Fetter, born February 16, 1814

6. Roderick Griffith, born December 8, 1787, died May 26, 1817.

7. Hezekiah Griffith, Jr., born November 1, 1790, died August 13, 1840. Married September 1, 1813 to Lydia Mobley, born January 24, 1795 and had ten children:

a. John Griffith, born November 8, 1814.

b. Roderick R. Griffith, born July 21, 1816, died August 6, 1889. Married first Isabel Clark, and had three children. Married second Mary Tillman and had six children.

c. Anne E. Griffith, born June 15, 1815. Married to Jesse V. Bramwell.

d. Randolph Griffith, married Eliza J. Barfield.

e. Rebecca Griffith, born February 4, 1824. Married Ezra Bramwell.

f. Rachel Griffith, born June 13, 1827. Married to Samuel Hovens.

g. Catherine Griffith, born July 30, 1829, died July 24, 1851, single.
h. Hezekiah Griffith, 3rd, born May 2, 1832. Married to Mary Ann Stevens.
i. Alexander W. Griffith, born July 7, 1835
j. Lydia Griffith, born December 11, 1837. Married Joseph Renier.

8. Charles Greenberry Griffith, born July 3, 1792, died May 24, 1864. Married to Jane Johnson, and had ten children:
a. Sarah Griffith, born December 29, 1817. Married three times: A. Arnick; M. C. Maynard; and Smith Vowler.
b. James J. Griffith, born November 13, 1819, died November 7, 1855.
c. Margaret Griffith, born November 20, 1820. Married to McKeehan.
d. Samuel Griffith, born November 26, 1822. Married to Elizabeth Goltha.
e. Hezekiah Griffith, born August 19, 1824
f. Mary Griffith, born August 31, 1826. Married Johnson.
g. Anna Griffith, born November 31, 1828, died November, 1860. Married to J. Chase.
h. Charles Greenberry Griffith, Jr., born August 19, 1830. Married to McKeehan.
i. Rachel Griffith, born August 10, 1832. Married to W. C. Soper.
j. Jennie Griffith, born March 31, 1833.

9. Jane Griffith, born November 3, 1794

William Griffith
died 1699
The Immigrant
Chapter 2
*

*

Orlando Griffith
1688
*

*

Greenberry Griffith
1727
Chapter 9
*

*

Howard Griffith
1756
Chapter 11
*

*

* * * * * * * * *
*
* * Mordecai Griffith 1782
*
* * Jemima Jacob Griffith 1784
*
* * Greenberry Griffith 1787
*
* * Ruth Griffith 1789
*
* * Leah Griffith 1792
*
* * Howard Griffith, Jr. 1794
*
* * Eleanor Griffith 1798
*
* * Thomas Griffith 1801
*
* * Lebbeus Griffith 1804

CHAPTER 11

Howard Griffith
1757-1834

This son of Greenberry Griffith (1727) and Ruth Riggs (1730) was born June 18, 1757 in a part of Frederick County which later became Montgomery, died there January 4, 1834. Howard was a private in the 2nd Co., Middle Battalion, Militia, September 4, 1777, and Private 1st Class, 3rd Co., Middle Battalion, Militia, July 15, 1780. Married February 7, 1782 to Jemima Jacob, born December 1, 1759, died January 21, 1831, daughter of Mordecai Jacob and Jemima Isaac of Prince George's County. Howard left a will in Montgomery County dated January 25, 1831, probated January 21, 1834, recorded in liber T at folio 240; rerecorded in liber VMB 3 at page 532. He named several specific bequests, including daughter Leah, sons Mordecai J. and Howard; and a niece Rebecca Griffith. The residue of the estate was to be divided between the heirs of his deceased daughter Jemima Riggs and his surviving sons and daughters, including: Greenberry Griffith; Ruth Maynard; Leah Griffith; Eleanor Chiswell; Thomas I. Griffith; Lebbeus Griffith; each to receive one seventh interest. The one-seventh share going to the heirs of Jemima Riggs was to be divided between her children: Amon Riggs, Lydia Riggs and Eliza Riggs. They had nine children:

1. Mordecai Griffith, born November 15, 1782, of whom more as Child 1.
2. Jemima Jacob Griffith, born February 17, 1784, of whom more as Child 2.
3. Greenberry Griffith, born May 20, 1787, of whom more as Child 3.
4. Ruth Griffith, born August 20, 1789, and of whom more as Child 4.
5. Leah Griffith, born January 15, 1792, died May 17, 1835; buried at Mt. Olivet Cemetery, Frederick.
6. Howard Griffith, Jr., born June 7, 1794, died October 10, 1866, served in the War of 1812. Married November 20, 1817

in Frederick County to Ruth Plummer, who died May 18, 1885, daughter of Jesse Plummer and Ruth Griffith. They had ten children and lived in Baltimore.

7. Eleanor Griffith, born May 22, 1798, died October 28, 1870. Married first May 23, 1823 to John Augustine Chiswell, born December 2, 1792 in Montgomery County, died August 21, 1840; buried at Monocacy cemetery. He was the son of Joseph Newton Chiswell (1747) and Eleanor White (1750) and inherited from his father a bridle, saddle and clothing, a desk and bookcase, and the residue of the books. After the death of John Augustus Chiswell, Eleanor was married second January, 1843 to the Reverend William Marvin. Children were born to the first marriage:

a. Howard Griffith Chiswell, born July 6, 1824, died March 28, 1899; buried at Mt. Olivet Cemetery, Frederick. Not found in the 1850, 1860 or 1870 census.

b. John Augustine Chiswell, Jr., born January 29, 1830, died September 22, 1852. Married November 21, 1851 Sarah Rebecca Phillips, born April 10, 1830, died January 21, 1921; buried at Monocacy cemetery; daughter of Philip L. and Matilda Phillips. At least one child:

(1) John Augustine Chiswell, III, born December 30, 1851, died June 7, 1924 at Licksville, Maryland. Married October 25, 1876 to Susan Elizabeth Gott, born July 21, 1852, died December 4, 1926, daughter of Thomas Norris Gott (1818) and Eleanor White Chiswell (1822). They had children:

(a) Margaret White Chiswell, born January 11, 1879, died January 13, 1919; buried Monocacy

(b) Eugenia Gott Chiswell, born September 16, 1883, died March 6, 1933; buried at Monocacy; single.

(c) Mary Collinson Chiswell, born c.1886, died September 12, 1961, single.

(d) Eleanor Chiswell, born c.1900, died May 29, 1969 and married to Burke.

c. Jemima Eleanor Chiswell, born October 16, 1831, died June 19, 1916; buried at Mt. Olivet cemetery, Frederick.

Married November 30, 1854 to Nathan Maynard, born April 29, 1824, died July 17, 1888; buried at Mt. Olivet Cemetery, Frederick, with his wife and two daughters, son of Thomas Maynard and Ruth Griffith. Children:

(1) Fanny Maynard, born September 19, 1855, died June 27, 1935. Married to Barney Taylor Noland, born March 25, 1847, died October 11, 1925; buried at Mt. Olivet cemetery in Frederick; son of George W. Noland and Ruth Hannah Taylor.

(2) Frank N. Maynard, born March 25, 1857

(3) John Newton Maynard, born June 10, 1860, died November 9, 1938; buried at Mt. Olivet cemetery. Married March 27, 1890 to Jennie E. Bennett. Also apparently married to Mary Bowers, born December 15, 1867, died February 7, 1956; buried Mt. Olivet.

(4) Rachel Ann Maynard, born October 11, 1865, died January 24, 1927. Buried at Mt. Olivet, single.

(5) Eleanor Maynard, born July 7, 1870, died December 16, 1939. USA Nurses Corp. Buried at Mt. Olivet.

(6) Benjamin T. Maynard, born July 12, 1874

d. Sarah Newton Chiswell, born April 11, 1836, died November 26, 1892. Married in Frederick County by license dated September 13, 1856 to Howard Griffith Maynard, born February 3, 1817, died March 28, 1899; buried at Mt. Olivet Cemetery at Frederick, with his wife and four children. They had eleven children:

(1) Louis S. Maynard, born June 17, 1857, died September 11, 1879

(2) Nathan Maynard, born December 25, 1858

(3) Joseph T. Maynard, born December 12, 1860

(4) Ruth Eleanor Maynard, born June 4, 1863, died 1927

(5) John A. Maynard, born November 10, 1865

(6) Sarah H. Maynard, born July 30, 1868, died April 14, 1955

(7) Augusta C. Maynard, born February 24, 1871, died May 9, 1871

(8) Florence E. Maynard, born April 28, 1872

(9) Richard Maynard, born December 10, 1874

(10) William Maynard, born June 23, 1876

(11) George E. Maynard, born June 11, 1878

e. Joseph Newton Chiswell, born August 3, 1837. A copy of a family Bible clearly reports his birth year as 1827. Married first February, 1861 to Fannie Florence of Missouri and had at least one son. Married second to Mary Quinn and had a son also:

(1) Joseph Chiswell, born April 5, 1863

(2) Styles Chiswell, born c.1871

f. Augusta Ann Chiswell, born February 24, 1841, died October 12, 1921, single; buried at Mt. Olivet cemetery.

8. Thomas Griffith, born June 11, 1801

9. Lebbeus Griffith, born February 11, 1804, of whom more as Child 9.

CHILD 1

Mordecai Griffith
1782-1826

Mordecai Griffith was born November 15, 1782, and died July 27, 1826, the eldest son of Howard Griffith (1757) and Jemima Jacob (1759), and was the grandson of Greenberry Griffith. Married September 13, 1808 to Matilda Dorsey, born March 31, 1787, daughter of Nicholas Dorsey and Rachel Warfield (1759). They had children. After the death of Mordecai, Matilda was married secondly c.1840 to Thomas Guthrie of Kentucky, and died September 8, 1843 without having children from that marriage. The children were:

1. Nicholas Howard Griffith, born August 18, 1811, living as late as 1892 in Missouri. Married December 25, 1829 to Sarah M. Parrish, born August 18, 1812 in Shelbyville County, Kentucky, died February 23, 1864. She was a daughter of Benjamin Parrish and Sarah Harlow, who had moved from Virginia to Kentucky at an early date. Nicholas and Sarah had children, probably either in Kentucky or Missouri, and some of them later lived in Illinois:

a. Benjamin M. Griffith, born April 14, 1831; married June 1, 1859 to Alice Anna McElroy, born September 30, 1831 in Missouri. They had three children and lived in Illinois, where he was a Doctor, State Board of Health.

b. George J. Griffith, born January 30, 1833; married November 29, 1855 to Martha Downing, born September 10, 1835. They had seven children.

c. John Nicholas Griffith, born August 8, 1834, died March 3, 1885. Married October 29, 1859 to Amanda Hendricks, born February 24, 1843. Nine children.

d. Thomas D. Griffith, born May 27, 1837, died 1838

e. Sarah E. Griffith, born 1839, died April 19, 1857

f. Mary M. Griffith, born February 2, 1841; married February 16, 1869 to William Showse, born November 10, 1838. Two children.

g. Elizabeth Griffith, born July 8, 1842; married July 14, 1864 to Augustus W. Wehrman and had two children.

h. Almeda Griffith, born September 9, 1844; married January 24, 1865 to Frank Wetherford. Three children.

i. William David Griffith, born December 30, 1846

2. Erastus Griffith, born October 13, 1813, died September 2, 1819

3. Agrippa Griffith, a twin, born January 9, 1817, died 1825

4. Almeda Griffith, a twin, born January 9, 1817, died March 29, 1889. Married February 27, 1838 to Horatio N. Baskett, born July 6, 1809 and had ten children.

5. Jemima Griffith, born July 6, 1819, died October 6, 1821

6. Dorsey Griffith, born November 21, 1820, died August 18, 1821

7. Clarissa Griffith, born May 21, 1822; married October 21, 1838 to William Guthrie, born August, 1817. Seven children.

8. Joshua Dorsey Griffith, born January 20, 1824, died September 15, 1838

CHILD 2

Jemima Jacob Griffith
1784-1819

The daughter of Howard Griffith (1757) and Jemima Jacob (1759), was born February 17, 1784, died November 15, 1819, and was the eldest of their daughters. She was married November 20, 1804 to Henry Riggs, born July 23, 1772, son of Amon Edwin Riggs (1748) and Ruth Griffith (1747). They had children:
1. Howard Griffith Riggs, born October 17, 1805
2. Amon Riggs, born June 30, 1808; moved to Ohio.
3. Antoinette Riggs, born August 2, 1811
4. Lydia Griffith Riggs, born June 21, 1813
5. Eliza Riggs, born August 3, 1817
6. William H. Riggs, born November 8, 1819, an infant death.

CHILD 3

Greenberry Griffith
1787-1848

This son of Howard Griffith (1757) and Jemima Jacob (1759), was born May 20, 1787, died October 25, 1848. Titled Major Greenberry Griffith in some records, he commanded the Alexandria Artillery during the War of 1812. He was married February 24, 1814 in Frederick County, Maryland to Prudence Jones, born November 5, 1796, died December 7, 1881 in Poolesville, buried at Monocacy Cemetery at Beallsville. She was a daughter of Charles Jones of Ireland, who raised an Irish Brigade to fight in the American cause. She was found as head of household in the 1850 census of Montgomery County for the First District, presumably a widow, reported there as born in Virginia, owning six slaves, with five children at home. In the agricultural census of 1850, Prudence owned 100 acres of improved land and 200 acres unimproved, for a value of $1,800 in total. She owned 2 horses, 3 milch cows, 2 working oxen, 3 other cattle, 13 sheep and 16 swine. In the previous year, she had produced 30 bushels of wheat, 500 bushels of Indian corn,

80 bushels of oats, 600 pounds of tobacco, 40 pounds of wool, 20 bushels of Irish potatoes, 250 pounds of butter and 6 tons of hay.

Greenberry left a will in Montgomery County, dated September 3, 1844, probated December 5, 1848, recorded in liber HH 3 at folio 69; rerecorded in liber VMB 4 at page 506 in the Register of Wills office. It was fairly lengthy, naming his wife Prudence, and all the children with various bequests, as noted following. During her lifetime, should any of the slaves become "disobedient or unmanageable", Prudence was given authority to sell them and apply the money to the benefit of the children. They had children:

1. Jemima A. Griffith, born 1814, died July 21, 1872, single; buried at Monocacy Cemetery, Beallsville. In the 1850 census, reported as born c.1820. She was head of household in the 1870 census of Montgomery County for the Third District, Beallsville Post Office, listed as keeping house. Living with her was her youngest brother, Greenberry, born c.1838 and listed here following as the tenth child in this family. He was a farmer, and then owned $6,400 in real estate and $200 in personal property. Living with them was William Jones, born c.1860, no relationship stated.

2. Prudence Jane Griffith, born July 21, 1816, of whom more.

3. Emily Howard Griffith, born December 6, 1818, died October 1, 1903; married as his second wife in Montgomery County by license dated April 16, 1855 to Harry Woodward Dorsey Waters, born c.1813, who was first married to her sister Prudence Jane Griffith. No children.

4. Howard Griffith, born March 20, 1821, died March 5, 1897; lived at Beallsville, Montgomery County, Maryland; buried at Monocacy Cemetery. Under his father's will, he received the shotgun and flasks, and an equal share with his siblings in the entire estate after the death of his mother. Married first January 12, 1847 to Sarah Newton Chiswell, born September 18, 1822, buried March 19, 1859 at Monocacy Cemetery, the daughter of Captain William Chiswell and Sarah Fletchall, and had four children. He was married second December 24, 1877 in Hagerstown to Angelica C. Young, born February 14, 1830, died September 16, 1899; buried at Monocacy Cemetery with her husband. She was a daughter of John Young

(1790) and they were childless. Howard was head of household in the 1850 census of Montgomery County for the Third District, with $1,800 in real estate, his wife, and their first child. Howard was next found as head of household in the 1860 census of the county for the Third District, then a widow, with $5,750 in real estate and $9,500 in personal property. He then had four children living at home. Living with them was Prudence Griffith, his widowed mother, and Elizabeth Sibley, born c.1829, not otherwise identified. He was head of household in the 1870 census of the county for the Third District, Beallsville Post Office, with four of his children still at home. Living with them was Frances Griffith, born c.1797, not yet identified as to family relationship. He was next head of household in the 1880 census of the county for the Medley District, with his wife Angelica and two children, Georgia and William, both single. Living with them was his mother Prudence Griffith, a widow, 83 years of age. Howard Griffith left a will in Montgomery County, dated February 7, 1894, probated March 16, 1897, and recorded in liber GCD 2 at folio 430. To his wife Angelica C., he left his gray mare named Doll, his single buggy and harness, and the piano. To his two sons, Charles G. and William T., he left $5,000 in trust for the benefit of his wife during her lifetime, and at her death, to divide between the three children. Additionally, she was to have the use of the dwelling house, the land on that same side of the road, and the garden and orchard. His son Charles was to receive the plantation on which he was then living, valued at $22 per acre for purposes of equalizing the inheritances. William T. was to receive one-third at the death of Angelica, and he and his brother were to hold the remaining one-third, in trust, to the benefit of their sister Julia, wife of Richard H. Cissel. The sister Georgianna died before her father wrote his will, and was not mentioned. The children were:

a. Charles Greenberry Griffith, born July, 1849, and of whom more.

b. Georgianna Griffith, born September, 1851, died March 17, 1891. Married at the Methodist Church in Poolesville on January 24, 1882 to Francis Thomas Williams of

Poolesville, born August 30, 1845, died November 3, 1906; buried at Monocacy with his wife. No children.

c. Julia Griffith, born September 4, 1853, died December 11, 1924 at Rockville. Married October 28, 1875 in the Poolesville Presbyterian Church to Richard Humphrey Cissel, born June 14, 1849, died December 6, 1911; buried at Monocacy Cemetery with his wife. He was a member of the County Commissioners for the Fourth District, and appeared as head of household in the 1900 census of the county for the Sixth District, with his wife Julia, and seven children. He was listed by his middle name, Humphrey, and they had been married for twenty-seven years and she had been the mother of eleven children, with nine surviving. The children were:

(1) William Howard Cissel, born January 5, 1876, died April 5, 1900.

(2) Richard Thomas Cissel, a twin, born 1879

(3) Charles Leroy Cissel, a twin, born 1879, died August 8, 1922.

(4) Richard Humphrey Cissel, Jr., born 1881, died 1940

(5) George Newton Cissel, born April 3, 1883, died April 19, 1888.

(6) William Griffith Cissel, a twin, born December 18, 1884, died June 20, 1930; buried at Monocacy. Married to Pauline Claire Jones, born August 1, 1898, died May 5, 1978; buried at Monocacy; the daughter of John Augustus Jones (1870) and Edna Manakee (1871). A child:

(a) Lisa Lorraine Cissel, born August 6, 1924.

(7) Sarah Newton Cissel, a twin, born December 18, 1884, died December 22, 1946. Married to John Thomas Williams, born January 21, 1884, died May 20, 1972; buried at Monocacy. Two children:

(a) Julia Elizabeth Williams.

(b) Eleanor Newton Williams.

(8) Mary Eleanor Cissel, born October 4, 1887, died April 4, 1926. Married March 25, 1908 to Julian Boyd Waters, born 1878, and had children:

(a) Ella Virginia Waters.

(b) Lorraine J. Waters.

(c) Mary Poultney Waters.

(d) Julian Boyd Waters, Jr.

(9) Elmo Cissel, born 1888, died May 20, 1891.

(10) Eugene Wilbur Cissel, born March 16, 1890, died March 17, 1931. Married to Cecil Tschiffely, the daughter of Doctor Frederick Tschiffely, and had children:

    (a) Richard Humphrey Cissel, born c.1918. Married to Laura Bradley, born c.1906, died November 30, 1986 at home in Rockville. He married second to Cecelia Fisher; no children. Humphrey, or Hump, is a Land Surveyor, and from 1961 to 1965 was the partner of this author in the firm Hurley and Cissel Surveys, with offices in Rockville.

    (b) Ruth Cissel, married Walter Johnson, Jr.

    (c) Eugene Wilbur Cissel, Jr., born c.1924, died March 10, 1983 in Hagerstown, Maryland. Married to Mary Broschart, daughter of Doctor Broschart of Gaithersburg, and had children:

        1. Suzanne Cissel, married to Appleby.

        2. Dorothy Cissel, married to Marshall.

        3. Laura Cissel, married to Campbell.

        4. Lawrence M. Cissel.

(11) Albert Jones Cissel, born November 23, 1892. Married Lula May Ward, born January 1, 1897, died June 24, 1976 at Bethesda; buried at Darnestown, daughter of Harrison Gilmore Ward (1853) and Ara Matilda Thrift (1857). At least two children:

    (a) Albert Jones Cissell, Jr.

    (b) Howard G. Cissell.

(12) Griffith Cissel, born February, 1895.

d. William Thomas Griffith, born March 1, 1856, died April 17, 1931 at Hancock, Maryland; buried at Mt. Olivet, Frederick. He left a will in Montgomery County, dated January 4, 1929, probated June 9, 1931 and recorded in liber PEW 20 at folio 149. The will is very brief and simple, leaving everything to his wife to do with as she pleases. He was not listed in the 1850 census, and was living at home at the time of the 1860 census, there listed at the age of 4, or born c.1856, rather than 1846, which has appeared in other reports. The 1856 date appears to be correct. Married January 16, 1883 at the home of the bride's parents near Jefferson, in Frederick County, to Elizabeth Darnall Dade, born 1858, died March 31, 1941, buried Monocacy Cemetery; only daughter of Columbus Dade (1831) and Ann Mary Jones (1833). He was head of household in the 1900 census of the county for the Third District, although there read incorrectly by initials only as W. D. Griffith, born March, 1856. His wife Elizabeth D was there, with two children. They had been married seventeen years, and she had been the mother of four children, only two surviving. Children, born at Poolesville:

(1) Mary Elizabeth Griffith, born June 16, 1886, died December 31, 1951; buried at Monocacy with her husband. Married November 16, 1910 Dr. Charles Thomas Pyles, born August 4, 1885, died December 20, 1948. Reportedly four children, including:

    (a) William Griffith Pyles, born March 4, 1913, died October 8, 1959; buried at Monocacy Cemetery. Married to Nellie Jenkins.

    (b) Elizabeth Dade Pyles, born February 1, 1916, died May 25, 1916; buried at Monocacy.

    (c) Charles Pyles, reported in the marriage announcement of Columbus Dade Griffith,

(2) William Howard Griffith, born July 11, 1887, died November 22, 1890.

(3) Columbus Dade Griffith, born December 22, 1888 and died November 25, 1943; buried at Monocacy. Married June 7, 1917 at Neelsville Church to Mary Alice Waters, born March 12, 1896, died July, 1943, daughter of Perrie Etchison Waters (1867) and Ella Virginia Harris (1864) of Germantown. Her

name is on the same stone at Neelsville Cemetery with her brother, Harold Gorman Waters (1891). Columbus and Alice had two children:

(a) Elizabeth Darnall Griffith, born February 17, 1917. Married first Elisha Sterling Chapin, Jr. and second to Edward Fitzgerald. No children.

(b) Ellen Waters Griffith, born May 15, 1924. Married first to Robert Alexander Pumphrey, born February 4, 1921 and had four children. Ellen married second November 17, 1973 to Lloyd Archibald Brewer, born July 7, 1918, died March 6, 1978; no children. Her children from the first marriage were:

1. Ellen Irene Pumphrey, born September 18, 1946. Married September 23, 1971 to Ralph Frederic Nelson and had one child:
   a. Sandra Elizabeth Nelson.

2. William Reuben Pumphrey, III, born October 18, 1948. Married April 4, 1971 to Martha Witherspoon Sphar, and had three children:
   a. William Alexander Pumphrey.
   b. John Sphar Pumphrey.
   c. Lucy Woodford Pumphrey.

3. Robert Alexander Pumphrey, Jr., born September 4, 1950. Married January 24, 1970 Sally Ann Holm, and had two children:
   a. Kirk Griffith Pumphrey.
   b. Traci Ann Pumphrey.

4. Richard Griffith Pumphrey, born April 23, 1952. Married June 22, 1974 to Kathryn Ann Mitchell and had two children:
   a. Benjamin Griffith Pumphrey.
   b. Meredith Ann Pumphrey.

(4) Infant Griffith, stillbirth September 2, 1890.

5. Charles Greenberry Griffith, born November 1, 1823. Served as Judge of the Orphans' Court of Baltimore. Under his fa-

ther's will, he received the watch and clock tools, and an equal share with his siblings in the entire estate after the death of his mother. Married first to Fannie Knowles, daughter of Hazard Knowles and had a son. Married second to Mollie Burns and had a son:

  a. Hazard K. Griffith, lived in Atlanta, Georgia.
  b. Charles Griffith.

6. Leah Griffith, born March 21, 1826, died December 1, 1891; buried with her husband at Monocacy Cemetery at Beallsville. Married in Montgomery County by license dated April 26, 1847 Captain George Walter Chiswell, born March 6, 1819, died June 10, 1882, son of William Augustus Chiswell (1783) and Sarah Newton Fletchall (1787). The young couple are first found in the 1850 census of the Third District, with his mother living with them, and two children. George is also shown as the owner of four slaves. They are next found in the 1860 census for the same district, with his mother still living with them, and five children. They are finally found in the 1870 census, with the same five children still at home. Their children were:

  a. William Greenberry Chiswell, born February 13, 1848, died December 27, 1903; buried Monocacy cemetery. Married November 11, 1880 to Lulu Helen Lyons, born April 12, 1859, died January 28, 1920 Washington, D. C. and buried at Monocacy. They had children:

    (1) Charles Lewis Chiswell, born April 10, 1883, died December 22, 1966. Married to Pearl Day.
    (2) Catherine Christell Chiswell, born March 18, 1885, died June 26, 1966. Married July 25, 1936 as his second wife, to Thomas Lloyd Grubb.
    (3) Leah Griffith Chiswell, born November, 1887, died October 28, 1938. Married twice.
    (4) George William Chiswell, a doctor, born September 23, 1892, died January 9, 1957; buried at Monocacy cemetery. Married September 2, 1922 to Carrie Geneva Bodmer, born December 16, 1893 at Poolesville, died March 14, 1978; buried at Monocacy.

(5) Byron Walling Chiswell, born August 6, 1894, died January 22, 1974; buried at Monocacy.

(6) Lulu Mae Chiswell, born January 13, 1897, died August 24, 1966. Married to William Charles Raynor and had at least a daughter.

(7) Marie Antoinette Chiswell, born April 20, 1899, died March 4, 1979.

b. Sarah Prudence Chiswell, born April 10, 1850, died January 21, 1921; buried at Monocacy, single.

c. Elizabeth Ellen Chiswell, born November 23, 1852, died July 17, 1951 at Poolesville; buried at Monocacy cemetery, single.

d. Joseph Thomas Chiswell, born September 18, 1855, died May 2, 1912; buried at Monocacy Cemetery with his wife in her father's plot. Married November 29, 1887 to Verlinda Catherine Young, born June 7, 1864. This is the same individual as Linda Young, born c.1864, died February 9, 1914, daughter of Isaac Young (1828), and Margaret R. (Young) Young, a twin, (1829). Joseph and Linda appeared in the 1900 census for Poolesville, married for twelve years, six children, all then living. There were more children:

(1) Isaac Young Chiswell, born September 2, 1888 and died July 8, 1962; buried at Arlington National Cemetery. Married to Lillie D.

(2) Charles Newton Chiswell, born August 20, 1890.

(3) Olivia Marguerite Chiswell, born July 18, 1892, died July 12, 1983, buried at Monocacy

(4) Leanora Chiswell, born April 30, 1894, died December 9, 1947. Married July 19, 1919 to John William Myers, born 1900. Four children.

(5) Bessie Clotworthy Chiswell, born September 16, 1895, died September 20, 1958, single.

(6) Joseph Thomas Chiswell, born November 9, 1897 and died January 20, 1898; buried at Monocacy

(7) Carroll Thomas Chiswell, born March 28, 1899, died April 16, 1982; buried at Monocacy Cemetery. Married July 14, 1936 to Mary Elizabeth Fyffe,

daughter of Isaac Fyffe (1839) and Elizabeth Darby (1874); no children.

(8) Ruby Agatha Chiswell, born July 29, 1904, died January 17, 1911; buried at Monocacy.

7. Joseph Thomas Griffith, born June 1, 1828, died November 20, 1910 at Poolesville. Under his father's will, he received (with his brother Francis M.) his father's library, and an equal share with his siblings in the entire estate after the death of his mother. His obituary in the *Sentinel* styles him as Captain, a Confederate veteran, commissioner of revenue for Clark County, Virginia for eighteen years, survived by two daughters and two sons. Married April 4, 1854 to Jane Rebecca Willson, born April 15, 1834, daughter of John Clark Willson. Lived in Berryville, Virginia, and had at least seven children. One of them was:

a. C. W. Griffith, born c.1856, died July 26, 1886 near Berryville. His obituary in the Sentinel stated that he was a son of Captain J. T. Griffith, apparently the individual discussed here.

8. Francis Moore Griffith, born June 14, 1831, died January 20, 1908. Under his father's will, he received (with his brother Joseph T.) his father's library, and an equal share with his siblings in the entire estate after the death of his mother. Married at Arlington, Virginia on February 9, 1859 to Elizabeth Dickerson, born June 26, 1836, died April 6, 1904; buried at Monocacy Cemetery with her husband and other family members; only daughter of Nathan Cooke Dickerson (1809) and Christine Ashe Hempstone (1813). In the 1860 census of the Second District, he was listed as owning $3,000 in real estate and $2,100 in personal property, and they had one child. This is perhaps the same as F. M. Griffith found in the 1867-1858 Slave Census of the county, as the owner of one slave, Isaac W. Snowden, aged nineteen, who left with the military, without compensation. They next appeared in the 1870 census for the Third District, Barnesville Post Office, with three children, and Francis M. was listed as a country merchant. The family was found in the 1880 census for the Third District, with Francis M. listed as Frank a clerk in an office. Elizabeth and

six children were at home. In the 1900 census for the Eleventh District, Francis and Elizabeth appear, with the statement that they have been married 41 years, that he is a merchant, that they have had eight children, six of whom are then living, and three of them are still at home. Elizabeth Dickerson Griffith left a will in Montgomery County dated January 24, 1898, probated August 29, 1905 and recorded in liber HCA 4 at folio 224. She referred there to a deed from her husband dated May 16, 1884, in which he conveyed to her the land, with the store and dwelling combined located thereon, reserving the right to him to remain there for life. That property was bequeathed to her children, subject to her husband's rights. The will also named for personal bequests the three youngest children, and the Executors were the oldest son Nathan C. D. Griffith, then living in Chicago, and son-in-law Doctor L. Wilson Davis of Baltimore. Francis Moore Griffith left a will in the county, dated October 29, 1907, probated March 3, 1908 and recorded in liber HCA 8 at folio 2. He mentioned five children, apparently all who were still living, leaving each a personal bequest, including such items as a walking stick, a silver watch, library books, mathematical instruments, and gold framed eye glasses. The children were:

a.   Nathan Cook Dickerson Griffith, born October 24, 1859, died February 16, 1905 in Chicago, single, buried at Monocacy; not at home in the 1880 census. He is perhaps the same person read as Nathan L. Griffith, of the proper age, listed as a clerk in the store of John A. Belt during the 1880 census of the county for the Cracklin District. In the 1904 obituary of his mother, he was living in Chicago

b.   William Howard Griffith, born February 15, 1862, died c.1864.

c.   Mary Harrison Griffith, born May 18, 1864, died January 24, 1937; buried at Monocacy with her husband. Married August 29, 1889 to Doctor Leonidas Wilson Davis, born October 18, 1862, died May 18, 1947, a dentist, son of Isaac Howard Davis (1818) and Catherine S. Miles (1822). In the obituary of her mother in 1904, she and her husband were living in Baltimore.

d. Clarence Edgar Griffith, born April 25, 1867. Head of household in the 1900 census of the First District, a merchant, with wife Louise H., born February, 1873, and one child:
    (1) Matilda Ober Griffith, born February, 1900
e. Francis Moore Griffith, Jr., born June 10, 1870, and died December 8, 1889 in Manchester, Virginia. Buried at Monocacy Cemetery, Beallsville, Maryland.
f. Harold Clark Griffith, born January 7, 1874; at home in 1900
g. Bessie Estelle Griffith, born June 17, 1877; at home in 1900. Perhaps the same Bessie E. Griffith who was married August 17, 1904 at Beallsville to Herbert M. Hurtt (records of St. Peter's Church at Poolesville).
h. Charles Byron Griffith, born February 20, 1880; at home in 1900. The *Sentinel* of January 19, 1917 announced that Doctor Charles Byron Griffith, formerly of Montgomery County, now makes his home in Chicago.

9. David Porter Griffith, born January 22, 1835, died January 9, 1903 at his home in Middlebrook, near Gaithersburg; buried at Monocacy Cemetery. Under his father's will, he received an equal share with his siblings in the entire estate after the death of his mother. Of considerable more interest, however, his father left to him his artillery sword. Married in the county March 7, 1860 to Margaret Virginia Keys, born November 26, 1838, died December 10, 1930, daughter of Chandler Keys; buried at Rockville. They were divorced in the county October 4, 1895, and he was married second September 21, 1897 to Mrs. Carrie Iona Reicher of Chicago. Listed only as David, he was head of household in the 1880 census of the county for the Medley District, with his wife Margaret. He was there listed as clerking in a store, and they had two children, both in school. His household was listed next door to that of his brother Frank, reported just above. In the 1900 census of the county for the Fourth District, Margaret was head of household, a widow, with the four children all at home. She was listed as having been the mother of four children, all surviving. Margaret Virginia Griffith left a will in Montgomery

County, dated December 8, 1930, probated December 22, 1930 and recorded in liber PEW 20 at folio 45. To her daughters Rose V. and Emily Jane, she left a twelve-acre woodlot on the road from Westmore Station to Horner's Lane bordered on the south by Lincoln Park Subdivision at Rockville. The four children were left all the rest, equally divided between them. Children were:

a. Rose V. Griffith, born January 29, 1861, died February 13, 1953.

b. Emily Jane Griffith, born March 9, 1863, died March 26, 1943 at Barnesville; buried at Rockville Union Cemetery. Emily left a will in Montgomery County, dated November 4, 1940 at Barnesville, probated April 6, 1943 and recorded in liber JWN 2 at folio 110. She mentioned both of her sisters, Clara A. Griffith and Rose V. Griffith, and left to the latter all her interest in the 55 acres on Westmore Road inherited from their mother. She also named three cousins: Emily Darby Brown; Elizabeth Brown Allnutt; and Mary Shaw Brown.

c. William Thomas Griffith, born December 6, 1864, died August 31, 1934, single, buried at Monocacy. He left a will in Montgomery County dated November 30, 1933, probated December 11, 1934, recorded in liber HGC 5 at folio 421, in which he left his entire estate to his youngest sister Clara A. Griffith.

d. Clara Angeline Griffith, born October 19, 1866, died May 30, 1961; buried at Rockville with her mother.

10. Greenberry Griffith, born November 28, 1838, single. Jemima A. Griffith, born c.1814, was head of household in the 1870 census of Montgomery County, Third District, Beallsville Post Office, listed as keeping house. Living with her was her youngest brother, Greenberry, born c.1838 and listed here as the tenth child in this family. Greenberry received the most interesting legacy of all, and apparently the most important to his father. He was to have "*the gold medal that was presented to me by the brother officers and soldiers of the Alexandria Artillery, their token of respect and regards for me as their commander. I wish it kept sacred and handed down to pos-*

terity uninjured and not defaced." Greenberry was a farmer, and then owned $6,400 in real estate and $200 in personal property. Living with them was William Jones, born c.1860, no relationship stated.

Prudence Jane Griffith
1816-1853

This daughter of Greenberry Griffith (1787) and Prudence Jones (1796), was born July 21, 1816, and died December 21, 1853. Married in Montgomery County by license dated January 23, 1837, as his first wife, to Harry Woodward Dorsey Waters, born c.1813 in Montgomery County, died c.1880, son of Nathaniel Magruder Waters (1786) and his wife Achsah Dorsey (1789). He was married second by license dated April 16, 1855 to her sister Emily Howard Griffith, born December 6, 1818, died October 1, 1903 and buried at Monocacy Cemetery with other family members.

Harry Woodward Dorsey Waters was not found in any census records of Montgomery County after his reported marriages. We did, however, find him listed simply as Dorsey Waters, head of household in the 1850 census of the New Market District of Frederick County, but with no listing of his age. His wife Prudence J. was there, as were four children. The census also indicated that he then owned eleven slaves, of various ages, without naming them. He then owned 160 acres of improved land and 40 acres unimproved, valued at $8,000 total. He owned 6 horses, 5 milch cows, 5 other cattle, 27 sheep and 30 swine. During the previous twelve months, he had produced 380 bushels of wheat, 20 bushels of rye, 625 bushels of Indian corn, 300 bushels of oats, 70 pounds of wool, 15 bushels of Irish potatoes, 300 pounds of butter, and 30 tons of hay. Children were born to the first marriage only, and included:

1. Nathaniel Magruder Waters, born c.1839; 1850 census of Frederick County. Married to Leah Ellen Maynard, daughter of Benjamin Maynard and Eliza M. R. Claggett. Leah left a will in the county dated September 12, 1905 at New Market, probated February 25, 1907. She left her entire estate to her sister Ruthanna Jones, in trust for the use and benefit of her husband, Nathaniel M. Waters. One child:

a. Emily Jane Waters, died young.
2. Greenbury Griffith Waters, born c.1842; 1850 census of Frederick County. Served in Co. K, First Regiment, Virginia Cavalry, under Captain Gus Dorsey. Died in military prison in 1864 as a prisoner of war.
3. Prudence Waters, an infant death.
4. Tilghman Waters, died September, 1885. Married to Drusilla Hammond, daughter of Burgess Hammond. One child:
   a. Henry Hammond Waters.
5. Susanna Magruder Waters, born June 24, 1845, died c.1933 in Baltimore County. Married October 20, 1869 to William Nevins Worley, born October 31, 1834, died c.1912, and had children. This family group appears in *The Riggs Family of Maryland*, by John Beverley Riggs, printed 1989 in Baltimore. However, that report presents our subject's name as Sue Magruder Waters, and her parents as Henry and Prudence (Griffith) Waters. We are dealing with the same individuals, but this book demonstrates the care with which the genealogist must approach each source in reporting proper names. They had children:
   a. Edith May Worley, born March 14, 1871; married to Phillip Asfordby Beatty, son of Doctor Joseph E. Beatty and Emily Frapnell.
   b. Dorsey Waters Worley, born December 27, 1872; married to Inez Biggs Hinton and had children:
      (1) Dorsey Waters Worley, Jr.
      (2) William Nevins Worley, captain, married Marianne Treo and had at least one son:
         (a) William Nevins Worley, III, married to Joan Roberta Worley.
   c. John William Worley, born January 1, 1875; married to Laura Higgins.
   d. Helen James Worley, born February 20, 1877; died c.1945.
   e. Nathan Maynard Worley, born September 18, 1878; married to Corinna Moorman and had children:
      (1) Wilbur Moorman Worley, married Martha Higgins and had children:

(a) Curtis Worley.

(b) Sue Waters Worley.

(2) Marion Worley, married Nathaniel Mantiply and had children:

(a) Mary Corinna Mantiply.

(b) Betty Jean Mantiply.

(3) Virginia Worley.

f. Edgar Brewer Worley, born January 27, 1883

g. Sue Waters Worley, born August 31, 1885

6. Achsah Dorsey M. Waters, born July 4, 1848, died April 14, 1890; buried at Mt. Olivet Cemetery, Frederick. Married to Roderick Dorsey Hobbs, who is perhaps the same born February 25, 1830, died November 9, 1894 and buried at Mt. Olivet Cemetery in Frederick. They had at least a son:

a. Edward Dorsey Hobbs, born October 4, 1877, died December 2, 1918; buried at Mt. Olivet. Married Edna Pearl East, and had at least one child:

(1) Edward Dorsey Hobbs, Jr.

7. Prudence Jane Waters, born September 6, 1853, died January 27, 1923; buried at Monocacy. Apparently a second use of the name after the infant death, but reported in *The Riggs Family of Maryland* as Jennie P. Waters. Born to the first marriage, named for her mother, and was married to Charles McGill Williams, born October 9, 1852, died January 16, 1924; also buried at Monocacy; son of Walter Williams and Miss Dyson. Prudence may have been his second wife. He appeared as head of household in the 1880 census of the Medley District, reported there as born c.1853, with a wife and one child. However, the wife was reported as Virginia, born c.1854, and the son was Charles, born c.1878. We next found the elder Charles as head of household in the 1900 census of the Third District, correctly reported as born October, 1852. There, his wife was listed as Prudence J., born September, 1853. They were reported as married for twenty-four years and Prudence had been the mother of nine children, eight of them surviving, and eight listed at home. Living with them was Emily H. Waters, mother-in-law, at the age of eighty-one years, who was the step-mother of Prudence. The report in the 1900 census that

Charles and Prudence were married c.1876 suggests that we may have misread the 1880 census with the name Virginia as his wife, or that there is more to Prudence's name than we have found. The children were:

a. Charles McGill Williams, Jr., born August, 1877; the child who was found in the 1880 census.

b. Dorsey Waters Williams, born August 9, 1880, died June 1, 1971; buried at Monocacy with his parents.

c. Elizabeth Howard Williams, born January 6, 1883, died February 9, 1954; buried at Monocacy. Married May 8, 1907 to George William Brewer, born September 3, 1878, died November 12, 1950 at Poolesville; buried at Monocacy. He was a son of William George Brewer (1850) and Ida White (1852). They had children, all born at Poolesville, Montgomery County, Maryland:

   (1) Charles McGill Brewer, born July 16, 1908, died March 31, 1984. Married November 5, 1938 in Barnesville to Lucille Banghardt Weller, born December 21, 1917. Three children, including:
       (a) Jennie Brewer, born August 14, 1946
       (b) Elizabeth Ann Brewer, born August 27, 1948

   (2) Betty Williams Brewer, born November 28, 1909, died September 22, 1992 in Harrisonburg, Virginia. Married March 10, 1933 Doctor John Randolph Eggleston, born January 6, 1905 in Arkansas, died October 22, 1981 in Danville, Virginia. They had two children:
       (a) Robert Bolling Eggleston: August 5, 1935
       (b) Peyton Archer Eggleston: August 14, 1939

   (3) George William Brewer, born March 9, 1913. Married August 17, 1932 to Lena Elizabeth Jones, born October 21, 1915 at Dickerson, daughter of Louis John Jones and Nellie Jane Titus. Two children:
       (a) Bettie Jane Brewer, born May 29, 1933
       (b) Mary Joan Brewer, born December 7, 1935

   (4) Jane Waters Brewer, born August 13, 1916, died December 31, 1962. Married October 12, 1940 to Charles Winfield Carlisle, born December 29, 1913

at New Windsor, Maryland, son of John Englar Carlisle and Anna Belle Caylor. Two children:
  (a) George William Carlisle: November 3, 1942
  (b) Charles Winfield Carlisle: April 10, 1947
d. Rodger Walter Williams, born May 23, 1885, died July 5, 1970, a doctor. Married May 24, 1910 Mabel Stuart White, born June 6, 1887, baptized May 7, 1902, died July 15, 1920 at Lynchburg, Virginia. She was a daughter of Mansfield Smith White (1859) and Ella Roberta Whitmore (1857). They had children:
  (1) Ella Whitmore Williams, born April 16, 1911. Married September 5,1936 to Joseph Everette Fauber, Jr., born August 15, 1908. Children:
    (a) Joseph Everette Fauber, III: March 15, 1938.
    (b) Rodger Williams Fauber: November 14, 1941.
  (2) Rodger Walter Williams, Jr., born February 25, 1914. Married February 25, 1941 to Mary Shaw Brown, born August 3, 1917, daughter of William Clifton Brown and Emily P. Darby. Children:
    (a) Rodger Walter Williams, III, born December 20, 1942.
    (b) William Clifton Williams: September 11, 1945.
e. Prudence Jane Williams, born May 14, 1887, died September 1, 1978; buried at Monocacy. Married October 24, 1917 to Henry White Allnutt, born January 14, 1875 in Dawsonville, died September 20, 1956; buried at Monocacy cemetery. He was a son of Benjamin White Allnutt (1837) and Rachel Ann White (1835). At least one son:
  (1) Benjamin White Allnutt, born August 19, 1919, died June 2, 1976. Army Air Force Captain; China/India-Burma Theater during second world war.
f. Emily Byron Williams, born December 6, 1889 and died March 15, 1981. Married to Thomas Cummings Oxley, born January 7, 1889, died December 13, 1980; buried at Monocacy with his wife and her family members.
g. Arthur White Williams, born September 28, 1892, died September 21, 1976; buried at Monocacy with parents.

Married March 28, 1917 in Montgomery County to Julia Nannette White, born December 5, 1892, died May 1, 1940; buried at Monocacy but not with her husband. She was a daughter of Lawrence Allnutt White (1854) of *Inverness* and Annie Oliver Belt (1853). Children:

(1) Julia Nannette Williams, born March 27, 1918

(2) Lawrence McGill Williams, born May 21, 1924

h. Carrie Wheeler Williams, born there April 11, 1895, died June 28, 1987; buried at Monocacy. Married November 9, 1916 in Poolesville to Edwin Ruthvin Allnutt, Jr., born May 26, 1892, died December 28, 1958; buried at Monocacy. He was the son of Edwin Ruthvin Allnutt (1854) and Hester Anna Chiswell (1858). Children:

(1) Anna Chiswell Allnutt, born March 31, 1918. Married August 14, 1942 at Macon, Georgia, to Harry Rimmer, and had three children.

(2) Carrie Williams Allnutt, born October 25, 1919. Married November 9, 1940 to Wiley Gaither Griffith, born June 11, 1914 at Laytonsville, son of Greenberry Gaither Griffith (1874) and Cornelia Isabelle Warfield (1877). Two children, born at Frederick, Maryland:

(a) Marilyn Ann Griffith, born January 11, 1947. Married June 12, 1971 to Michael Lloyd Newman, born 1945.

(b) Barbara Jean Griffith, born January 20, 1951.

(3) Edwin Ruthvin Allnutt, III, born July 9, 1925, died November 30, 1938.

(4) Jane Waters Allnutt, born February 11, 1930. Married September 24, 1948 to Ralph Stanley Price, born October 20, 1920. Two children.

(5) Emily Williams Allnutt, born December 16, 1932. Married October 2, 1954 at Darnestown to Ernest Randolph Dudley, born September 10, 1931. They had three children.

Charles Greenberry Griffith
1849-1931

This son of Howard Griffith (1821) and Sarah Newton Chiswell (1822) was born July, 1849 at Beallsville in Montgomery County, died November 5, 1931 at the home of his son-in-law and daughter, Mr. and Mrs. T. Magruder Veirs, near Rockville; buried at Monocacy Cemetery (*Sentinel* obituary). Married November 28, 1874 at Poolesville to Caroline Virginia Hempstone, born July 3, 1853 at *Hanover Farm* near Beallsville, died April 26, 1914, buried at Monocacy Cemetery with her husband. She was a daughter of Armistead T. Hempstone (1814) and Harriet B. Luckett (1821). Charles was a Montgomery County Commissioner, a state legislator, a farmer, a miller, and the owner of *Charline Manor*. He appears as head of household in the 1880 census for the Medley District of Montgomery County, born c.1849, with Lina, and their first two surviving children. Charles G. next appears in the 1900 census of the Eleventh District, with his wife and eight children. It is said there that he and Lina have been married 25 years, that he is a cattle dealer, owning his farm free and clear, and that they have had 12 children, nine of them then living. Also living with them is Harry D. Hempstone, listed as single and a brother-in-law, proving the relationships. The children now identified are:

1. Bettie Griffith, a twin, born August 29, 1875, died same day; buried at Monocacy Cemetery.
2. Willie Griffith, a twin, born August 29, 1875, died November 23, 1876; buried at Monocacy Cemetery.
3. Harriet Griffith, born January 15, 1877, died March 9, 1949; buried at Monocacy. Married to Alvin Nathan Bastable of Baltimore, Maryland; born October 14, 1837.
4. Howard Griffith, born June 22, 1878, died December 27, 1942 and was a former postmaster of Silver Spring. Married first at the home of the bride October 18, 1899 to Lutie Brewer, born August 19, 1876, died February 20, 1904, daughter of William George Brewer (1850) and Ida White (1852); buried at Monocacy with her husband. Married second to Margaret Elizabeth Perry, born February 17, 1879, died December 10, 1959, daughter of Richard Humphrey Williams Perry (1827)

and Margaret Bell Waters (1849); also buried at Monocacy Cemetery. Howard was head of household in the 1900 census of the county for the Eleventh District, with his wife Lutie, apparently less than a year after their marriage, with no children listed. At least two children were born to the first marriage; eight to the second:

a. Blanche Newton Griffith, born August 6, 1900. Married October 4, 1930 to Morrison MacDowell Clark, born February 8, 1898, died March 4, 1975 in Chevy Chase, Maryland. No children.

b. Esther Rebecca Griffith, born June 19, 1902, died October 30, 1985; buried at Arlington National Cemetery. Records of Poolesville Presbyterian Church report her date of birth as February 2, 1902. Married 1950 to Frederick J. Edwards, died May 16, 1966; buried at Arlington National Cemetery.

c. Charles Howard Griffith, born August 30, 1907 at Poolesville, died February 19, 1997 in Richmond, Virginia; buried at Monocacy Cemetery, Beallsville. Married first June 6, 1930 at the home of the bride in Batesville, Arkansas to Mary Elizabeth Terry, born October 15, 1907; and divorced. He married second July 27, 1946 to Gustava LaMond, born August 30, 1914 at Pine Bluff, Arkansas, died July 7, 1997 in Newport News, Virginia; buried at Monocacy Cemetery at Beallsville. One child from the first marriage and two from the second:

(1) Charles Howard Griffith, Jr., born October 18, 1931 and killed 1954 in the Korean War.

(2) James LaMond Griffith, born July 27, 1946; married April 2, 1970 to Linda Null; four children.

(3) Howard Griffith, born December 28, 1954. He was a minister, married December 15, 1979 to Jacqueline Shelton and had two children.

d. Margaret Waters Griffith, born January 28, 1910. Married June 20, 1929 to John Cope Livingston, born July 5, 1908. Three children:

(1) Elizabeth Ann Livingston, born January 18, 1931. Married April 7, 1955 to Samuel John Irvine, III, born March 9, 1933. Four children:
    (a) Samuel John Irvine, IV: May 15, 1956
    (b) William Bruce Irvine; September 24, 1959
    (c) Margaret Lee Irvine: October 5, 1961
    (d) Laura Irvine, born May 11, 1963
(2) John Cope Livingston, Jr., born February 8, 1935 and married September 8, 1956 Carol Frances Shaeffer, born January 24, 1937. Children:
    (a) John C. Livingston, III: November 29, 1958.
    (b) Frank William Livingston: March 7, 1962
    (c) Terry Suzanne Livingston: July 9, 1963
(3) Howard Griffith Livingston, born October 21, 1941. Married September 18, 1965 to Sharon Ann Beall, born June 1, 1944, divorced after two children. Married second June 30, 1992 to Janet Hammond.

e. Mabel Elizabeth Griffith, born January 22, 1912. Married first June 18, 1932 to Townley Gamble, born March 20, 1908, died December 29, 1953. Married second July 19, 1958 to James Hemenway Littlepage, born December 3, 1910. One child from her first marriage; none from the second:
    (1) Joan Griffith Gamble, born April 26, 1938. Married September 3, 1960 to James Howe Brown, Jr., and divorced.

f. Thomas Perry Griffith, born January 22, 1913, died April 7, 1986, of Frederick; buried at Monocacy. Married three times: first September 20, 1937 to Lucille Ferris; second to Lorraine Dronenburg, born January 22, 1920, divorced; and third November 4, 1957 to Elizabeth Lochner McNulty. Two children from his first marriage; none from the second; two from the third:
    (1) Lucinda Griffith, born September 18, 1938. Married October 7, 1958 to George Walter Sconyers, Jr., born December 16, 1933. Three children:
        (a) George Walter Sconyers, III: July 3, 1959
        (b) Steven William Sconyers: April 11, 1962

        (c)   Anne Lucy Sconyers: September 28, 1964

    (2)   Pamela Griffith, born October 10, 1947

    (3)   John L. Griffith, reported as a son in the obituary of his father.

    (4)   Isabel Perry Griffith, born April 22, 1959

    (5)   Laura Lochner Griffith, born December 14, 1961

g.   William Bastable Griffith, born January 28, 1918. Married April 18, 1947 to Barbara Smith Shetterly, born c.1922, died May 5, 2000 at Beallsville; apparently her second marriage. Her obituary mentions a son, Russell B. Shetterly, and a daughter:

    (1)   Mary Patricia Griffith, born May 26, 1948; married to Wilson.

h.   Mary Ann Griffith, born January 15, 1921. Married June 23, 1942 to George Overton Kephart, born February 16, 1920, and had children:

    (1)   George Overton Kephart, Jr.: July 7, 1944

    (2)   Elizabeth Perry Kephart: November 28, 1945

    (3)   Ann Frazer Kephart: April 8, 1949

i.   Daughter Griffith, married Morrison M. Clark of Chevy Chase.

j.   Daughter Griffith, married Fred Edwards.

5.   Armistead Hempstone Griffith, born January 29, 1881, died November 7, 1943; buried at Monocacy Cemetery, Beallsville, with his wife and other family members. Married October 28, 1914 at Darnestown Presbyterian Church to Sarah Marcylean Hersberger, born November 14, 1883, died March 3, 1967 at her home on Upton Street in Rockville; daughter of Aaron Hersberger of Poolesville; buried at Monocacy Cemetery at Beallsville. The spelling of the bride's surname is questionable; it has been found as Hersberger, Hersperger, or Herspberger. Aaron was a census taker in the Third District during 1900, and he spelled it Hersberger. One daughter:

a.   Ann Marcylean Griffith, born May 11, 1918, died June 18, 1993. Married January 16, 1947 at Rockville to John Auchinvole Backus, born July 20, 1908 in New York. One child:

    (1)   Sarah Ann Backus, born June 9, 1954.

6. Sarah Newton Griffith, born June 14, 1884, died October, 1963. Married January 16, 1909 to her cousin, Charles Byron Sellman, born January 22, 1881, died February 28, 1947; buried at Monocacy Cemetery, Beallsville, son of Charles Sellman (1848) and Lucy Veirs (1854). Two children:
   a. Charles Griffith Sellman, born October 1, 1912
   b. Richard Brooke Sellman, born February 12, 1915 and died February 8, 1997. Married to Margaret Burns, born May 31, 1917, died October 9, 1985; both buried at Monocacy.
7. Lutie Griffith, born c.1884, died January 11, 1933, single, buried with her parents at Monocacy Cemetery.
8. Susan Boyd Griffith, born June 23, 1886 on the family farm near Beallsville, died June 15, 1975; buried at Monocacy Cemetery with her husband. Married December 29, 1908 at St. Peter's Church in Poolesville to Frank Isaac Davis, born September 4, 1885, died February 7, 1960, son of Horace Morsell Davis (1851), of Poolesville and Mary Emma Williams (1855). He was Clerk of the Montgomery County Police Court, and the County Sheriff from 1946 to 1950. Susan was a public school music teacher, and her father and grandfather both served in the Maryland Legislature. Five children, born at Poolesville, Maryland:
   a. Carolyn Virginia Davis, born October 12, 1909, died July 25, 1910; buried at Monocacy cemetery.
   b. Charles Horace Davis, born November 20, 1911, died November 28, 1987 at Frederick; buried at Monocacy. His stone also bears the name of Mabel Coatsworth Davis, probably his wife.
   c. Infant Davis, stillbirth September 9, 1913; buried at Monocacy cemetery.
   d. Harriet Griffith Davis, born October 6, 1917, married June 1, 1946 to Gerald James Fahey and lived in Detroit.
   e. Frank Isaac Davis, Jr., born February 18, 1919 and married to Elizabeth Virginia Battle.
9. Elizabeth Griffith, born January 29, 1889 at Beallsville, died at Rockville August 23, 1968. Married December 22, 1920 to

Thomas Magruder Veirs, born November 9, 1894, died April 18, 1976. At least one son:
a. Thomas Magruder Veirs, Jr., born June 5, 1924. He operates T. M. Veirs & Sons Excavating Company near Rockville. Married October 27, 1943 to Harriett O'Neill Stokes, born July 27, 1924. Nine children:
  (1) Harriett Stokes Veirs, born March 27, 1945
  (2) Marguerite Valerie Veirs, born April 17, 1946
  (3) Thomas Griffith Veirs, stillbirth June 4, 1951
  (4) Thomas Magruder Veirs, IV; December 14, 1953
  (5) Katherine Elizabeth Veirs; December 27, 1957
  (6) Richard O'Neil Veirs, born May 15, 1960
  (7) Mary Celeste Veirs, born May 5, 1961
  (8) John Griffith Veirs, born May 2, 1962
  (9) Mary Teresa Veirs, born May 13, 1964
10. Harry Walling Griffith, born January 3, 1890, died November 15, 1936 at Raleigh, North Carolina; buried at Monocacy. Married August 4, 1914 to Florence Ayers, born January 27, 1893, died May 13, 1975. Two children:
a. Dorothy Hempstone Griffith, born February 13, 1916. Married September 7, 1940 to Harold Edwin Carter, born August 23, 1914, and had two children.
b. Robert Clifton Griffith, born May 5, 1919
11. Raymond Griffith, died March 18, 1892, aged 8 months and 10 days; buried at Monocacy Cemetery.
12. Ruth Griffith, born August 19, 1894 at Beallsville, died at Rockville June 9, 1964. Married November 17, 1915 to Charles Clifton Veirs, born February 18, 1888, died November 20, 1973 at Rockville, son of Charles Veirs (1859) and Rose Lyddane (1858). Children, born there:
a. Charles Clifton Veirs, Jr., born April 6, 1917, died September 16, 1979. Married August 20, 1949 Mary Anne Dawson, born August 10, 1925; three children:
  (1) Charles Clifton Veirs, III, born April 12, 1951
  (2) Frazier Peter Veirs, born March 27, 1955
  (3) Anne Dawson Veirs, born November 20, 1955
b. Alvin Bastable Veirs, born March 12, 1922, died October 23, 1994. Owner of A. B. Veirs and Sons Paving Com-

pany of Rockville. Married June 29, 1944 to Barbara Ann Smith, born October 3, 1925. Eight children:

(1) Alvin Bastable Veirs, Jr., born April 12, 1945
(2) Barbara Ann Veirs, born June 30, 1946
(3) Charles Smith Veirs, born July 3, 1947
(4) James Hunter Veirs, born November 12, 1949
(5) Joan Griffith Veirs, born December 14, 1950
(6) Michael Guthrie Veirs, born December 20, 1953
(7) William Anthony Veirs, born January 30, 1958
(8) Daniel Howard Veirs, born February 11, 1960

c. Carolyn Griffith Veirs, born January 11, 1924. Married December 11, 1943 C. Reginald Smith, divorced. Married second October 26, 1946 to William Chase Mudgett, Jr. She had one child born to her first marriage and two to the second:

(1) Carol Ann Smith, born June 8, 1944
(2) William Chase Mudgett, III, born August 9, 1947
(3) Kevin Mudgett, born February 27, 1957

CHILD 4

Ruth Griffith
1789-1855

This daughter of Howard Griffith (1757) and Jemima Jacob (1759), was born August 20, 1789 in Montgomery County, died October 14, 1855; buried at Mt. Olivet Cemetery in Frederick with her husband. Married February 13, 1812 to Thomas Maynard, born c.1776, died July 24, 1830, and had children:

1. Rachel Ann Maynard, born November 24, 1813. Married in Frederick County by license dated August 21, 1833 to John McElfresh, son of Philip McElfresh and Lydia Griffith (1755).
2. Howard Griffith Maynard, born February 3, 1817, died March 28, 1899; buried at Mt. Olivet Cemetery at Frederick, with his wife and four children. Married in Frederick County by license dated September 13, 1856 to Sarah Newton Chiswell, born April 11, 1836, died November 26, 1892. Eleven children, of whom at least four were buried with them:

a. Louis S. Maynard, born June 17, 1857, died September 11, 1879
b. Nathan Maynard, born December 25, 1858
c. Joseph T. Maynard, born December 12, 1860
d. Ruth Eleanor Maynard, born June 4, 1863, died 1927
e. John A. Maynard, born November 10, 1865
f. Sarah H. Maynard, born July 30, 1868, died April 14, 1955
g. Augusta C. Maynard, born February 24, 1871, died May 9, 1871
h. Florence E. Maynard, born April 28, 1872
i. Richard Maynard, born December 10, 1874
j. William Maynard, born June 23, 1876
k. George E. Maynard, born June 11, 1878
3. Benjamin Maynard, born August 28, 1819, died August 16, 1868; buried at Mt. Olivet Cemetery in Frederick with his wife and one son. Married in Frederick County by license dated September 21, 1843 to Eliza M. R. Clagett, born May 6, 1823, died August 31, 1886.
a. Howard G. Maynard, born July 9, 1853, died July 9, 1878; buried at Mt. Olivet.
4. Jemima Maynard, born March 5, 1822; married L. Shull.
5. Nathan Maynard, born April 29, 1824, died July 17, 1888; buried at Mt. Olivet Cemetery, Frederick, with his wife and two daughters. Married November 30, 1854 to Jemima Eleanor Chiswell, born October 16, 1834, died June 19, 1916, daughter of John A. Chiswell and Eleanor Griffith. Children:
a. Fannie Maynard, born September 19, 1855
b. Frank N. Maynard, born March 25, 1857
c. John N. Maynard, born June 10, 1860. Married March 27, 1890 to Jennie E. Bennett.
d. Rachel Ann Maynard, born October 11, 1865, died January 24, 1927. Buried at Mt. Olivet.
e. Eleanor Maynard, born July 7, 1870, died December 16, 1939. USA Nurses Corp. Buried at Mt. Olivet.
f. Benjamin T. Maynard, born July 12, 1874
6. Thomas Maynard. Probably the same Thomas Maynard who was born February 2, 1826, died March 6, 1908; buried at

Mt. Olivet Cemetery in Frederick with a wife and five children. Married Frederick County by license dated January 29, 1855 to Henrietta E. Stevenson, born December 11, 1830, died July 16, 1862. Five children buried with them:

a. Nettie Maynard, died September 9, 1867 at four months.
b. Thomas Maynard, died September 9, 1868; three months
c. Helen Virginia Maynard, born 1869, and died August 18, 1877
d. Katie Maynard, born 1874, died March 1, 1875
e. Fleet Maynard, born 1876, died July 13, 1877

7. Leah Maynard. Probably the same as Leah Ellen Maynard, who was married in Frederick County by license dated May 17, 1849 to John A. Fleet. She was born March 9, 1829, died October 12, 1882, and is buried at Mt. Olivet, Frederick.

CHILD 9

Lebbeus Griffith
1804-1889

This son of Howard Griffith (1757) and Jemima Jacob (1759) was born February 11, 1804 in Montgomery County, died February 5, 1889; buried at New Market Methodist Church Cemetery. A short biography of Lebbeus and his family appears in *History of Western Maryland*, by J. Thomas Scharf, first published in 1882. Typical of the time period, when such publications were quite popular, and in the style commonly used by Scharf, the article begins on page 604, Volume I, and describes in flowing terms the contributions that Lebbeus Griffith, in particular, and the Griffith family, in general, made to the development of Montgomery and Frederick Counties. The article includes a rather handsome portrait of Lebbeus, showing a stern gentleman, with a long, flowing white beard and mustache. It is recommended reading, with many family facts, written over one hundred years closer to the facts than we are today. How often the genealogist expresses the wish that we might have talked with our grandparents about the family; here we have the possibility provided to us.

Lebbeus reportedly moved into Frederick County about 1827, and was first married January 27, 1829 in Frederick County to Mary Eleanor Griffith, born August 28, 1805, died June 30, 1835, youngest daughter of Colonel Philemon Griffith (1756) and Eleanor Jacob (1762), and had two children. In 1882, Lebbeus was living on the farm formerly owned by Colonel Philemon Griffith, who died there in 1839.

Lebbeus was married second March 12, 1839 to Sarah Ann Wood, daughter of Reverend John Wood and Ruth H. Burgess and had five children. Head of household in the 1850 census of Frederick County for the New Market District, he was a farmer with $5,000 in real estate. His second wife, Sarah A., was there, born c.1818, and there were five children, Philemon and Jemima from the first marriage, and Lebbeus, Prudence and Alverda from the second. Sarah Ann died January 29, 1853, and Lebbeus was married third January 26, 1858 to Ruth S. Warfield, daughter of Seth Warfield and Lydia Meredith, and had eight more children. He was a slave holder, and an extensive farmer.

Lebbeus left a will in Frederick County, dated June 16, 1888, probated March 12, 1889 and recorded in liber HL-1 at folio 119. He specifically leaves to his wife Ruth S. Griffith the set of parlor furniture, bedroom furniture, personal property, his riding mare and the buggy and harness. Further, he leaves his flock of sheep to his wife Ruth and her four children, jointly. He and Ruth were reportedly the parents of eight children; perhaps only four of them were then surviving. To his sons Seth W. Griffith, Robert E. L. Griffith and Clarence M. Griffith, he left five hundred dollars each. To his daughter Florence C. Griffith, he left five hundred dollars and a half dozen hair-seat, walnut chairs; a marble top wash stand, and the sewing machine. Finally, he concludes with the statement that in consideration of the legacies to his children named in the will, he releases "all my other children" from the effect of any debts they owe him, from advancements, notes, and other obligations.

According to Scharf, Lebbeus was the father of a total of sixteen children from his three marriages, including these:
1. Philemon Howard Griffith, born May 7, 1830, died September 12, 1900, buried at Mt. Airy Methodist Church with his wife. Married December 11, 1855 to Elizabeth H. Wood, born Oc-

tober 5, 1838, died December 12, 1913 at the home of her daughter, Mrs. Edwin Waters, near Goshen; daughter of the Reverend John Wood. They reportedly lived at New Market in Frederick County. Children:

a. Harry C. Griffith, born September 28, 1856; perhaps the same Harry Griffith who died March 19, 1883; buried at New Market.

b. Philemon Howard Griffith, Jr., born April 1, 1858. Perhaps married and the father of, at least:
   (1) Frances Ruth Griffith, born January 24, 1893

c. William C. Griffith, born December 9, 1859

d. Lebbeus Griffith, born January 21, 1862, died August 21, 1863; buried with his parents.

e. Tanjore T. Griffith, born January 12, 1865, died July 2, 1935; buried at Mt. Olivet, Frederick. Married to Sarah Dorsey, born December 23, 1866, died January 31, 1958 at White Plains, New York; buried with her husband, daughter of Doctor Harry Woodward Dorsey, Jr. (1831). At least three children:
   (1) Dorsey J. Griffith, married Hilda Bowen and had at least two children:
      (a) Mary E. Griffith.
      (b) Elizabeth Griffith.
   (2) Howard T. Griffith, married Cecelia Hedgeman.
   (3) Mary Griffith, married to Joseph Stansfield and had at least a daughter. At the time of her mother's death, they were living in Scarsdale, New York. Daughter:
      (a) Sarah Dorsey Stansfield.

f. Mary E. B. Griffith, born January 15, 1868, of whom more.

g. Linda Griffith, born April 14, 1870, died January 11, 1939; buried at Mt. Olivet in Frederick, with her husband. Married to Charles Julian Reich, born August 15, 1849, died March 2, 1914.

h. Lena Griffith, born February 18, 1872

i. Guy Griffith, born February 18, 1875

2. Jemima Eleanor Griffith, born June 24, 1832. Married November 26, 1856 to Doctor Basil B. Crawford, born c.1833. Lived at Laytonsville, and had children:
   a. Howell Crawford, born October 15, 1857, died August 18, 1881, single.
   b. Varena Crawford, born June 11, 1860, died September 16, 1863
   c. Mary A. Crawford, born August 26, 1862. Married to Thomas Banks and lived in Howard County; children.
   d. Lebbeus Crawford, born February 8, 1865, died July 3, 1865
   e. Basil B. Crawford, Jr., born November 23, 1866, died December 11, 1868
   f. Eldred Crawford, born December 12, 1868, died June 18, 1870
   g. Arthur Crawford, born February 18, 1871, died August 31, 1881
   h. A. Blanche Crawford, born January 28, 1873
   i. Nellie B. Crawford, born October, 1875, died August 29, 1881
3. Festus Agrippa Griffith, born November 25, 1834. Listed in an old family Bible with the other two children here, and may have died young.
4. Ruth Griffith, born December 11, 1839, died February 11, 1845
5. Lebbeus Griffith, Jr., born March 4, 1842, died December 10, 1887 at New Market, buried at Monrovia Friends Cemetery, Frederick County. He has been reported as single, but *Names In Stone*, by Jacob Mehrling Holdcraft, reports a wife buried with him. She was Rachel, born c.1843, died November 28, 1937 at 94 years.
6. Prudence Griffith, born May 30, 1845, died August 7, 1853
7. Alverda Griffith, born August 9, 1848. The obituary of Alverda appearing in the *Montgomery County Sentinel* states that she died November 15, 1915 near Laytonsville, and that she was then aged 78 years, which would place her birth as c.1837, which is eleven years earlier than her birth date reported from other sources. Cemetery records at Goshen Meth-

odist Church report her birth as c.1848, which is probably correct. There is no question of her identify; the obituary reports the name of her husband and the married names of three surviving daughters. Married to Harry Griffith, born April 4, 1839, died November 24, 1920; buried at Goshen Cemetery; son of Ulysses Griffith (1810) and Julia Riggs (1811), and had children. Their family is reported in detail under their father's name in the chapter devoted to the descendants of Henry Griffith of 1767, which see.

8. Sarah Ann Griffith, born October 14, 1850, died February 11, 1917 at her home near Etchison. Married to William H. Griffith, born 1847, died December 29, 1923 at his home near Etchison; buried at the Laytonsville cemetery, son of Walter Griffith (1820) and Mary W. Riggs (1819). In the 1870 census of the First District of Montgomery County, he and his wife Sarah, and their first child, were living with his widowed mother. William H. was head of household in the 1880 census of the county for the Cracklin District, with Sarah A., and five children. Head of household in the 1900 census of the First District (although we transcribed his name as William A. Griffith and he was there reported as born January, 1843), with his wife Sarah A. and two sons. They had been married thirty-one years and she had been mother of seven children, six surviving. Children were:

a. Mary W. Griffith, born c.1870

b. Lyde Griffith, born May 28, 1871, died July 21, 1915 in the Laytonsville District. His *Sentinel* obituary assigns him the name of N. Lyde Griffith, the only time we have seen evidence of a first name. Married in Gaithersburg, Montgomery County, at Ascension Episcopal Church by license dated December 4, 1894 to Julia Morgan Snouffer, born July, 1875, died May 21, 1951, the daughter of G. Fenton Snouffer. He was head of household in the 1900 census of the county for the First District, with his wife Julia. They had been married for six years, and she had been the mother of two children, both surviving, but only one at home. Living with them was Henry (A.)

Griffith, born August 29, 1825, single, listed as a cousin. The one child listed at home was:

(1)   Mary Ann Griffith, born March 6, 1896.

c.   Louisa Hood Griffith, born c.1874, died November 27, 1922 of heart trouble and pneumonia at her home at Laytonsville, leaving her husband and three children; buried at Laytonsville (*Sentinel* obituary). Married November 22, 1898 at St. Bartholomew's Church in Laytonsville to her cousin Thomas Cranmer Griffith, born April 14, 1866, died June 1, 1924 at his home in Laytonsville; buried at Laytonsville Cemetery, son of Uriah Henry Griffith (1825) and Henrietta E. Wilcoxen (1821). They had children, discussed under their father's name, which see.

d.   Alverda Griffith, born c.1876, died December 28, 1946, buried with her husband; at Laytonsville Cemetery. Married November 9, 1893 at Hawlings Episcopal Church to Frank Griffith, born December 18, 1869, died 1903, son of Judge Charles Harrison Griffith (1840) and Hester Boone Dorsey (1843). The *Sentinel* announced that they would live in Howard County. At least these children:

(1)   Mary Louise Griffith, born October 13, 1896

(2)   William Franklin Griffith, born January 27, 1899

(3)   Charles Harrison Griffith, born July 23, 1903

e.   William L. Griffith, born c.1878, buried October 27, 1934 (records of St. Bartholomew's Church). Married December 3, 1903 at Rockville to Nellie M. Allnutt, born c.1879, daughter of William J. Allnutt of near Laytonsville. Her obituary in the *Gaithersburg Gazette* reported that she died November 5, 1971, wife of the late William L. Griffith, buried at Laytonsville. They had children, not necessarily in this order:

(1)   Nellie Griffith, married to Hardell.

(2)   Anna Griffith, married to Waters.

(3)   Helen Griffith, married to Kramer.

(4)   Sarah Jane Griffith, born 1905, died October 12, 1925; buried with her parents.

(5) Ruth H. Griffith, born 1921, died 1921; buried with her parents.

(6) Margaret Wood Griffith, born June 6, 1912, died November 16, 1976 at Montgomery General Hospital, single. Buried at Laytonsville.

(7) Mary Griffith, married to Collins.

f. Walter Griffith, born July 11, 1886. An obituary in the *Sentinel* reported the death of Walker Griffith (sic) on December 31, 1925 in a Washington hospital, son of the late William H. Griffith, leaving a wife, the former Nettie Griffith, and naming a brother and two sisters, which match the family here reported. Buried at Laytonsville Cemetery.

9. Mary Ellen Griffith, born January 29, 1853, died June 2, 1853

10. Harry Griffith, born September 28, 1856, perhaps died young

11. Ida May Griffith, born November 22, 1858, and died May 9, 1883. Married as his first wife to Edwin Waters, born February 23, 1859, died August 15, 1938; buried at Goshen Methodist Church; named in his father's will of 1906. He was a son of Zachariah Maccubbin Waters (1832) and Sarah Virginia Magruder (1835). No children, and he was married secondly to her niece, Mary E. B. Griffith, born January 15, 1868, died c.1941; also buried with her husband.

12. Seth Warfield Griffith, born January 9, 1860, died November 4, 1935; buried at Salem Cemetery, Brookeville with his wife. In the 1900 census of Montgomery County for the Eighth District, he was listed as single, living alone. Married July 30, 1907 in Richmond, Virginia to Mrs. Elizabeth (Hopkins) Miller. In January of 1907, the *Sentinel* reported that Seth W. Griffith, of Abbeville, South Carolina, was visiting relatives in Brookeville, Maryland. The *Sentinel* reported the death of Eliza on February 22, 1930, stating that she left two daughters and had been twice married; her first marriage being to Sheriff William B. Miller. Cemetery records of St. John's Episcopal in Olney report her birth as September 28, 1850. The daughters were perhaps from that first marriage: Bessie Hutton (Mrs. Josiah J. Hutton); and Mrs. Ernest Wiggins. Seth W. Griffith left a will in Montgomery County, dated October 28, 1935 in

the Town of Brookeville, probated November 15, 1935; recorded in liber HGC 11 at folio 199. To Mrs. Lillian D. Tillotson of Brookeville he left Lot 49 on Market Street. We have not identified her as yet. The will mentions bequests to a number of his nieces and nephews, naming brothers and sisters of the testator.

13. Florence C. Griffith, born May 8, 1861, died 1933; buried with her husband in Forest Oak Cemetery at Gaithersburg. Married in Frederick County October 15, 1889 to Francis B. Etchison, born c.1864, son of Lysander Etchison (1831), and had children, named in the will of her brother Seth:
   a. Ruth Anna Etchison, married to Belt and apparently also to Watson. In the will of her uncle Seth W. Griffith, she is referred to as Ruth Anna Belt, but also as mother of:
      (1) Jack Mitchell Watson.
   b. Frank Lester Etchison.
   c. Bowie Griffith Etchison.

14. Robert E. Lee Griffith, born July 15, 1862. Married to Eliza Warfield, daughter of Garrison Warfield (1822) and Caroline Lewis (1835). There were three children, all named in the will of their uncle Seth W. Griffith:
   a. Forest India Griffith; married to Myers.
   b. Forrest Lee Griffith, married, with at least one son:
      (1) Forrest Lee Griffith, Jr.
   c. Katherine Griffith, married to Lauterback.

15. Clarence M. Griffith, born November 17, 1864, died April 8, 1924, buried at Forest Oak Cemetery in Gaithersburg, with his wife. His *Sentinel* obituary states that he died as the result of a fall, leaving his widow and two daughters, although we have identified only one girl. Married at Trinity Methodist Church in New Market, Frederick County December 24, 1889 to Grace Etchison, born January 5, 1869 at New Market, died April 8, 1946 at Boyds, daughter of Lysander Etchison (1831). The 1900 census of Montgomery County, for the Second District, carries a household headed by Clarence R. Griffith (sic), with a wife Grace and two children, which is apparently this family. However, Clarence R. is there listed as having been born November, 1855, ten years earlier than that re-

ported above. The 1855 date does not appear to be accurate. The couple had been married ten years, and she had been the mother of three children, only two surviving. The obituary of their son Clarence Gorman reports that he was survived by a brother and two sisters, both of them identified only by their husband's names: Mrs. Alexandria C. Gawlis, and Mrs. Walter M. Royal, Jr. The obituary of their mother names the same two daughters, as well as the two surviving sons. Clarence M. Griffith left a will dated April 5, 1924, written at Georgetown University Hospital, three days before his death. The will was probated May 20, 1924 and recorded in liber PEW 2 at folio 184, leaving his entire estate to his wife Grace, to do with as she pleases. The known children were:

a.   Gladys May Griffith, born May, 1891; referred to in the will of her uncle Seth W. Griffith as married to Alexander C. Gawlis.

b.   Elizabeth Etchison Griffith, who died at the age of 3 years, 3 months and 4 days.

c.   Clarence Gorman Griffith, born May 31, 1899 in Boyds, died February 28 1967 at his home on East Diamond Avenue in Gaithersburg. Married November 29, 1922 at Clarksburg to Addie Maria King, born May 8, 1893, and died April 30, 1962, daughter of James Edward King (1854) and Addie Cassandra Hurley (1859). Gorman Griffith was postmaster of Gaithersburg for a number of years. He and his wife are buried at Forest Oak in Gaithersburg. No children.

d.   Robert Leland Griffith. This may be the child referred to as Seth Robert Griffith in the will of his uncle Seth W. Griffith. He was born c.1908 and died August 5, 1970; buried at Glenwood Cemetery, Silver Spring, Maryland. His obituary reports that he was employed by the Civil Aeronautics Board, and died of cancer at Kensington Gardens Sanitarium. He was survived by his wife Margaret and two daughters. Also named were two surviving sisters. His children were:

(1)   Claire Ann Griffith, married James Roupas.

(2)   Sarah Griffith, married Ronald G. Tipton.

e. Mary Ann Griffith; referred to in the will of her uncle Seth W. Griffith; perhaps married Walter M. Royal, Jr.

16. Varena Griffith, an infant death.

Mary E. B. Griffith
1868-

This daughter of Philemon Howard Griffith (1830) and Elizabeth H. Wood (1838), was born January 15, 1868 at New Market, in Frederick County, Maryland. Married January 22, 1889 at Trinity Methodist Church in New Market, as his second wife, to Edwin Waters, born February 23, 1859, died August 15, 1938; buried at Goshen Methodist Church; named in his father's will of 1906. He was a son of Zachariah Maccubbin Waters (1832) and Sarah Virginia Magruder (1835). He was first married to Mary's aunt, Ida May Griffith, born c.1858, and died May 9, 1883 at Baltimore at the age of 24 years, 5 months and 17 days; and is buried at the Goshen cemetery, daughter of Lebbeus Griffith and his wife Ruth S. Warfield. Head of household in the 1900 census of Montgomery County for the Twelfth District, he had a wife Mary E., born January, 1867, and two children. Married for eleven years, she had been the mother of three children, with two surviving. The children were:

1. Edwin Griffith Waters, born October, 1889. Married to Nellie Mullen of Frederick.

2. Sarah Virginia Waters, born May, 1895, and married January 20, 1921 at Christ Episcopal Church, Rockville, (or in Laytonsville?) to Dawson Vachel Hammond, Jr., of Walkersville, born December 12, 1887. At least two daughters:
   a. Virginia Hammond, born December 24, 1921.
   b. Charlotte Hammond.

3. Linda Alverda Waters, born June 30, 1900 at the family farm at Goshen, along Seneca Creek, died January 6, 1981; buried in the Friends Cemetery at Sandy Spring, Montgomery County, Maryland. Her obituary described how her parents, during the Civil War, drove their herd of cattle into Seneca Creek until just their heads were above water to save them from the Confederate Army. She had attended St. Mary's Seminary in southern Maryland and was a volunteer worker at

Montgomery General Hospital, where she died, after suffering a heart attack at her *Longmead Farm* home. Married April 3, 1919 to Frank Forsythe Willson, born December 30, 1897, died March 16, 1986, the son of George Arthur Willson (1868) and Sarah Forsythe of Layhill. Unfortunately, at the wedding, Elizabeth Earl Willson (1903), sister of the groom, was fatally injured when her dress caught on fire at the wedding. Frank was a member of the Sandy Springs Lions Club and the Enterprise Club of Sandy Spring; and was buried with his wife. Children:

a. Frank Forsythe Willson, Jr., born May 12, 1920, married first June 15, 1946 to Lois Jane Ely, born September 26, 1925 and had one child. Married second February 5, 1960 to Anne Elizabeth McGarry, born December 21, 1935, and had three children:

    (1) Constance Willson, born April 2, 1947

    (2) Frank Forsythe Willson, III, born August 31, 1961

    (3) Anne Elizabeth Willson, born September 7, 1963, married September 18, 1987 to Robert F. Gilroy.

    (4) John Earl Willson, born August 5, 1966

b. Barbara Waters Willson, born November 17, 1922; married to Armando and lived in New Jersey.

c. Edwin Gilpin Willson, born July 10, 1928 at Silver Spring, died July 15, 1990 at his home at Sykesville. He was a builder of fine homes in Montgomery County, during the late 1950s when this author was employed in the office of the Montgomery County Surveyor. He was first married July 19, 1952 to Betty Harris, born November 10, 1924, by whom he had five children and was divorced. Married second May 1, 1978 to Patricia Kingma Parrish, divorced, and married a third time to Catherine C., who survived him. He had a stepson, Augustus A. Conaway, and five children. His children were:

    (1) Edwin Gilpin Willson, Jr., born April 11, 1953 and married April 12, 1979 to Betsy 'Bonnie" Bonifant, born July 3, 1946 in Washington, and died May 26, 1994 at Montgomery General Hospital. Buried at St. Peter's Catholic Church at Olney. She was the

daughter of Doctor Alfred Dement Bonifant and his wife Betsy of Silver Spring and had first been married to Lynn Thomas Callahan, III, by whom she had a daughter, Melissa Callahan. She was a member of the women's tennis association of the Argyle Country Club. and she and Gil had twin children:

    (a) Jennifer Willson, born December 3, 1979

    (b) Jeffry G. Willson, born December 3, 1979

(2) Kimberly Willson, born July 11, 1954, married April 7, 1981 M. Jeffery St. Clair. One child:

    (a) Zenocrate Sophia Willson: July 22, 1982

(3) Carter Harris Willson, born July 12, 1955 and married July 18, 1981 Stephany Roche. At least a child:

    (a) Brooke Hayward Willson: August 25, 1984

(4) Brian Forsythe Willson, born September 21, 1956.

(5) Drew Kimbal Willson, born January 2, 1959.

William Griffith
died 1699
The Immigrant
Chapter 2
*

Charles Griffith
1693
Chapter 3
*

Sarah Griffith
1730
(md Azel Warfield)
*

Anne Warfield
1762
Chapter 12
*
*

* * * * * * * * *
*
* * Samuel Waters
*
* * Charles Alexander Waters
*
* * Walter Warfield Waters
*
* * Elizabeth Waters 1794
*
* * Charlotte Waters 1795
*
* * Catherine Waters 1797
*
* * Azel Waters 1799
*
* * Ignatius Waters 1801
*
* * Richard Waters
*
* * Louisa Ann Waters 1808
*
* * Samuel Waters 1818

CHAPTER 12

Anne Warfield
1762-1850

This daughter of Azel Warfield (1726) and Sarah Griffith (1730) was born June 28, 1762, perhaps in Anne Arundel County, and died c.1850 in Montgomery County. She was apparently married in Anne Arundel County to Ignatius Waters, son of Richard Waters (1715) and Elizabeth Williams. He was born in what is now Montgomery County and died there in the 1820s, apparently intestate. In some records, he was reportedly married in Anne Arundel County by license dated June 14, 1790 to Nancy Warfield, daughter of Azel Warfield and Sarah Griffith. However, in *Genealogy of the Griffith Family*, by William and Sarah Maccubbin Griffith, published 1892, they report that Ignatius Waters was married to Anne Warfield, (not Nancy), born June 28, 1762, youngest daughter of Sarah Griffith, which appears to be correct. Further, in *Early Families of Southern Maryland*, Volume 1, by Elise Greenup Jourdan, there is no mention of a daughter Nancy having been born to Azel Warfield and Sarah Griffith. Nor is such a daughter reported by Harry Wright Newman in *Anne Arundel Gentry*, considered the definitive work on families of that area and period.

In his father's will, Ignatius was referred to as Nacy, inherited all the personal estate, received the property known as *Back Pond* on Seneca Creek, and was named Executor of the will. On June 1, 1829, Ann Waters, as widow of Ignatius, together with several of her adult children, sold 404 acres of *Waters' Conclusion* to Walter W. Warfield. Anne (or Ann) Waters left a will in Montgomery County dated February 23, 1846, probated May 25, 1850, and recorded in liber HH 3 at folio 169. To three of her Smith grandchildren, she left 40 acres of land on the south side of the road from Seneca Bridge to Mechanicsville. The remainder of the dwelling plantation known as *Waters' Conclusion* was left to her two daughters, Charlotte Waters and Louisa Ann Meriwether. Ignatius was father of at least eleven children:

1. Samuel Waters, who died as an infant.

2. Charles Alexander Waters, married in Montgomery County by license dated February 2, 1822 to Teresa Murphy of Baltimore. In various deeds of the county it is evident that he at one time owned the 404 acres of *Waters' Conclusion* and 55 acres of *Wildcat Spring*, as well as sixteen negroes, livestock and farm implements. He is said to have served in the War of 1812, and is buried in Bonnie Brae Cemetery, Baltimore.

3. Walter Warfield Waters, married in Montgomery County by license dated January 2, 1826 to his cousin, Elizabeth Ann Warfield, the daughter of James Warfield (1751) and Ann Gassaway. Moved to Tennessee.

4. Elizabeth Waters, born February 17, 1794, died March 16, 1824. She married December 6, 1814 to Philemon McElfresh Smith of Hyattstown, born February 2, 1794, died March 14, 1879; son of John Smith and Rachel McElfresh, and had at least three children named in her mother's will, who jointly received 40 acres of land on the south side of the public road leading from Seneca Bridge to Mechanicsville. Philemon M. Smith was named postmaster of Hyattstown on May 30, 1837, and was married three times. After the death of Elizabeth Waters, he was married second to Arra, who died in 1838; and third to Miranda, who died in 1880. He and his three wives are all buried at Hyattstown Methodist Church. He was found as head of household in the 1850 census of the Second District of Montgomery County, with his third wife, and three of his children, all born too late to have been children of Elizabeth Waters, and therefore not of the Waters lineage. She may have had children, and probably did, during the ten years she was married to Philemon Smith, and they may have included one or more of these:

   a. John Hamilton Smith.

   b. Ignatius Waters Smith.

   c. Philemon McElfresh Smith. An obituary in the *Sentinel* reports that he died in April, 1891, after being struck by a train, leaving a wife and an infant child. It appears from the language of the obituary that the individual killed was perhaps a son of this Philemon McElfresh Smith.

5. Charlotte Waters, born September 18, 1795, died August 27, 1883, single. Under her mother's will, she received jointly with her sister Louisa Ann Meriwether the dwelling plantation called *Waters' Conclusion*. She was head of household in the 1850 census of Montgomery County for the First or Cracklin, District, listed next door to her cousin, Richard Rawlings Waters (1794). In the 1850 census, Charlotte was also listed as owning six slaves. There were three others living with her: Louisa A. Meriwether, born c.1808; Annie Meriwether, born c.1842; and Albert G. Meriwether, born c.1854. Louisa was her sister, widow of Albert Gallatin Meriwether, and the two children were hers. In the 1850 census, Charlotte Waters was listed as owning 60 acres of improved land and 60 acres unimproved. She owned 3 milch cows, 1 other cattle, and 5 swine. In the previous year, she had raised 75 bushels of Indian corn, 90 bushels of oats, and 100 pounds of butter. Charlotte was next found as head of household in the 1860 census of the First District, with Annie and Albert Meriwether still living with her, both born in the District of Columbia. In the 1870 census of the First District, Charlotte was head of household, owning $2,000 in real estate and $500 in personal property. Living with her still was Albert G. and Annie W. Meriwether. In the 1880 census of the Cracklin District, Albert G. Merriwether (sic) was listed as head of household, with Annie W. Merriwether listed as sister, and Charlotte Waters listed as aunt; all of them listed as single. Charlotte Waters left a will in Montgomery County, dated 1859, probated September 11, 1883 and recorded in liber RWC 6 at folio 333. She named her niece Anna M. Meriwether and her nephew Albert C. Meriwether, the children of her sister Louisa Ann Meriwether; leaving them her entire estate.

6. Catherine Waters, born June 20, 1797, died February 29, 1836; buried in the family graveyard at the Dorsey home near Laytonsville. Married February 19, 1833 as the second of his three wives to Joshua Warfield Dorsey; no children; lived near Laytonsville. He is perhaps the Joshua W. Dorsey reported in a *Sentinel* obituary as in his 93rd year (born c.1783), who died June 6, 1875.

7. Azel Waters, born December 14, 1799 in Montgomery County; married by license dated May 9, 1821 in Baltimore County to Eleanor Howard, daughter of Joseph Howard of Anne Arundel County. One record we have seen lists her name as Ercilla Holland, but that does not appear to be confirmed. Azel sold the property he had inherited in Montgomery County, and lived in either Baltimore or Anne Arundel. They had children:
   a. Mary Ann Waters.
   b. Joseph Howard Waters.
   c. Washington Waters.
   d. Rachel Howard Waters.
   e. Isabel E. O. Madden Waters.
8. Ignatius Waters, born September, 1801, and commonly known as Nacy. Married in Montgomery County by license dated February 8, 1825 to Harriet White, daughter of John White of Georgetown; reported by St. Peter's Church records at Poolesville. She died soon after the birth of her only child, and he moved about 1830 with his son to Coshocton County, Ohio. He was married second to Catharine Smith and had a second son. He again moved his family to Hancock County, Indiana, where he died December 17, 1877. His wife died there July 15, 1868. The children were:
   a. William Henry Waters, born November, 1826 and baptized July 15, 1827 at St. Bartholomew's Episcopal Church in Olney. Reported in church records as a son of Nacy and Harriet Waters, and perhaps the only child born to the first marriage.
   b. John White Waters, born December 16, 1828 and baptized January 12, 1829 (Prince George's Parish Records). Married twice. He was a doctor, and lived in Lexington, Illinois. Married in 1857 to Nannie Park of Pennsylvania, and had a son:
      (1) Frank Park Waters, who lived in Chicago.
   c. Samuel Richard Waters, born April 12, 1842; married in Hancock County, Indiana December 22, 1864 to Catharine Juliet Seachrist. Samuel served in the Union Army during the Civil War.

9. Richard Waters, who died as an infant.
10. Louisa Ann Waters, born June 27, 1808, died June 27, 1857; married July 1, 1838 to Albert Gallatin Meriwether and had children, both born in the District of Columbia:
    a. Annie W. Meriwether, born c.1842
    b. Albert G. Meriwether, born c.1844. Head of household in the 1880 census of the Cracklin District of Montgomery County, he was listed as single, with his sister Annie W. Merriwether (sic), also single, living with him and keeping house. Living with them was their aunt, Charlotte Waters, single. According to his obituary in the *Sentinel*, he died September 18, 1892 at his home at Goshen, born in Georgetown, but lived in Montgomery County for a number of years.
11. Samuel Waters, born c.1818, died c.1883; a second use of the name after the early death of the first Samuel, and of whom more following.

Samuel Waters
1818-1883

This son of Ignatius Waters and Anne Warfield was born c.1818 and died c.1883. Commonly known as Seneca Sam Waters, he was reportedly married in Montgomery County by license dated January 10, 1833 to his cousin, Mary Deaver Waters, daughter of Thomas Waters (died c.1847) and Sarah Deavers. Our sources appear to be somewhat confused in this family, other reports indicating a marriage c.1848, which perhaps is more nearly correct, based on ages. The will of her brother Samuel D. Waters refers to Mary's husband as Samuel Waters of S of Howard County. They had at least the one son mentioned in the will of Mary's sister, Charity Waters, and apparently three other sons, as well as three infant deaths also. The four sons who lived to maturity were:
1. Richard Waters, born c.1836, died January 3, 1904 and buried at the Columbia Primitive Baptist Church. His obituary in the *Sentinel* states that he was survived by his wife, nee Hutton, and three sons. It also lists three surviving brothers, all included here following. Head of household in the 1880 census

of Montgomery County for the Fifth District, this Richard Waters was a farmer. Married in the county by license dated December 21, 1859 to Lavinia Hutton, born c.1839. She was present in the census, and they then had five children at home. They were not found in Montgomery County census records prior to 1880. Lavinia was a daughter of Enoch B. Hutton (1811) and Elizabeth Ann Jones (1816), and in the 1850 census of the First District, was living with her parents. The Hutton household was then listed four dwellings removed from the household of Richard Rawlings Waters (1794), so we can assume some early contact between the two families. Head of household in the 1900 census of Montgomery County for the Fifth District, Richard and Lavinia had then been married forty-one years, and she had been the mother of six children, three surviving, and two living at home. Also in the household was Richard Cissel, born November, 1891, grandson; and Lavinia C. Cissel, born November, 1889, granddaughter. Children:

a. William H. Waters, born November, 1860. This child was not listed in the household of Richard Waters (1836) in any census record, but the obituary of Richard includes a son named William. In the 1900 census of the Fifth District, William H. was found as head of his own household, and listed next door to the household of Richard Waters. Head of household in the 1900 census of Montgomery County for the Fifth District, this William H. Waters was reported as born November, 1860 in Virginia, with both parents being born there as well, which is apparently an error on the part of the census taker. His wife was Alice E., born October, 1865 in Maryland, and they had then been married sixteen years. She had been the mother of six children, four of them surviving. The *Sentinel* reported that William H. Waters and Alice E. Turner, both of Montgomery County, obtained a marriage license in Washington on December 1, 1884. Their children included:

(1) Nellie E. Waters, born October, 1885

(2) William H. Waters, born June, 1889

(3) Leroy Waters, born August, 1894

(4) Lawrence Waters, born March, 1896

b. Frank W. Waters, born c.1861

c. Mary E. Waters, born c.1863; reported as Betty in *Sentinel* obituary, eldest child of Richard and Mary Waters; died August 17, 1883 near Burtonsville in her 20th year.

d. Louisa Waters, born c.1865

e. Enoch B. Waters, born c.1867

f. Willie H. Waters, born c.1878

2. Thomas A. Waters, named as a brother in the obituary of Richard, and there described as Thomas Waters of S., born November 1, 1835 in Maryland, and died March 12, 1914 in Washington; buried at Monocacy Cemetery at Beallsville with his wife. His obituary in the *Sentinel* states that he died at the home of his daughter, Mrs. W. J. Giddings, at 3227 11th Street, NW, and was buried at the Primitive Baptist Church at Petworth, D. C. (not Monocacy). The obituary names his surviving children, and two surviving brothers. The obituary, however, names his widow as the former Margaret Dawson, which is perhaps an error. He was head of household in the 1860 census of Montgomery County for the Fifth District, living alone, with $3,000 in real estate and $1,400 in personal property. He was next found as head of household in the 1870 census of Montgomery County for the Fifth District, with $2,000 in real estate and $2,000 in personal property. He is apparently the same Thomas Waters who was married in the county by license dated December 5, 1864 to Martha Maria Dawson. She was born March 4, 1842, died May 12, 1903; buried at Monocacy cemetery, the daughter of Doctor Benoni Dawson (1797) and his wife Sarah Ann Newton Jones (1808) of the Barnesville area in the Third District. Martha was at home in the 1870 census, and they then had three children. The 1800 census of the Fifth District included a household headed by Thomas Waters of S. with his wife Martha D., and six children. The terminology "of S." provides a clue to his father, as in Samuel, which is the case here. Martha D. Waters left a will in the county, dated April 6, 1903 at Takoma Park, probated February 16, 1904, and recorded in liber HCA 4 at folio

113. She named each of her eight children, leaving each of them five dollars. The residue of the estate was left to her husband, Thomas Waters. Her obituary in the *Sentinel* reported that she died May 14, 1903 at the home of Doctor Charles H. Waters of Washington Grove, leaving her husband, Thomas Waters of S. and five sons. Thomas was at one time Sheriff of Montgomery County, and served in the House of Delegates. The children were:

a. Benoni Dawson Waters, born September 1, 1865, and obviously named for his maternal grandfather. In 1903, lived in Takoma Park; in 1915 in Mabton, Washington.

b. George Washington Waters, born November 8, 1867. In 1903 lived in Oregon. Married October 2, 1894 to Ida Houston, born in California and had children. In 1915, they were living near Boise, Idaho. The children were:
    (1) Walter Waters.
    (2) Errol Waters.
    (3) Alice Waters.

c. Mary Adelaide Waters, born February 24, 1870, died at Burnt Mills, Maryland. Married February 18, 1896 to William Johnson Giddings, born c.1861 in Washington, D. C., died September 21, 1945; and had children. He was a son of Charles Glenville Giddings (1834) and Dorcas Ann Hempstone (1835). The wedding service was performed by the Reverend Charles H. Waters at Trinity Episcopal Church in Takoma Park. The children were:
    (1) Carrie Deaver Giddings.
    (2) William Campbell Giddings.
    (3) Susan Dawson Giddings.

d. Henry Wilkerson Waters, born January 25, 1872, died April 26, 1872

e. Walter Warfield Waters, born December 31, 1873, died August 13, 1959; buried in the Giddings plot at St. Mark's Cemetery in Fairland.

f. Sarah Jones Waters, born April 6, 1876. The *Sentinel* of some unreported date in 1915 reported that Sarah had been visiting her brothers in the west, listing them with their then places of residence, which is of some interest:

Benoni D. Waters of Mabton, Washington; Frederick L. Waters of Vancouver, in British Columbia; George W. Waters, about eighty miles from Boise, Idaho, and his wife, the former Ida Huston of Stockton, California, and their three children.

g. Robert Thomas Dawson Waters, born June 17, 1878. In 1903 lived in Oregon.

h. Frederick Lewis Waters, born December 19, 1880. died June 25, 1957; buried at Union Cemetery, Burtonsville, where cemetery records list him simple as Fred L. Waters. Married November 11, 1923 to Alice Henrietta Waters, born May 24, 1894, the daughter of William Plummer Waters (1853) and Carrie Belle Childs (1854). In 1903, he lived in the Klondike, Alaska. In 1915 he was reported in Vancouver, British Columbia. They had one stillbirth son, and a daughter:

   (1) Carri Belle Waters, born December 9, 1924 in the District of Columbia. Married April 18, 1953 to Paul R. Conway and had children:

      (a) Robert Porter Lewis Conway, born February 16, 1955

      (b) Paul Raymond Conway, born June 14, 1959

      (c) Candace Alison Patricia Conway, born January 21, 1965.

i. Joseph Henry Waters, born December 20, 1884, died by drowning July or September 28, 1925 at Pittsburg; buried at Monocacy cemetery near Beallsville. Married November 20, 1912 at Barnesville to Mary Hilleary Shreve, born January 8, 1890, daughter of Daniel Trundle Shreve and Effie Charity Hammond (1867) of Dickerson. *Sentinel* gives the marriage date as June 5, 1912, at Christ Episcopal Church in Barnesville; church records report June 7, 1912; which is probably correct. Children:

   (1) Doris Hammond Waters, born c.1915, died January 2, 1916; buried at Monocacy with her father.

   (2) Charles Henry Waters.

3. Samuel Deaver Waters, Jr., born c.1846 in Maryland, died September 1, 1922; buried in the family lot at Columbia Bap-

tist Church cemetery near Burtonsville. His obituary in the *Sentinel* states that he was the last of four brothers, the other three being Thomas, Richard and Charles. The obituary describes their father as being Judge "Seneca" Samuel Waters. Head of household in the 1880 census of Montgomery County for the Fifth District, this Samuel D. Waters was a miller by profession. In his marriage license dated December 11, 1871 in the county, he was styled Samuel D. Waters, Jr., married to Ella M. Bond. She was born c.1853, the daughter of James L. Bond (1818), a miller from Virginia; appearing with her parents and several siblings in the 1870 census of the Fifth District. In 1880, Samuel and Ella were listed next door to her parents, and had two children. According to the *Sentinel*, Ella M. Waters, wife of Samuel D. Waters of Burnt Mills, died May 24, 1895 in Washington. Ella died May 24, 1895, buried at Columbia Primitive Baptist Church near Columbia Road, and he was married second in the county by license dated September 6, 1898 to Ida Sherwood Greer, at the home of his brother Dr. Charles Waters, Fairview Seminary, Gaithersburg (*Sentinel* report). He appeared as head of household in the 1900 census of Montgomery County for the Fourteenth District, in Takoma Park Town, there reported as a hardware merchant, with a wife Ida S., born April, 1862 in North Carolina, of Virginia parents. The census reported that they had been married for twenty years (which is probably incorrect) and that she had been the mother of two children, both living. Both had probably been married before, and there was one child living with him, apparently hers from a first marriage: Robert E. Greer, born December, 1891 in the District of Columbia; his father born in Maryland, and his mother in North Carolina. Children of Samuel D. Waters included:

a. Carrie Deaver Waters, born c.1875, died August 4, 1895; buried at Columbia Primitive Baptist Church near Laurel. The *Sentinel* obituary states that her mother died about ten weeks earlier. Notice the use of the uncommon name Deaver as a middle name here, being the same as that of her great grandmother, if we have the relationships correct. Married July 14, 1894 to Doctor John Latane Lewis

230

of Kensington, Maryland. He was born c.1865 and after her death, married secondly March 23, 1899 to Mary Elliot Chichester of Stafford County, Virginia. The *Sentinel* announcement of her wedding states that Carrie Waters was the daughter of Samuel D. Waters of Burnt Mills, and that the ceremony was performed by her uncle the Reverend Doctor Charles Waters.

b. Robert L. Waters, born c.1878. The *Sentinel* of April 19, 1901 reported that Robert L. Waters, "the only son of Judge Samuel D. Waters" was married April 17, 1901 to Sue Davis, daughter of Major and Mrs. Garrett M. Davis of Washington. They were married at Ascension Church in Washington, and would live in Olympia, Washington. That is perhaps this individual. Her obituary lists her as Susan Davis Waters, wife of Robert L. Waters, and daughter of Gerrard and Elizabeth Davis (not Garrett Davis). She died April 25, 1923 at her home in Takoma Park, and was buried at Rock Creek Cemetery in Washington, leaving her father, her husband and four children:

    (1) Elizabeth R. Waters.
    (2) Samuel D. Waters.
    (3) Gerrard D. Waters.
    (4) Robert Lee Waters.

c. Inez Bond Waters, born December, 1893, died June 29, 1894 at seven months.

4. Charles Henry Waters, born July 1, 1849, of whom more.

Charles Henry Waters
1849-1920

This son of Samuel Waters (1818) was born July 1, 1849 in Montgomery County. Notice above that in the announcement of the wedding of Samuel Deaver Waters, Jr. and Ida Greer, the *Sentinel* reported that the wedding was held at the home of Dr. Charles Waters, brother of the groom. Note further here following reference to the father of Charles H. Waters being Samuel Waters, thus establishing the family relationships. Head of household in the 1880 census of Montgomery County for the Fifth District, Village of

231

Spencerville, Charles H. Waters was born July 1, 1849, and was a physician. He died January 21, 1920 at his home, 1503 Rhode Island Ave., NW, in Washington, D. C., and is buried at Monocacy Cemetery near Beallsville, with his wife and several family members. The obituary in the *Sentinel* stated that he was survived by his wife, two sons in Washington, two sons in Akron, Ohio, and five daughters. The daughters were listed as being Mrs. J. Lawn Thompson; Mrs. J. B. Clark; Mrs. H. B. Haddox; Eleanor Waters; and Lucy Waters. Note following that Eleanor Waters was reported as an infant death in 1890; there may have been a second one of that name. His wife Ella O. Yates was born February 21, 1848 in Luray, Virginia, and they then had four children. They were married December 20, 1871, and her father was the Reverend Paul Yates, a Baptist Minister of Rappahannock, Virginia. She died June 2, 1921 and is also buried at Monocacy. Living with them were several other individuals, including Samuel Waters, born c.1809, listed as father and retired farmer. Charles H. Waters served as Pastor of the Columbia Primitive Baptist Church from August, 1882 until his death, and was known in many records as Elder Charles H. Waters. He was next found as head of household in the 1900 census of Montgomery County for the Ninth District, with his wife Ella. He was there listed as a teacher, may have been operating a school, and they are listed in a double household. He and Ella have been married for twenty-nine years, and she has been the mother of thirteen children, nine of them surviving and at home. The other half of the double household is headed by Captain J. B. Adams (1865), with his wife; two sons; Doctor H. B. Haddox (1860), a boarder; and seven servants. The obituary of Ella Yates Waters appeared in the *Sentinel* of June 10, 1921, naming all nine of her surviving children.

A biography of Dr. Charles H. Waters appeared in *Portrait and Biographical Record of the Sixth Congressional District, Maryland* by Chapman Publishing Company, originally published in 1898, reprinted 2001 by Heritage Books. It states that he was the founder of Fairview Academy, located at Dawsonville, but moved to Gaithersburg about 1895. There, he built a new school for girls on Monument View Hill, about a mile and a half from the town (a location with which this author is not familiar). He was for some time an associate editor with the *Zion's Advocate*, published in Virginia by the Baptist Association. In 1880, he was ordained a minister of the Baptist Church, thus serving in three different professions at one time: medicine, religion and education! Children:

1. Alice May Allnutt Waters, born September 22, 1873; died September 17, 1893 at Dawsonville; buried at Monocacy. See *Sentinel* obituary.
2. Mary Lee Waters, born June 27, 1875; a teacher at her father's academy. Died June 11, 1869 and buried at Monocacy with her husband. He was Doctor Horace Boliver Haddox, born January 10, 1867 at Rappahannock County, Virginia, died February 24, 1930. They were married December 3, 1901, with her father officiating. H. B. Haddox was first found in the 1900 census of the Ninth District of Montgomery County, single, born c.1860 (although there listed as born in Maryland, which is perhaps incorrect), living in the household of his future wife's father, Charles Henry Waters, and listed as a boarder. In the same plot at Monocacy is a daughter, and his obituary provides the names of three children:
    a. Dorothy Haddox, born May 5, 1903, died July 23, 1990. Married to Edwin Langhorn Yates, born January 5, 1903, died April 14, 1972; buried with his wife.
    b. Daughter Haddox, married to Merrell Tyree, and lived in California.
    c. Horace Haddox.
3. Paul Yates Waters, born c.1878; a teacher; died June 5, 1940; buried at Monocacy. Although the census does not support it, some references suggest that Paul and his sister Mary Lee were twins. Married April 22, 1908 to Alta Jenkins, daughter of Mr. and Mrs. A. Caldwell Jenkins of Washington. She died September 13, 1967; buried at Monocacy with her husband.
4. Charles Lewis Henry Waters, born March 11, 1879, died June 17, 1931 at his home in Washington; buried at Monocacy, single. A teacher and later a doctor. His obituary in the *Sentinel* named brothers and sisters then surviving.
5. Anna Letitia Waters, born February 12, 1881; a teacher, died May 25, 1960; buried at Monocacy with her husband. Married

June 3, 1912 to Doctor Joseph Lawn Thompson, and had at least one son:

    a.   Joseph Lawn Thompson, Jr., born March 30, 1909, died December 8, 1994; buried with his mother at Monocacy Cemetery. Married to Cassie Parker.

6.   Elizabeth B. Waters, born September 21, 1882 and married August 21, 1911 to James B. Clark from Texas, with her father officiating at the wedding. She was a teacher.

7.   Lucy Gardiner Waters, born December 18, 1883, died January 15, 1950; buried at Monocacy with her sister Anna. Married October 29, 1921 at St. Matthew's Church in Washington to Augustus Lonergan, who was a Congressman from Hartford, Connecticut. They had at least one daughter:

    a.   Ruth Ellen Lonergan, born February 3, 1923

8.   Perry Davis Waters, born June 26, 1885, died April 22, 1888; buried at Monocacy.

9.   William Clark Waters, born August 9, 1886. Clark was named in the obituary of his brother Doctor Charles L. Waters. Living in New York City as of 1931.

10.   Allnutt Hess Waters, born February 22, 1888 and died August 27, 1889 at the age of 1 year, 6 months and 5 days; buried at Monocacy.

11.   Eleanor Allnutt Waters, born September 16, 1889, died August 9, 1890 at the age of 10 months and 23 days.

12.   Samuel Deaver Waters, born January 17, 1891. Samuel Deaver Waters is buried at Monocacy in a plot owned by Ralph Alexander Gilchrist (who is his brother-in-law). He is there marked as born c.1891, died September 10, 1964, presumably this individual.

13.   Eleanor Yates Waters, born February 27, 1893; an apparent second use of the name following the early death in 1890. Named in the 1920 obituary of her father. She died April 5, 1951; buried at Monocacy with her husband. He was Ralph Alexander Gilchrist, born c.1896, died March, 1983. Eleanor was mentioned in the obituary of her father and her brother, Doctor Charles L. Waters.

14.   Alice L. H. Waters, an apparent second use of the given name Alice. The obituary of Doctor Charles L. Waters named a sis-

ter as being Mrs. J. Brent Clarke. James Brent Clark (sic) died December 4, 1966 in Washington and is buried at Monocacy with a wife. She was Alice L. H. Clark, died February 3, 1962 at Washington.

CHAPTER 13

Miscellaneous Griffith Family Members

In the course of research, a number of bits of information about members of the Griffith family has been uncovered, but not connected with the lineage under study. They are generally in the same geographic area, however, and very possibly belong to the same family groups, if we could but identify them. They are shown here for further consideration. All individuals listed in the left-hand column bear the Griffith surname, either by birth or marriage. All events occurred in Montgomery County, Maryland, unless otherwise specified in the information presented.

Unknown Griffith

Obituary of one of the sons of this unknown father reveal the name of a sister and a brother in the same family, in Montgomery County, the three being:
1. Frederick M. Griffith.
2. Helen Griffith, married to Darnell.
3. Vernon T. Griffith, apparently first married to Sarah Schwab, daughter of Harry G. Schwab. Her obituary stated that she died March 11, 1964 at Sibley Memorial Hospital in Washington, wife of Vernon T. Griffith, and mother of William M. Griffith. The obituary of Vernon T. Griffith of Germantown states that he died January 10, 1970 at Suburban Hospital, Bethesda, Maryland, the husband of Louise P. Griffith (apparently a second marriage), brother of the two siblings reported here, and father of the one son. Vernon and his first wife Sarah were both buried at Arlington National Cemetery. The one known son was:
   a. William M. Griffith.

David Griffith
died 1788

This David Griffith left a will in Frederick County dated April 8, 1788, probated May 28, 1788 and recorded in liber GM 2 at folio 271. He leaves to his wife Hannah the plantation, toward raising the children until the youngest son, David, arrives at the age of twelve years. At that event, the property was to be sold and divided in three portions. The wife was to receive one-third, and the remaining two-thirds was to be divided between the children, the three sons Philip, John and David to have a third part more than the daughters, Jean and Elizabeth, with daughter Mary to be equal with each son. Daughter Margaret was to receive the sum of five dollars, and the wife was to also receive her riding mare, with saddle and bridle, and one milch cow. The children were:

1. Philip Griffith.
2. John Griffith.
3. David Griffith.
4. Jean Griffith.
5. Elizabeth Griffith.
6. Mary Griffith.
7. Margaret Griffith.

Joseph W. Griffith
1798-

Head of household in the 1850 census of Frederick County for the Buckeystown District, Joseph W. Griffith was born c.1798. He then had a wife Mary M. Griffith, born c.1788, and three children:

1. Frances Griffith, born c.1830
2. Mary J. Griffith, born c.1834
3. Susan C. Griffith, born c.1836

Individual	Event
Abraham	Married in Frederick County by license dated September 5, 1796 to Elizabeth Thompson.

Ann Groomes	Born July 27, 1908; record of St. Bartholomew Episcopal Church, Laytonsville.
Drusilla	Married in Frederick County by license dated February 3, 1803 to Robert Pile.
Elizabeth	Married in Frederick County by license dated May 5, 1807 to Samuel Hoot.
Elizabeth	Died 1860, buried in the family cemetery on *Edgehill Farm*, near Laytonsville.
Ellen Ann	Married September 5, 1822 to Basil Owings of Anne Arundel County. St. Bartholomew's Episcopal Church, Laytonsville.
Francis Ruddell	Born July 22, 1920, died October 4, 1920; buried Montgomery Chapel, north of Damascus and son of T. C. and M. E. Griffith.
Goldsboro S.	Full name Goldsboro Sappington Griffith. Born August 3, 1903 at Baltimore, son of Claude and Mary Griffith; died October 2, 1884. Wife Helen Griffith predeceased him; one daughter, Deon G. Neff of Etchison.
Harriet M.	Born November 1, 1877, died December 20, 1956, formerly of Seneca. Buried Mt. Carmel Cemetery at Sunshine.
Helen Allnutt	Born c.1910, records of St. John's Episcopal Church at Olney.
Isaac	Born c.1782, died May 2, 1827 at 45 years old. Styled Captain; see *Jacob Englebrecht Death Ledger of Frederick County, Maryland 1820-1890*, by Edith Olivia Eader and Trudie Davis-Long.
John	Married November 7, 1826 to Martha Gaither, St. Bartholomew's Episcopal Church.
Julia	Mrs., confirmed March 4, 1832; buried April 16, 1886. St. Bartholomew's Episcopal Church.
Kenneth Louis	Died April 24, 1999 at Rockville; wife Ernestine P.; daughter Nancy Frederickson (wife of Alan Frederickson); father of William Griffith, and the late Alan Griffith. Six siblings;

	and grandfather of Amanda Frederickson, Chris Oliver and Shawn Griffith.
Leona Rabbitt	Died September 6, 1989 of University Park, Maryland. Wife of the late Doctor G. Allen Griffith. Buried at Rockville Cemetery.
Margaret	Born c.1764, maiden name Tice, died September 16, 1829 at age 65 years. Widow of Richard Griffith. See: *Jacob Englebrecht Death Ledger of Frederick County.*
Margaret E.	Born December 2, 1908, died September 10, 1972; buried Rockville Cemetery.
Mary	Mrs.; born August 14, 1768; records of St. Bartholomew's Episcopal Church.
Mary Lee	Born June 16, 1914; records of St. John's Episcopal Church, Olney.
Mary Virginia	Married June 8, 1902 to Posey; records of the Rockville Methodist Circuit.
Myrtle	Born March 6, 1937; Columbia Primitive Baptist Church.
Robert E.	Of Germantown, Captain USArmy; the son of J. Cleveland Griffith of Darnestown; married February 14, 1947 at Darnestown to Jane Beall of Germantown, daughter of Arthur W. Beall.
Thomas	Born September 15, 1803, died January 28, 1870; buried *Edgehill Farm*, near Laytonsville.
Thomas	Married November 1, 1825 to Elizabeth Griffith. Records of St. Bartholomew's Episcopal Church.
Thomas C.	Married May 4, 1912 to Maud E. Easton at the Kemptown Methodist parsonage.

BIBLIOGRAPHY

Adams, Katharine Beall. *Maryland Heritage-A Family History.* Hillsboro, NC Privately printed 1983

Allen, Dorothy Edmonstone Zimmerman. *Zimmerman, Waters and Allied Families.* Undated, private printing. Cumberland College, Lebanon, Tennessee.

Andrews, Mathew Page. *Tercentenary History of Maryland.* Three volumes. Chicago & Baltimore. S. J. Clarke Publishing Co. 1925.

Aud, Kathleen L. and Susan E. *Our Ancestors,* 1972, Washington, D. C. Federal Lithography Co. Privately published. Montgomery County Historical Society library, Rockville, Md.

Baltz, Shirley V. & George E. *Prince George's County, Maryland, Marriages and Deaths in Nineteenth Century Newspapers. Volumes 1 and 2.* Bowie, Md. 1995. Heritage Books, Inc.

Barnes, Robert. *Maryland Marriages, 1634-1777*

_____. *Maryland Marriages, 1778-1800*

_____. *Marriages and Deaths From the Maryland Gazette 1727-1839.* Baltimore. Genealogical Publishing Co. 1973

_____. *Colonial Families of Anne Arundel County, Maryland.* Westminster, Maryland: Family Lines Publications, 1996.

_____. *Marriages and Deaths from Baltimore Newspapers.* Three volumes. Baltimore. Genealogical Publishing Co. 1978

Beall, Frederick Carroll. *Robert Beall, the Scotsman, Immigrant.* Privately printed booklet. 1976. Copy at Montgomery County Historical Society Library, Rockville, Md.

Beatty, Edith Worley. *The Waters Book.* Undated, apparently privately printed. Copy at Montgomery County Historical Society Library, Rockville, Md.

Bowie, Effie Gwynn. *Across The Years in Prince George's County.* Baltimore, Md. Genealogical Publishing Company. Original 1947. Reprint 1996.

Bowman, Tressie Nash. *Montgomery County Marriages, 1796-1850*

Brown, Helen W. *Index of Marriage Licenses, Prince George's County, Maryland 1777-1886.* Baltimore, Md. Genealogical Publishing Co. Reprint. 1995

_____. *Prince George's County Maryland Indexes of Church Registers 1686-1885, Volume 2.* Westminster, Md. Family Line Publications. 1994

Brumbaugh, Gaius Marcus. *Maryland Records, Colonial Revolutionary, County and Church, Volumes 1 and 2.* West Jordan, Utah. Reprint. Stemmons Publishing Co. Original 1915

Burke, Sir Bernard, Ulster King of Arms. *The General Armory of England, Scotland, Ireland and Wales, Volumes 1, 2 & 3..* Bowie, Md. Heritage Books, Inc. 1878, Reprint 1996

Buxton, Allie May. *Family of Harry and Rosa Hurley.* Manuscript; Montgomery County Historical Society, Rockville, Maryland.

_____. *The Family of Isaac Moxley.* Damascus, Md. 1984

_____. *Nehemiah Moxley, His Clagettsville Sons and Their Descendants.* Chelsea, Michigan. BookCrafters. 1989

Carothers, Bettie Sterling. *1776 Census of Maryland.* Westminster, Md. Family Line Publications. 1992

Carroll County Genealogy Society, Md. *Carroll County Cemeteries, Volume Three: Southwest.* Westminster, Maryland 1992.

Cavey, Kathleen Tull-Burton. *Tombstones and Beyond, Prospect U. M. Church Cemetery and Marvin Chapel Church Cemetery.* Westminster, Maryland: Family Lines Publications, 1995

Chapman. *Portrait and Biographical Record of the Sixth Congressional District, Maryland.* Chapman Publishing Company, New York. 1898

Chesly, Nelle Offutt. *The Offutt Family.* Privately printed, 1977. Seven volumes, three-ring binders. Library of the Montgomery County Historical Society, Rockville, Md.

Coldham, Peter Wilson. *The Bristol Register of Servants Sent to Foreign Plantations 1654-1686,* Genealogical Publishing Company, Baltimore. 1988

_____. *The Complete Book of Emigrants, 1607-1660,* Genealogical Publishing Co., Baltimore, 1987

Condon, Julia N. and Thomas. *Gassaway Sellman of Maryland.* 1961, private printing. Montgomery County Maryland Historical Society library.

Darby, Rodney H. *All About Darbys,* Privately published, Rockville, Maryland. 2000

Day, Jackson H. *The Story of the Maryland Walker Family, In-cluding the Descendants of George Bryan Walker and Eliza-beth Walker Beall.* 1957, privately printed manuscript.

_____. *James Day of Browningsville, and his descendants, A Maryland Family.* Columbia, Md, private printing, 1976.

Dern, John P. and Grace L. Tracey. *Pioneers of Old Monocacy, The Early Settlement of Frederick County, Maryland 1721 to 1743.* Baltimore. Genealogical Publishing Co. 1987

Dern, John P. and Mary Fitzhugh Hitselberger. *Bridge in Time, The Complete 1850 Census of Frederick County, Maryland.* Redwood City, CA. Monocacy Book Company. 1978

Dorsey, Maxwell J. and Jean Muir. *The Dorsey Family.* Not dated, private printing. Copy in the Montgomery County Historical Society library, Rockville, Maryland.

Eader, Edith Oliver & Trudie Davis-Long. *The Jacob Engelbrecht Marriage Ledger of Frederick County, Maryland 1820-1890.* Monrovia, Md. Paw Prints, Inc. 1994.

_____. *The Jacob Engelbrecht Death Ledger of Frederick County, Maryland 1820-1890.* Monrovia, Md. Paw Prints, Inc. 1995.

_____. *The Jacob Engelbrecht Property and Almshouse Ledgers of Frederick County, Maryland.* Monrovia, Md. Paw Prints, Inc. 1996.

Elgin, Dorothy and Sween, Jane C. *Chiswell Family.* 1982, not published, family group sheets. Montgomery County Histori-cal Society library, Rockville, Md.

Ferrill, Matthew & Gilchrist, Robert. *Maryland Probate Records 1635-1777.* Volume 9.

Flowers, Susanne Files & Edith Olivia Eader. *The Frederick County, Maryland Will Index 1744-1946.* Monrovia, Md. Paw Prints, Inc. 1997

Frain, Elizabeth R. *Monocacy Cemetery, Beallsville, Montgomery County, Maryland.* Lovettsville, Va. 1997, Willow Bend Books.

Fry, Joshua & Jefferson, Peter. *Map of Virginia, North Carolina, Pennsylvania, Maryland, New Jersey 1751.* Montgomery County, Md Library, Atlas Archives.

Gaithersburg, Maryland, City. *Gaithersburg, The Heart of Montgomery County*. Privately printed. 1978

Geibel, Bruce Burgee. *The Burgee Families*. Woodstock, Georgia. Privately printed June 15, 2000.

Gilland, Steve. *Frederick County Backgrounds*. Westminster, Maryland: Family Lines Publications, 1995.

_____. *Early Families of Frederick County, Maryland and Adams County, Pennsylvania*. Westminster, Maryland: Family Lines Publications, 1997.

Goldsborough. *Maryland Line in the Confederacy*.

Green, Karen Mauer. *The Maryland Gazette, Genealogical and Historical Abstracts, 1727-1761*. Galveston, TX The Frontier Press. 1989

Griffith, R. R. *Genealogy of the Griffith Family, The Descendants of William and Sarah Maccubbin Griffith*. Baltimore, The Press of William K. Boyle & Son. 1892

Gurney, John Thomas, III. *Cemetery Inscriptions of Anne Arundel County, Maryland. Volume 1* . Pasadena, Md. Anne Arundel Genealogical Society. 1982, 1994.

_____. *Cemetery Inscriptions of Anne Arundel County, Maryland. Volume 2*. Chelsea, MI. BookCrafters. 1987

Haney, Ritchie Lee. *1920 Census for Damascus, Montgomery County, Maryland*. From personal notes of his father, Ritchie E. Haney, census-taker. Damascus, Md. Private. 1997

Hartzler, Daniel D. *Marylanders in the Confederacy*. Westminster, Maryland: Family Lines Publications, 1994.

Holdcraft, Jacob Mehrling. *Names in Stone; 75,000 Cemetery Inscriptions From Frederick County, Maryland*. Ann Arbor, Michigan. 1966. Reprinted with "More Names in Stone" in two volumes, Genealogical Publishing Co., Baltimore, 1985

Hopkins, G. M. *Atlas of Fifteen Miles Around Washington, Including the County of Montgomery, Maryland*. Baltimore, Md. Garamond/Pridemark Press, Inc. for the Montgomery County Historical Society. Original 1879. Reprint, 1975

Hurley, William Neal, Jr. Numerous family genealogies and census compilations; see page iv, Introduction of this study.

Jourdan, Elise Greenup. *Early Families of Southern Maryland. Volumes 1 through 10.* Westminster, Md. Willow Bend Books. 1993 to 2001

_____, *Colonial Records of Southern Maryland.* Westminster, Md. Willow Bend Books. 2000

Kelleher, Polly P., et al. *John Pigman and his Descendants.* Not dated, privately printed. Copy in Montgomery County Historical Society library at Rockville, Maryland.

Lord, Elizabeth M. *Burtonsville, Maryland Heritage, Genealogically Speaking*

Malloy, Mary Gordon; Sween, Jane C.; Manuel, Janet D. *Abstract of Wills, Montgomery County, Maryland 1776-1825.* Westminster, Md. Family Line Publications. 1977.

_____, *Abstract of Wills, Montgomery County, Maryland 1826-1875.* Westminster, Md. Willow Bend Books. 2000.

Malloy, Mary Gordon; Jacobs, Marian W. *Genealogical Abstracts, Montgomery County Sentinel, 1855-1899.* Rockville, Md. Montgomery County Historical Society. 1986.

Manuel, Janet Thompson. *Montgomery County, Maryland Marriage Licenses, 1798-1898*

Maryland Hall of Records. *Wills, estates, inventories, births, deaths, marriages, deeds and other reference works relative to counties of Maryland.*

_____. *Maryland Calendar of Wills.* All volumes.

_____. *Maryland Historical Society Magazine.*

_____. *Vestry Book of St. John's Episcopal Parish Church, 1689-1810.* Original.

Meyer, Mary Keysor. *Divorces and Names Changed in Maryland By Act of the Legislature 1634-1867.* Mt. Airy, Md. Pipe Creek Publications, Inc. 1991

Montgomery County Court Records. *Wills, inventories of estate, deeds.* Rockville, Maryland.

Montgomery County Historical Society, Rockville, Maryland. *Folder files; census, church, correspondence, newspaper, manuscripts, library, and family records.*

_____. *Queen Anne Parish Records, 1686-1777*

_____. *King George Parish Records 1689 - 1801*

_____. *King George Parish Records 1797-1878*

245

_____. *St. Paul's at Baden, Parish Records*

_____. *Frederick County Maryland Marriage Licenses*

_____. *Montgomery County Marriages*

_____. *1850 Census, Montgomery County, Maryland*

_____. *1860 Census, Montgomery County, Maryland*

_____. *1870 Census, Montgomery County, Maryland*

_____. *1880 Census, Montgomery County, Maryland*

_____. *1850 Census, Prince George's County, Maryland*

_____. *1850 Census, Frederick County, Maryland*

_____. *Pioneers of Old Monocacy*

_____. *Mt. Olivet Cemetery, Frederick, Md.* Computer printout of burial records.

Moore, L. Tilden. *Index to Administration Account Records of Frederick County, Maryland 1750-1816.* Westminster, Md. Family Line Publications. 1996

_____, *Marriages and Deaths, Newspapers of Frederick And Montgomery Counties, Maryland.* Bowie, Md. Heritage Books, Inc. 1991 Morrow and Morrow. *Marriages of Washington County, Maryland, An Index, 1799-1866.* DAR library, Washington, D. C.

Myers, Margaret Elizabeth. *Marriage Licenses of Frederick County, Maryland 1778-1810.* Westminster, Md. Family Line Publications. Second Edition, 1994

_____. *Marriage Licenses of Frederick County, Maryland 1811-1840.* Family Line Publications. 1987

_____. *Marriage Licenses of Frederick County, Maryland 1841-1865.* Family Line Publications. 1988

_____. *George Zimmerman and Descendants of Frederick County, Maryland 1714-1987.* Family Line Publications. 1987.

Newman, Harry Wright. *Anne Arundel Gentry, A Genealogical History of Some Early Families of Anne Arundel County, Maryland. Volumes One, Two and Three.* Annapolis, Md. Privately printed. 1979

_____. *Charles County Gentry.* Baltimore, Md. Genealogical Publishing Co. 1971 and 1990 reprints from 1940 original publication.

_____. *Mareen Duvall of Middle Plantation*. Private printing 1952. Baltimore, Md. Port City Press, Inc. Reprint 1984

_____. *The Maryland Dents*. Richmond, Virginia. The Dietz Press. 1963

Omans, Donald James and Nancy West. *Montgomery County (Maryland) Marriages 1798-1875*. Compiled by Potomack River Chapter, National Society of Colonial Dames. Athens, Georgia. 1987. Iberian Publishing Co.

Peden, Henry C., Jr. *Revolutionary Patriots of Prince George's County 1775-1783*. Westminster, Md. Family Line Publications. 1997

_____. *Revolutionary Patriots of Montgomery County, Maryland 1776-1783*. Westminster, Md. Family Line Publications. 1996

_____. *Revolutionary Patriots of Calvert & St. Mary's Counties, Maryland 1775-1783*. Westminster, Md. Willow Bend Books. 2001

_____. *Revolutionary Patriots of Caroline County, Maryland 1775-1783*. Westminster, Md. Willow Bend Books. 2001

_____. *Revolutionary Patriots of Anne Arundel County, Maryland 1775-1783*. Westminster, Md. Willow Bend Books. 2000.

_____, *Quaker Records of Southern Maryland, Births, Deaths, Marriages and Abstracts From the Minutes, 1658-1800*. Westminster, Md. Family Line Publications. 1992

_____, *Quaker Records of Northern Maryland, Births, Deaths, Marriages and Abstracts From the Minutes, 1716-1800*. Westminster, Md. Willow Bend Books. 2001

_____, *More Maryland Deponents 1716-1799*. Westminster, Md. Family Line Publications. 1992

_____, *Colonial Maryland Soldiers and Sailors, 1634-1734*. Westminster, Md. Willow Bend Books. 2001

_____, *A Collection of Maryland Church Records*. Westminster, Md. Willow Bend Books. 2001

Powell, Henry Fletcher. *Tercentenary History of Maryland*, in four volumes. Chicago-Baltimore. The S. J. Clarke Publishing Company. 1925

Powell, John W. *Anne Arundel County, Maryland Marriage Records 1777-1877.* Pasadena, Md. Anne Arundel Genealogical Society. 1991

Prince George's County, Md Genealogical Society. *Index to the Probate Records of Prince George's County, Maryland, 1696-1900.* Bowie, Md. 1989.

_____. *Prince George's County Land Records, Volume A, 1696-1702.* Bowie, Maryland, 1976

_____. *1850 Census, Prince George's County, Maryland.* Bowie, Maryland, 1978

_____. *1828 Tax List Prince George's County, Maryland.* Bowie, Maryland, 1985.

Reinton, Louise Joyner. *Prince George's County, Md. Piscataway or St. John's Parish (now called King George's Parish. Index to Register, 1689-1878.*

Richardson, Hester Dorsey. *Side-lights on Maryland History, with Sketches of Early Maryland Families.* Cambridge, Md. Tidewater Publishers. 1967

Ridgely, Helen W. *Historic Graves of Maryland and the District of Columbia.* West Jordan, Utah. Reprint. Stemmons Publishing Co. Original Grafton Press, New York, 1908.

Riggs, John Beverley. *The Riggs Family of Maryland.* Baltimore, Maryland. 1989.

Russell, Donna Valley. *Western Maryland Genealogy.* Volumes 1 thru 12. Catoctin Press, Middletown, Md. 1985-1996

_____, *Selby Families of Colonial America.* Middletown, Maryland, Catoctin Press, 1990.

Sargent. *Stones and Bones, Cemetery Records of Prince George's County, Maryland.*

Scharf, J. Thomas. *History of Maryland.* Three Volumes. Hatboro, Pennsylvania. Tradition Press. 1967

_____. *History of Western Maryland, Volume 1.* Baltimore, Md. Genealogical Publishing Co., Inc. 1995

_____. *History of Western Maryland, Volume II.* Baltimore, Md. Genealogical Publishing Co., Inc. 1995

_____. *History of Western Maryland, Index to Volumes I and II.* By Helen Long (which see). Baltimore, Md. Genealogical Publishing Co., Inc. 1995

_____. *History of Delaware 1609-1888, Volume II.* Westminster, Md. Family Line Publications. Reprint. Original Philadelphia. L. J. Richards & Co. 1888

Schildknecht, Calvin E. *Monocacy and Catoctin, Volumes 1 thru 111.* Gettysburg, Pa. 1994

Skinner, Vernon L., Jr. *Provincial Families of Maryland, Volume 1.* Westminster, Md. Willow Bend Books. 2000.

_____, *Abstracts of the Prerogative Court of Maryland, 1726-1729*

Skordas, Gust. *Early Settlers of Maryland*

Tracey, Grace L. and Dern, John P. *Pioneers of Old Monocacy, The Early Settlement of Frederick County, Maryland 1721 to 1743.* Baltimore. Genealogical Publishing Co. 1987

VanHorn, R. Lee. *Out of the Past.*

Warfield, J. D. *The Founders of Anne Arundel and Howard Counties, Maryland.* Baltimore. Kohn & Pollock. 1905. Reprinted 1995, Heritage Books, Bowie, Md.

Warfield, Thomas Ord. *Warfield Records,* By Evelyn Ballenger. Annapolis, Md 1970.

Weiser, Frederick Sheely. *Records of Marriages and Burials in the Monocacy Church in Frederick County, Maryland, and in the Evangelical Lutheran Congregation in the City of Frederick, 1743-1811.* National Genealogical Society. 4th Printing, 1993

_____. *Frederick, Maryland Lutheran Marriages and Burials 1743-1811.* Washington, D. C. National Genealogical Society. Fourth printing, 1993

Welsh, Luther W., A.M., M.D. *Ancestral Colonial Families, Genealogy of The Welsh and Hyatt Families of Maryland and Their Kin.* Lambert Moon Printing Co., Independence, Missouri. 1928.

Western Maryland Genealogy. *Frederick County (Md) Wills, Unprobated Wills, Will Book A1, 1744-1777.* Middletown, Md.

Wilcox, Shirley Langdon. *1828 Tax List Prince George's County, Maryland.* Prince George's County Genealogical Society. Special Publication No. 6. 1985

_____. *1850 Census Prince George's County, Maryland.* Prince George's County Genealogical Society. Special Publication No. 4. 1978

_____. *Prince George's County Land Records Volume A, 1696-1702.* . Prince George's County Genealogical Society Special Publication No. 3. 1976

_____. *Index to the Probate Records of Prince George's County, Maryland 1696-1900.* . Prince George's County Genealogical Society. 1988

Williams, Mildred Corson. *Archibald Edmonston of Maryland.* No date, private printing. Montgomery County Maryland Historical Society library.

Williams, T. J. C. & Folger McKinsey. *History of Frederick County, Maryland, Volume 1.* Baltimore, Md. Genealogical Publishing Co., Inc. 1997

_____. *History of Frederick County, Maryland, Volume 2.* Baltimore, Md. Genealogical Publishing Co., Inc. 1997

Wright, F. Edward. *History of Washington County, Maryland, Index to Volumes 1 and 2.* Westminster, Md. Family Line Publications. 1992, 1995

_____. *Anne Arundel County Church Records of the 17th and 18th Centuries.* Westminster, Md. Family Line Publications. 1989, 1994

_____. *Marriages and Deaths in the Newspapers of Frederick and Montgomery Counties, Maryland. 1820-1830.* Westminster, Maryland: Family Lines Publications, 1992.

_____. *Marriages and Deaths From the Newspapers of Allegany and Washington Counties, Maryland.* Westminster, Md. Family Line Publications. 1993

_____. *Newspaper Abstracts of Frederick County 1811-1815.* Westminster, Md. Family Line Publications. 1992

_____. *Newspaper Abstracts of Frederick County, 1816 to 1819.* Westminster, Maryland: Family Lines Publications, 1993.

_____. *Newspaper Abstracts of Allegany and Washington Counties 1811-1815.* Westminster, Md. Family Line Publications. 1993

_____. *Maryland Eastern Shore Vital Records, Book 1, 1648-1725.* Westminster, Md. Family Line Publications. 1993

_____. *Maryland Eastern Shore Vital Records, Book 2, 1726-1750.* Westminster, Md. Family Line Publications. 1993

_____. *Maryland Eastern Shore Vital Records, Book 3, 1751-1775.* Westminster, Md. Family Line Publications. 1993

_____. *Maryland Eastern Shore Vital Records, Book 4, 1776-1800.* Westminster, Md. Family Line Publications. 1994

_____. *Maryland Eastern Shore Vital Records, Book 5, 1801-1825.* Westminster, Md. Family Line Publications. 1994

_____. *Washington County, Maryland Church Records of the 18th Century, 1768-1800.* Westminster, Md. Family Line Publications. 1988

_____. *Bible Records of Washington County, Maryland.* Westminster, Md. Family Line Publications. 1992

_____. *Frederick County Militia in the War of 1812.* Westminster, Md. Family Line Publications.

INDEX

All names appearing in the text are indexed, with each of the pages on which the individual appears. To distinguish between those persons with the same name, dates will generally follow the index entry. A plain date indicates the date of birth or nearly so; entries reading d/1789 indicate the date of death; m/1879 indicates the date of marriage. Some of the more common names, such as John, Sarah and others, will appear with no dates and numerous page references. Almost without exception, they will refer to more than one individual.

Barr, Marguerite, 77
Bartlett, Alice Riggs 1875, 66, 80
Bartlett, George W. B., 79
Bartlett, George W. B. 1850, 66
Bartlett, Vashti 1875, 80
Bartlett, Vashti R. 1875, 66
Barton, Richard, 86, 133
Baskett, Horatio N. 1809, 179
Bastable, Alvin Nathan 1837, 199
Batchelor's Choice, 3
Battle, Elizabeth Virginia, 203
Beall, Arthur W., 240
Beall, Bertha Marie 1901, 90
Beall, Jane, 240
Beall, Katherine, 77
Beall, Sharon Ann 1944, 201
Beard, Ada L., 136
Beasley, William J., 163
Beatty, Joseph E., Doctor, 194
Beatty, Phillip Asfordby, 194
Belt, Annie Oliver 1853, 198
Belt, Jeremiah 1724, 12
Belt, John A., 190
Belt, John Sprigg 1752, Captain, 12
Belt, No given name, 214
Bennett, Barry, 69
Bennett, Bradley Wayne 1989, 69
Bennett, Cory Thomas 1994, 69
Bennett, Dylan White 1996, 69
Bennett, Jennie E., 177, 206
Benson, Eugene, 74
Benson, Leroy, 74
Benson, Margaret 1884, 74
Benton, Catherine 1801, 164
Benton, William, 161
Benton, William W., 164
Berry, Charles L. 1860, 137
Berry, Horatio G. 1856, 137
Berry, John Dorsey 1824, 137
Berry, John Dorsey, Jr. 1864, 137
Berry, Martha, 5
Berry, Mary E. 1854, 137
Berry, Nena R. 1867, 137
Berry, Richard 1732, 105
Berry, Rosalie 1862, 137

Berry, Ruth, 105, 129, 135, 140, 143, 152
Berry, Samuel, 5
Berry, Winifred E. 1873, 137
Biondi, Harry, 83
Biondi, Stephen R., 83
Black Acre, 19, 20
Bodmer, Carrie Geneva 1893, 187
Boggs, Jane, 33, 172
Bond, Ella M. 1853, 230
Bond, James L. 1818, 230
Bonifant, Alfred Dement, Doctor, 218
Bonifant, Betsy, 218
Bonifant, Betsy 1946, 217
Boone, John, 26
Boone, John, Captain, 26
Borden, Charlotte, 159
Bordley's Choice, 43
Bosman, William, 1
Boss, James G. 1844, 82
Bostick, 96, 115
Bourne, Emily M. 1819, 129
Bourne, Mary A. 1849, 130
Bourne, No given name, 130
Bourne, Richard M. 1847, 130
Bowen, Hilda, 209
Bowers, Mary 1867, 177
Bowie, Anne, 97, 116
Boyd, Roland, 49
Bradley, Charles, 100
Bradley, George G., 100, 118
Bradley, Laura 1906, 184
Bradley, Laura G., 100
Bradley, Laura Worthington 1875, 100, 118
Bramwell, Ezra, 34, 172
Bramwell, Jesse V., 34, 172
Brashear, Thomas C., Colonel, 46
Brewer, Bettie Jane 1933, 196
Brewer, Betty Williams 1909, 196
Brewer, Charles McGill 1908, 196
Brewer, Elizabeth Ann 1948, 196
Brewer, George William 1878, 196
Brewer, George William 1913, 196
Brewer, Jane Waters 1916, 196
Brewer, Jennie 1946, 196

Brewer, Lutie 1876, 199
Brewer, Mary Joan 1935, 196
Brewer, William George 1850, 196, 199
Briggs, Marie Frances, 69
Brookfield, 168
Broschart, Mary, 184
Broschart, Mary Grace 1950, 76
Brown, Abraham F., Sr., 78
Brown, Alice C. 1829, 94
Brown, Amos d/1845, 93
Brown, Amos P. 1827, 94
Brown, Amos, Jr. 1810, 93
Brown, Annie Griffith 1811, 93
Brown, Elizabeth R. 1815, 94
Brown, Emily C., 50
Brown, Emily Darby, 192
Brown, Harriet A. 1821, 94
Brown, Henrietta 1825, 94
Brown, James Howe, Jr., 201
Brown, Louisa M. 1817, 94
Brown, Lydia H. 1831, 94
Brown, Mary E. 1823, 94
Brown, Mary Shaw, 192
Brown, Mary Shaw 1917, 197
Brown, Melvin E., Jr., 78
Brown, Ridgely 1833, Lt. Col., 95
Brown, Sarah R. 1818, 94
Brown, William, 29
Brown, William 1809, 93
Brown, William Clifton, 197
Brown, William N. 1814, 94
Browning, Drusilla 1800, 54
Browning, Jeremiah 1775, 54
Browning, Lavinia Winona 1857, 54
Browning, Nathan 1728, 160
Browning, Nathan, Jr. 1767, 160
Browning, Richard 1816, 54
Bryant, Raleigh D. 1829, 158
Burdette, Carrie M., 54
Burdette, Jacolyn 1939, 128
Burdette, Kimberly Dee, 68
Burdette, Millard Diehl 1885, 128
Burdette, Paul Douglas 1944, 128
Burdette, Paul Winfred 1905, 128
Burgee, Amon, Sr. 1865, 53

Burgee, Ann R. 1844, 52
Burgee, Clara E. 1888, 54
Burgee, Clayton 1830, 51
Burgee, Effa Ann 1879, 53
Burgee, Eli McSherry 1878, 54
Burgee, Eli Thomas, 54
Burgee, Eliza Ann 1825, 51
Burgee, Elizabeth 1846, 52
Burgee, Elizabeth 1852, 50
Burgee, Elizabeth Ellen 1822, 54
Burgee, Elizabeth Ruth 1817, 51
Burgee, Ellen, 51
Burgee, Ellen Jane 1834, 50
Burgee, Emily 1821, 51
Burgee, Emily 1854, 50
Burgee, Frederick Lewis 1847, 52
Burgee, Gabriel Lewis 1881, 54
Burgee, Grafton Lewis 1819, 51
Burgee, Guy 1870, 53
Burgee, Henry 1868, 53
Burgee, Henry B. 1841, 50
Burgee, Howard Edward 1889, 53
Burgee, James 1833, 50
Burgee, Joab Waters 1806, 50
Burgee, Joab Waters, Jr. 1850, 50
Burgee, John W. 1877, 52
Burgee, Leathe Ellen 1866, 53
Burgee, Letitia Ann 1844, 50
Burgee, Lydia O. 1850, 53
Burgee, Margaret 1885, 53
Burgee, Margaret A. 1850, 52
Burgee, Mary America 1857, 50
Burgee, Mary Ann 1819, 51
Burgee, Mary Eva 1890, 53
Burgee, McKendry Riley 1862, 53
Burgee, Miel, 51
Burgee, Miel Eldridge 1848, 52
Burgee, Miel, Jr. 1818, 51
Burgee, Nancy A. 1837, 50
Burgee, Ossie Delilah 1875, 54
Burgee, Ray Safford 1882, 53
Burgee, Susan A. 1833, 50
Burgee, Thomas 1847, 50
Burgee, Thomas A. 1839, 50
Burgee, Thomas H. 1808, 51
Burgee, Thomas, Jr. 1780, 49

Burgee, Thomas, Sr., 51
Burgee, Valira O. 1875, 53
Burgee, William Keefer 1872, 53
Burgee, Worthington 1880, 54
Burgess, Charlotte, 47
Burgess, Eleanor, 47
Burgess, John, 160
Burgess, John 1766, 47
Burgess, John H., 47
Burgess, Juliana, 47
Burgess, Nancy, 47
Burgess, Ruth, 47
Burgess, Ruth H., 208
Burgess, Sarah Ann, 47
Burgess, Washington, 47
Burgess, William P., 47, 160
Burke, No given name, 176
Burkett, Shelley, 78
Burns, Elizabeth 1816, 50
Burns, James, 50
Burns, Margaret 1917, 203
Burns, Mollie, 187
Bushy Park, 31
Butzer, Ephraim, 110

—C—

Caldwell, David, 48
Caldwell, Mary Ann Elizabeth, 48
Calfpen, 3
Callahan, Lynn Thomas, III, 218
Callahan, Melissa, 218
Campbell, No given name, 184
Canby, Martha Hughes 1845, 121
Canby, Thomas 1795, 121
Capell, Thomas, 4
Carlisle, Charles Winfield 1913, 196
Carlisle, Charles Winfield 1947, 197
Carlisle, George William 1942, 197
Carlisle, John Englar, 197
Carroll, Howard H., 70
Carroll, Thomas W., 70
Carroll, Thomas W., Jr., 70
Carter, Harold Edwin 1914, 204
Cassell, Mary Jane, 16, 145
Cauldfield, Adelaide, 90

Caylot, Anna Belle, 197
Caywood, William, 20
Chapin, Elisha Sterling, Jr., 186
Chapman, No given name, 10
Charline Manor, 199
Chase, Dudley, Reverend, 33, 172
Chase, J., 34, 173
Chase, Philander, 33, 171
Cheney, Mary, 107
Cherry Grove, 43
Chichester, Harriet R. 1859, 95
Chichester, Lydia 1894, 95
Chichester, Lydia Hanson, 95
Chichester, Lydia Hanson 1859, 95
Chichester, Margaret B. 1856, 95
Chichester, Mary Elliot, 231
Chichester, Mary R., 95
Chichester, Ridgely B. 1899, 95
Chichester, Robert H. 1893, 95
Chichester, Sarah 1895, 95
Chichester, Washington Bowie 1828, 94
Chichester, Washington Bowie, Jr. 1868, 95
Childs, Carrie Belle 1854, 229
Chiswell, Anna 1858, 198
Chiswell, Augusta Ann 1841, 178
Chiswell, Bessie Clotworthy1895, 188
Chiswell, Byron Walling 1894, 188
Chiswell, Carroll Thomas 1898, 188
Chiswell, Catherine Christell 1885, 187
Chiswell, Charles Lewis 1883, 187
Chiswell, Charles Newton 1890, 188
Chiswell, Eleanor 1900, 176
Chiswell, Eleanor White 1822, 176
Chiswell, Elizabeth Ellen 1852, 188
Chiswell, Eugenia Gott 1883, 176
Chiswell, George Walter 1817, Captain, 187
Chiswell, George William 1892, 187
Chiswell, Howard Griffith 1824, 176
Chiswell, Isaac Young 1888, 188
Chiswell, J. Eleanor 1834, 206
Chiswell, Jemima Eleanor 1831, 176

Clark, Katherine 1798, 32
Clark, Kitty 1798, 171
Clark, Lydia 1814, 32, 171
Clark, Mabel 1906, 30
Clark, Mary 1812, 32, 171
Clark, Morrison M., 202
Clark, Morrison MacDowell 1898, 200
Clark, Ridgely Brown 1882, 30
Clark, Robert 1809, 32, 171
Clark, Ruth Lavinia 1878, 29
Clark, Sarah 1804, 32, 171
Clark, Sarah J. 1826, 106
Clark, Spencer 1908, 30
Clark, Susan A., 50
Clark, Thomas Henry 1893, 30
Clarke, No given name, 164
Clements, Ann Eliza 1849, 75
Clements, Jane Alice 1910, 76
Clements, Jouette Henry 1883, 76
Coatsworth, Mabel, 203
Codwell, No given name, 77
Colliflower, Hattie M. 1876, 120
Colliflower, Hattie Maynard 1876, 102
Collins, No given name, 128, 213
Conaway, Augustus A., 217
Conklin, Jean Michele 1967, 128
Conklin, Richard, 128
Conklin, Richard Walter 1961, 128
Conway, Candace Alison Patricia 1965, 229
Conway, Paul R., 229
Conway, Paul Raymond 1959, 229
Conway, Robert Porter Lewis 1955, 229
Cooke, Alverda Griffith 1897, 91
Cooke, Nathan 1829, 91
Cooke, Zadoc Magruder 1865, 91
Crabb, Charles, 15
Crabb, Elizabeth Ridgely, 15, 63
Crabb, Emeline 1797, 18
Crabb, Jeremiah 1760, General, 15
Crabb, Jeremiah, General, 108
Crabb, Lydia Ridgely 1799, 18, 108
Crabb, Matilda 1795, 18

Crabb, Nancy, 15
Crabb, Richard, 15
Crabb, Sarah Griffith 1793, 15
Crawford, A. Blanche 1873, 210
Crawford, Arthur 1871, 210
Crawford, Basil B. 1833, Doctor, 210
Crawford, Basil B., Jr. 1866, 210
Crawford, Carrie, 86, 133
Crawford, Eldred 1868, 210
Crawford, Howell 1857, 210
Crawford, Lebbeus 1865, 210
Crawford, Mary A. 1862, 210
Crawford, Nellie B. 1875, 210
Crawford, Varena 1860, 210
Crutchley, Lydia M. 1870, 154
Crutchley, William E. 1868, 154
Cuseo, Angelo, Jr., 68
Cuseo, Michele, 68

—D—

Dade, Columbus 1831, 185
Dade, Drusilla 1821, 137
Dade, Elizabeth Darnall 1858, 185
Damascus Plains, 105
Daniel, Mansfield White 1918, 90
Daniel, William Aglionby 1878, 90
Darby, Alice Rebecca 1900, 72
Darby, Elizabeth 1874, 189
Darby, Emily P., 197
Darby, George Washington 1785, 42
Darby, Kezia 1742, 41
Darby, Remus R., 72
Darby, Rodney H., 42
Darby, Samuel 1760, 42
Darnell, No given name, 237
Davidge, Ann, 24
Davidge, Dinah, 31
Davidge, Robert, 24
Davidson, Halbert, 78
Davidson, Lorena Mae 1970, 78
Davidson, Ronald 1968, 78
Davidson, Salina Marie 1966, 78
Davidson, Timothy 1965, 78
Davis, Alice Katherine 1895, 139
Davis, Ann Maude 1886, 138

Frederickson, Amanda, 240
Frees, Jacob, 14
Freeze, Jacob, 14
Fyffe, Isaac 1839, 189
Fyffe, Mary Elizabeth, 188

—G—

Gaither's Spring, 46
Gaither, Ann, 62
Gaither, Elizabeth 1711, 39
Gaither, Elizabeth 1805, 69, 140
Gaither, Frederick, 69
Gaither, Mabel Olivia, 91
Gaither, Martha, 239
Gaither, Mary, 10
Gaither, No given name, 159
Gaither, Samuel R., 96, 115
Gallagher, Airy, 163
Gallagher, Lucy, 163
Gallagher, Norris, 163
Gallagher, T. D., 163
Gamble, Joan Griffith 1938, 201
Gamble, Townley 1908, 201
Gartrell, Jane, 69
Gartrell, Mary 1889, 138
Gartrell, Rebecca, 158
Gartrell, Ruth, 26
Gassaway, Ann, 222
Gassaway, Brice John, 11, 32
Gassaway, Henry, 11
Gassaway, Henry Charles, 11
Gassaway, Stephen Griffith, Reverend, 11
Gater, Widow, 20
Gawlis, Alexander C., 167, 215
Gawlis, Alexandria C., 166, 215
Geibel, Bruce Burgee, 52
Gibson, Elizabeth 1795, 56
Giddings, Carrie Deaver, 228
Giddings, Charles Glenville 1834, 228
Giddings, Susan Dawson, 228
Giddings, William Campbell, 228
Giddings, William J. 1861, 228
Gilbert, No given name, 51

Gilchrist, Ralph Alexander 1896, 234
Gilroy, Robert F., 217
Gilson, John E., 139
Glenwood, 149
Gloyd, Jacob Alexander 1833, 75
Gloyd, Lena Gertrude 1880, 75
Golden, Flora, 110
Goltha, Elizabeth, 34, 173
Gongo, Faith, 2
Gott, Susan Elizabeth 1852, 176
Gott, Thomas Norris 1818, 176
Green, Elena 1914, 138
Green, Elizabeth 1769, 24
Green, Thomas, Reverend, 47
Greenberry, Katherine, 8
Greenlee, No given name, 64
Greer, Ida Sherwood 1862, 230
Greer, Robert E. 1891, 230
Griffith's Adventure, 5, 9
Griffith's Burgh, 111, 124
Griffith's Island, 23, 24
Griffith's Lot, 7, 8
Griffith's Lott, 23
Griffith's Park, 5, 40
Griffith's Park Spring, 40
Griffith's Place, 38
Griffith's Range, 38
Griffith, A. Elizabeth 1827, 18, 108
Griffith, A. Wirtie 1881, 83
Griffith, Abraham, 4, 238
Griffith, Agnes, 133
Griffith, Agnes Riggs 1907, 86
Griffith, Agrippa 1796, 148, 152
Griffith, Agrippa 1817, 179
Griffith, Airy, 163
Griffith, Alan, 239
Griffith, Albert O. 1849, 65
Griffith, Albin 1828, 62
Griffith, Alexander W. 1835, 34, 173
Griffith, Alfred 1783, 104, 106
Griffith, Alfred 1832, 16, 146
Griffith, Alfred Bowie 1821, 130
Griffith, Alfred Charles 1864, 17, 146
Griffith, Alfred Crabb 1864, 17, 146
Griffith, Alfred d/1877, 106
Griffith, Alice, 3

Griffith, Alice 1873, 16, 146
Griffith, Alice M., 83
Griffith, Allen, 39
Griffith, Allen 1801, 58, 60
Griffith, Almeda 1797, 148, 152
Griffith, Almeda 1817, 179
Griffith, Almeda 1844, 179
Griffith, Alverda 1832, 109, 152
Griffith, Alverda 1848, 88, 210
Griffith, Alverda 1876, 72, 127, 212
Griffith, Alverda 1881, 91
Griffith, Amanda 1881, 83
Griffith, Amanda J. 1838, 18, 108
Griffith, Amanda S. 1842, 66, 79
Griffith, Amelia D., 62
Griffith, Amelia Dorsey 1795, 58, 59
Griffith, Angelina 1830, 136
Griffith, Angelina 1831, 107
Griffith, Angelina M. 1831, 135
Griffith, Ann, 3
Griffith, Ann 1759, 12
Griffith, Ann 1762, 36, 45
Griffith, Ann 1763, 12
Griffith, Ann 1766, 20
Griffith, Ann 1776, 32, 170, 171
Griffith, Ann 1788, 158
Griffith, Ann 1804, 25, 26
Griffith, Ann 1820, 114, 150, 153
Griffith, Ann England 1909, 64, 81
Griffith, Ann Groomes 1908, 239
Griffith, Ann Hall 1793, 11
Griffith, Ann L. 1847, 63, 81
Griffith, Ann Marcylean 1918, 202
Griffith, Ann R. 1797, 58, 60
Griffith, Anna, 128, 212
Griffith, Anna 1828, 34, 173
Griffith, Anna Maria 1838, 111
Griffith, Anne, 26
Griffith, Anne E. 1815, 34, 172
Griffith, Anne Eliza 1858, 137
Griffith, Anne Singleton 1872, 98, 117
Griffith, Annie, 163
Griffith, Annie Mary, 151
Griffith, Armistead Hempstead 1881, 202

Griffith, Artemus Riggs 1874, 102, 120
Griffith, Aurelia, 163
Griffith, Avarilla 1744, 3
Griffith, Barbara Ann 1955, 77
Griffith, Barbara Jean 1951, 74, 198
Griffith, Basil, 24, 26
Griffith, Basil Norris 1874, 163
Griffith, Basil, Jr., 26
Griffith, Bathsheba, 3
Griffith, Benjamin, 3
Griffith, Benjamin 1732, 12
Griffith, Benjamin d/1736, 3
Griffith, Benjamin M. 1831, 179
Griffith, Berry J. 1804, 111
Griffith, Bessie Estelle 1877, 191
Griffith, Betsy 1756, 12
Griffith, Betsy R., 86, 133
Griffith, Bettie 1875, 199
Griffith, Blanche Newton 1900, 200
Griffith, Brian C., 151
Griffith, C. W. 1856, 189
Griffith, Caleb 1759, 156, 157
Griffith, Carol Ann, 78
Griffith, Catherine, 23, 164
Griffith, Catherine 1732, 22, 24
Griffith, Catherine 1795, 158
Griffith, Catherine 1797, 13, 108
Griffith, Catherine 1829, 34, 173
Griffith, Catherine Greenberry 1769, 156, 160
Griffith, Catherine S. 1814, 106
Griffith, Charity 1875, 136
Griffith, Charles, 23, 163, 187
Griffith, Charles 1693, Captain, 6, 8, 23, 24, 30
Griffith, Charles 1758, 24
Griffith, Charles 1758, Lieutenant, 36, 45
Griffith, Charles A. 1796, 25
Griffith, Charles A. 1827, 151
Griffith, Charles Byron 1880, 191
Griffith, Charles Greenberry 1744, 14, 15
Griffith, Charles Greenberry 1771, 12

Griffith, Elizabeth 1800, 96, 113, 115
Griffith, Elizabeth 1842, 179
Griffith, Elizabeth 1868, 100, 118, 125
Griffith, Elizabeth 1889, 203
Griffith, Elizabeth d/1860, 239
Griffith, Elizabeth Darnall 1917, 186
Griffith, Elizabeth Etchison, 167, 215
Griffith, Elizabeth G. 1847, 75
Griffith, Elizabeth G. R. 1800, 11
Griffith, Elizabeth Greenberry 1799, 159
Griffith, Elizabeth m/1825, 240
Griffith, Elizabeth Ridgely 1764, 14, 15
Griffith, Elizabeth Ridgely 1799, 47
Griffith, Elizabeth Waters 1897, 66
Griffith, Ellen, 60
Griffith, Ellen Ann m/1822, 239
Griffith, Ellen Cuyler 1872, 135
Griffith, Ellen Waters 1924, 186
Griffith, Emeline 1829, 16, 145
Griffith, Emeline C. 1832, 16, 146
Griffith, Emeline M. 1811, 158
Griffith, Emily 1877, 16, 146
Griffith, Emily Howard 1818, 181, 193
Griffith, Emily Jane 1863, 192
Griffith, Emily M. 1819, 130
Griffith, Emma 1842, 109, 153
Griffith, Emory 1876, 16, 146
Griffith, Ephraim Jackson 1820, 159
Griffith, Erastus 1813, 179
Griffith, Ernestine P., 239
Griffith, Esther Rebecca 1902, 200
Griffith, Ethel 1875, 83
Griffith, Ethna Lena, 78
Griffith, Ezekiel 1720, 19
Griffith, Fannie M. 1851, 162
Griffith, Father Sydney 1938, 76
Griffith, Festus 1838, Captain, 44, 100, 119
Griffith, Festus Agrippa 1834, 153, 210
Griffith, Flavilla 1814, 164
Griffith, Florence, 29

Griffith, Florence Anderson 1877, 86, 134
Griffith, Florence C. 1861, 166, 214
Griffith, Florence May 1862, 110
Griffith, Forest India, 214
Griffith, Forrest Lee, 214
Griffith, Forrest Lee, Jr., 214
Griffith, Frances 1797, 182
Griffith, Frances 1830, 238
Griffith, Frances Ann 1830, 109, 152
Griffith, Frances I. 1871, 101, 119
Griffith, Frances Ruth 1893, 209
Griffith, Francis, 4
Griffith, Francis Moore 1831, 189
Griffith, Francis Moore, Jr. 1870, 191
Griffith, Francis Ruddell 1920, 239
Griffith, Frank 1869, 72, 127, 212
Griffith, Frank Riggs 1899, 102, 120
Griffith, Franklin 1840, 101, 119
Griffith, Frederick M., 237
Griffith, G. Allen, Doctor, 240
Griffith, Genevieve, 86, 133
Griffith, Genevieve Magruder 1921, 87, 134
Griffith, George, 5
Griffith, George 1838, 109, 153
Griffith, George 1839, 109, 153
Griffith, George d/1680, 4
Griffith, George H., Doctor, 60
Griffith, George J. 1833, 179
Griffith, Georgianna 1851, 182
Griffith, Gilbert 1853, 129
Griffith, Gladys May 1891, 167, 215
Griffith, Goldsboro Sappington 1903, 239
Griffith, Greenberry, 178
Griffith, Greenberry 1727, 11, 32, 157, 164, 171, 175
Griffith, Greenberry 1787, 174, 175, 180, 193
Griffith, Greenberry 1794, 159
Griffith, Greenberry 1802, 158
Griffith, Greenberry 1838, 181, 192
Griffith, Greenberry Gaither 1874, 73, 198

Griffith, Jane Ann 1952, 64, 81
Griffith, Jean, 238
Griffith, Jefferson 1801, 109
Griffith, Jefferson, Jr. 1846, 111
Griffith, Jeffrey M. 1829, 135
Griffith, Jeffrey Magruder 1881, 87, 134
Griffith, Jeffrey Magruder, Jr. 1913, 87, 135
Griffith, Jemima 1784, 148, 149
Griffith, Jemima 1819, 179
Griffith, Jemima A. 1814, 181, 192
Griffith, Jemima Eleanor 1832, 153, 210
Griffith, Jemima Jacob 1784, 41, 174, 175, 180
Griffith, Jennie 1833, 35, 173
Griffith, Jennie R., 151
Griffith, Jeremiah Crabb 1825, 18, 108
Griffith, Joanna, 86, 133
Griffith, John, 3, 4, 24, 45, 150, 159, 238
Griffith, John 1728, 22, 24
Griffith, John 1770, 20
Griffith, John 1808, 25
Griffith, John 1814, 34, 172
Griffith, John 1828, 113
Griffith, John A. 1830, 151
Griffith, John Belford 1780, 33, 170, 172
Griffith, John F., 72
Griffith, John Hammond 1754, 36, 44
Griffith, John Jefferson 1865, 110
Griffith, John L., 163, 202
Griffith, John m/1826, 239
Griffith, John McElfresh 1827, 162
Griffith, John Nicholas 1834, 179
Griffith, John Riggs 1773, 156, 161, 164
Griffith, John Samuel 1818, 114
Griffith, John Summerfield 1829, 18, 108
Griffith, John William 1848, 159
Griffith, John Worthington 1908, 75

Griffith, John Worthington, III 1972, 76
Griffith, John Worthington, Jr. 1943, 76
Griffith, Johnson, 151
Griffith, Jonas, 3
Griffith, Jonathan Worthington 1879, 74, 75
Griffith, Joseph H. B. 1831, 18, 108
Griffith, Joseph Milligan Worthington 1964, 77
Griffith, Joseph Thomas 1828, 189
Griffith, Joseph W. 1798, 238
Griffith, Joshua, 20
Griffith, Joshua 1730, 11
Griffith, Joshua 1764, 36, 46
Griffith, Joshua Dorsey 1824, 179
Griffith, Joshua, Jr. 1769, 12
Griffith, Joyce Jean 1942, 78
Griffith, Julia 1853, 183
Griffith, Julia d/1886, 239
Griffith, Julia Louisa 1897, 127
Griffith, Julia Marie 1947, 77
Griffith, Julia Riggs 1869, 89
Griffith, Julian 1846, 82
Griffith, Julian, Jr. 1873, 82
Griffith, Juliet, 44
Griffith, Katey 1765, 12
Griffith, Katherine, 214
Griffith, Kathryn, 87, 134
Griffith, Kenneth Louis, 239
Griffith, Kirke M. 1875, 85, 132
Griffith, Lafayette F. 1828, 136
Griffith, Laura Lochner 1961, 202
Griffith, Leah 1792, 174, 175
Griffith, Leah 1826, 187
Griffith, Leania Subina 1859, 159
Griffith, Lebbeus, 88, 153, 216
Griffith, Lebbeus 1804, 125, 153, 166, 174, 178, 207
Griffith, Lebbeus 1862, 209
Griffith, Lebbeus, Jr. 1842, 210
Griffith, Lemuel 1795, 113, 148, 150, 153
Griffith, Lena 1872, 209
Griffith, Leona Rabbitt, 240

Griffith, Philip, 26, 163, 238
Griffith, Philip 1792, 159
Griffith, Philip G. M. 1820, 161
Griffith, Priscilla, 20
Griffith, Priscilla 1744, 3
Griffith, Priscilla 1877, 135
Griffith, Prudence Jane 1816, 181, 193
Griffith, Rachel, 20, 26
Griffith, Rachel 1749, 36, 42
Griffith, Rachel 1761, 12
Griffith, Rachel 1766, 156, 160
Griffith, Rachel 1786, 11
Griffith, Rachel 1827, 34, 172
Griffith, Rachel 1831, 163
Griffith, Rachel 1832, 35, 173
Griffith, Rachel 1843, 210
Griffith, Rachel Warfield 1802, 113, 153
Griffith, Randolph, 34, 172
Griffith, Raymond 1892, 204
Griffith, Rebecca, 3, 164, 175
Griffith, Rebecca 1822, 159
Griffith, Rebecca 1827, 34, 172
Griffith, Reginald 1883, 84
Griffith, Remus 1786, 47
Griffith, Rezin, 151
Griffith, Richard, 4, 240
Griffith, Richard H. 1787, 104, 107, 129
Griffith, Richard H., Jr. 1828, 84, 130
Griffith, Ridgely 1806, 158
Griffith, Robert, 24
Griffith, Robert 1793, 158
Griffith, Robert Clifton 1919, 204
Griffith, Robert Cole 1944, 76
Griffith, Robert E. Lee 1862, 214
Griffith, Robert E. m/1947, 240
Griffith, Robert Emory 1843, 111
Griffith, Robert Leland 1908, 167, 215
Griffith, Robert Union 1861, 159
Griffith, Roderick 1787, 33, 170, 172
Griffith, Roderick R. 1816, 34, 172
Griffith, Roger, 163
Griffith, Romulus Riggs 1803, 58, 60

Griffith, Rosalie 1869, 110
Griffith, Rose V. 1861, 130, 192
Griffith, Ruth, 176, 177
Griffith, Ruth 1747, 36, 40, 180
Griffith, Ruth 1763, 156, 160
Griffith, Ruth 1770, 36, 47, 48
Griffith, Ruth 1789, 47, 174, 175, 205
Griffith, Ruth 1797, 158
Griffith, Ruth 1836, 110
Griffith, Ruth 1839, 210
Griffith, Ruth 1894, 204
Griffith, Ruth Berry 1840, 111
Griffith, Ruth E. 1849, 162
Griffith, Ruth Elizabeth 1814, 164
Griffith, Ruth H. 1784, 104, 107
Griffith, Ruth H. 1921, 128, 213
Griffith, Ruth Hammond 1784, 148, 149
Griffith, Ruth Matilda 1835, 18, 108
Griffith, S. Rebecca 1828, 162
Griffith, Samuel, 4, 5
Griffith, Samuel 1737, 3
Griffith, Samuel 1752, Captain, 15, 18, 36, 44, 71, 105, 111, 129, 135, 140, 143, 152
Griffith, Samuel 1822, 34, 173
Griffith, Samuel 1832, 110
Griffith, Samuel B. 1780, 104, 106
Griffith, Samuel C. 1867, 16, 145
Griffith, Samuel Christopher 1823, 130
Griffith, Samuel d/1741, 2
Griffith, Samuel R. 1828, 107
Griffith, Samuel, Jr., 2, 5
Griffith, Sarah, 4, 5, 26, 71, 167, 171, 215
Griffith, Sarah 1721, 22, 23
Griffith, Sarah 1730, 22, 24, 30, 221
Griffith, Sarah 1734, 3
Griffith, Sarah 1741, 36, 38
Griffith, Sarah 1749, 20, 23
Griffith, Sarah 1778, 33
Griffith, Sarah 1780, 170, 171
Griffith, Sarah 1790, 58, 59
Griffith, Sarah 1792, 104, 108, 140
Griffith, Sarah 1799, 148, 152

Griffith, Sarah 1802, 25
Griffith, Sarah 1817, 34, 173
Griffith, Sarah 1879, 16, 146
Griffith, Sarah Ann 1803, 148, 152
Griffith, Sarah Ann 1815, 158
Griffith, Sarah Ann 1835, 109, 152
Griffith, Sarah Ann 1850, 72, 211
Griffith, Sarah Catherine 1843, 159
Griffith, Sarah Crabb 1866, 17, 146
Griffith, Sarah E. 1839, 179
Griffith, Sarah E. 1865, 71
Griffith, Sarah Howard 1718, 9
Griffith, Sarah Jane 1905, 128, 212
Griffith, Sarah Maude 1872, 91
Griffith, Sarah Newton 1884, 203
Griffith, Sarah Ridgely 1792, 92, 93
Griffith, Sean Michael 1965, 77
Griffith, Seth Robert, 167, 215
Griffith, Seth Warfield 1860, 213
Griffith, Shawn, 240
Griffith, Shepherd 1872, 136
Griffith, Shirley L., 72
Griffith, Sophia 1691, 6, 8
Griffith, Stephen, 11
Griffith, Susan Boyd 1886, 203
Griffith, Susan C. 1836, 238
Griffith, Susan M. 1840, 111
Griffith, Susan Matilda 1888, 87, 135
Griffith, Susannah R. 1813, 130
Griffith, Suzanne Clements 1938, 76
Griffith, T. C., 239
Griffith, Tanjore T. 1865, 209
Griffith, Thomas, 5, 40, 44
Griffith, Thomas 1731, 3
Griffith, Thomas 1791, 158
Griffith, Thomas 1801, 174, 178
Griffith, Thomas 1803, 240
Griffith, Thomas Asbury 1846, 159
Griffith, Thomas C. m/1912, 240
Griffith, Thomas Cranmer 1866, 67,
    127, 212
Griffith, Thomas Cranmer, Jr. 1906,
    67
Griffith, Thomas D. 1837, 179
Griffith, Thomas d/1666, 4

Griffith, Thomas David 1871, 100,
    118
Griffith, Thomas G. 1803, 92, 96, 115
Griffith, Thomas G., Jr. 1831, Cap-
    tain, 97, 116
Griffith, Thomas H., 151
Griffith, Thomas m/1825, 240
Griffith, Thomas Perry 1913, 201
Griffith, Thomas Riggs 1820, 145
Griffith, Ulysses 1810, 58, 61, 78, 88,
    131, 211
Griffith, Ulysses 1871, 64, 81
Griffith, Ulysses 1876, 83
Griffith, Ulysses, IV 1908, 64, 81
Griffith, Ulysses, Jr. 1843, 64, 80
Griffith, Ulysses, V 1954, 64, 81
Griffith, Uriah 1808, 58, 61
Griffith, Uriah H. W. 1857, 65
Griffith, Uriah Henry 1825, 61, 62,
    127, 212
Griffith, Uriah W. 1825, 80
Griffith, Ursula d/1853, 65
Griffith, Varena, 216
Griffith, Vernon T. d/1970, 237
Griffith, Vernon Tschiffely 1903, 73
Griffith, Victor, 163
Griffith, Victor B. 1879, 163
Griffith, Virginia 1840, 79
Griffith, Virginia 1871, 82
Griffith, Virginia M. 1901, 66
Griffith, Walker 1886, 128, 213
Griffith, Walter 1781, 104, 106
Griffith, Walter 1783, 33, 170, 172
Griffith, Walter 1820, 114, 211
Griffith, Walter 1823, 124
Griffith, Walter 1886, 128, 213
Griffith, Washington 1842, 75
Griffith, Washington 1868, 72
Griffith, Wiley Gaither 1914, 74, 198
Griffith, William, 4, 20, 26, 163, 239
Griffith, William 1718, 22, 23, 36
Griffith, William 1768, 20
Griffith, William 1788, 159
Griffith, William A. 1843, 125, 211
Griffith, William B., 139
Griffith, William Bastable 1918, 202

271

Mobley, Walter W. 1869, 100, 118, 125
Mobley, William B. 1843, 100, 118, 125
Mobley, William B. 1896, 100, 118, 125
Molesworth, John, 53
Moneysworth, 160
Moore, John Basil, 50
Moore, Ranna Stevens, 159
Moore, Stevens, 159
Moore, Theresa, 50
Moorman, Corinna, 194
Moxley, Ezekiel, 151
Moy, Richard, 4
Mt. Ararat, 4
Mudgett, Kevin 1957, 205
Mudgett, William Chase, III 1947, 205
Mudgett, William Chase, Jr., 205
Mullen, Nellie, 216
Mullican, Harwood, 83
Mullinix, Thomas Pratt 1844, 162
Mullinix, Thomas Pratt, Jr., 162
Munford, Howard, Major, 137
Murphy, Annie Charlotte, 54
Murphy, Benjamin, 57
Murphy, Teresa, 222
Mussetter, Christian, Captain, 41
Mussetter, Christopher, 57
Mussetter, John 1801, 57
Mussetter, Rebecca, 41
Myers, John William 1900, 188
Myers, Milcah Amelia, 121
Myers, No given name, 214
Myers, Olivia Riggs 1862, 121
Myers, William H. 1831, 121
Myers, William H., Jr., 121

—N—

Narrow Neck, 23
Neel, James, 87, 134
Neel, Laura H. 1850, 122
Neel, Lillian 1883, 87, 134
Neel, Thomas 1872, 122

Neff, Deon G., 239
Nelson, Ralph Frederic, 186
Nelson, Sandra Elizabeth, 186
New Design Place, 38
Newman, Michael Lloyd 1945, 74, 198
Nickens, No given name, 72
Niles, Marguerite Alice 1890, 76
Noland, Barney Taylor 1847, 177
Noland, George W., 177
Norris, John, 163
Norris, Rachel Ann 1835, 162
Norwood's Fancy, 23
Norwood, Arianna, 153
Null, Linda, 200

—O—

O'Bryan, Thomas W. 1844, 56
O'Neill, No given name, 141
Oakley, 120
Ober, Lucretia 1806, 61, 62
Ober, Martha J. 1809, 69
Ober, Matilda 1812, 61
Ober, Robert, 61, 69
Offutt, Drew Griffith 1969, 76
Offutt, Jeffrey Worthington 1962, 76
Offutt, Pamela Elaine 1857, 76
Offutt, Ralph Worthington, Jr. 1937, 76
Orme, Charles, 15
Orme, Elizabeth 1801, 15
Orme, James 1808, 15
Orme, Jeremiah C. 1806, 15
Orme, Nancy Crabb 1815, 15
Orme, R., Doctor, 15
Orme, Sarah Griffith 1804, 15
Orme, Walter A., 16, 146
Orphans' Inheritance, 23
Owens, Margaet 1842, 144
Owens, Thomas 1881, 144
Owing's Contrivance, 8
Owings, Alice Dorsey 1898, 28
Owings, Basil, 239
Owings, Basil 1798, 60
Owings, Gillis, 145

Owings, L. I. G., 28
Owings, L. J. G., 145
Owings, Minnie, 145
Owings, Richard Henry, 60
Owings, Ruth, 145
Owings, Samuel, 145
Owings, Samuel Dorsey 1868, 28
Owings, Thomas, 145
Owings, Willie, 145
Oxley, Thomas Cummings 1889, 197

—P—

Palmer, Amy Nichole 1986, 90
Palmer, Eliza 1834, 130
Palmer, Stephen Joseph 1987, 90
Palmer, Steven, 90
Park, Nannie, 224
Parker, Cassie, 234
Parrish, Benjamin, 178
Parrish, Patricia Kingma, 217
Parrish, Sarah M. 1812, 178
Partnership, 32
Penner, Elizabeth, 155
Penniman, William, 95
Perry, Margaret Elizabeth 1879, 199
Perry, Richard Humphrey Williams
  1827, 199
Peters, No given name, 163
Pfeiffer, Jo, 77
Philip, John Oliver, 56
Phillips' Swamp, 2
Phillips, Matilda, 176
Phillips, Philip L., 176
Phillips, Sarah Rebecca 1830, 176
Pigman, Sarah, 106
Pile, Robert, 239
Pindell, Eric Dorsey 1942, 139
Pindell, Louis Spencer 1941, 138
Pindell, Stuart MacIntosh 1914, 138
Pindell, Stuart MacIntosh, Jr. 1938,
  138
Pitts, Anne Maria 1810, 46
Pitts, Charles H., 46
Pitts, John Lusby 1808, 45
Pitts, Jonathan 1772, Reverend, 45

Pitts, Nicholas, 45
Pitts, Thomas, 45
Pitts, Thomas Griffith 1812, 46
Pitts, William, 46
Plummer, Anna, 160
Plummer, Ellen W., 160
Plummer, Greenberry Griffith, 160
Plummer, Jesse, 160, 176
Plummer, Jesse Baker 1803, 160
Plummer, Lydia C., 47
Plummer, Lydia G., 160
Plummer, No given name, 152
Plummer, Philip, 160
Plummer, Ruth, 160, 176
Plummer, Sarah, 160
Plummer, Thomas Griffith, 160
Poole, Ann 1773, 96
Poole, Cordelia, 57
Poole, Filmore W. 1852, 114
Poole, Mabel, 141
Poole, Maggie L. 1857, 114
Poole, Sebastian 1879, 114
Posey, No given name, 240
Poss, Otis, 29
Postley, Mary T. 1838, 141
Pressman, Victor M., 73
Price, Eli, 52
Price, Ralph Stanley 1920, 198
Prospect Hill, 27
Prost, Marie Antoinette, 50
Pumphrey, Benjamin Griffith, 186
Pumphrey, Ellen Irene 1946, 186
Pumphrey, John Sphar, 186
Pumphrey, Kirk Griffith, 186
Pumphrey, Lucy Woodford, 186
Pumphrey, Meredith Ann, 186
Pumphrey, Richard Griffith 1952, 186
Pumphrey, Robert Alexander 1921,
  186
Pumphrey, Robert Alexander, Jr.
  1950, 186
Pumphrey, Traci Ann, 186
Pumphrey, William Alexander, 186
Pumphrey, William Reuben, III 1948,
  186
Purdum, Charles Riggs 1807, 42

Purdum, Eleanor Riggs 1820, 42
Purdum, Henrietta Maria 1809, 42
Purdum, James Henning 1847, 56
Purdum, James W. 1819, 42
Purdum, John 1739, 41
Purdum, John Riggs 1816, 42
Purdum, John Rufus 1827, 42
Purdum, Keziah 1816, 42
Purdum, Mamie 1886, 56
Purdum, Mary 1805, 42
Pyles, Charles, 185
Pyles, Charles Thomas 1885, Doctor, 185
Pyles, Elizabeth Dade 1916, 185
Pyles, William Griffith 1913, 185

—R—

Ralston, Mary, 160
Randall, Martha Lewis 1919, 139
Raynor, William Charles, 188
Read, Emma, 158
Read, Matthew, 4
Refuge, 2
Reich, Charles Julian 1849, 209
Reicher, Carrie Iona, 191
Reid, Anthony Eugene 1959, 78
Reid, Jacquelyn 1982, 78
Reid, Lisa 1981, 78
Reid, Paul Xavier, III 1963, 78
Reid, Paul Xavier, Jr. 1940, 78
Renier, Joseph, 34, 173
Resurvey on Daniel's Small Tract, 52
Retirement, 59, 61, 69, 70, 78, 86, 87, 134
Reynolds, Sarah, 7
Richardson's Joy, 23
Richardson, Mary 1767, 157
Ridgely, Anne 1771, 93, 115
Ridgely, C., 26
Ridgely, Charles Greenberry 1735, 46, 93
Ridgely, Elizabeth, 24, 31, 44
Ridgely, Elizabeth 1765, 46
Ridgely, Elizabeth 1766, 11
Ridgely, Elizabeth 1769, 46

Ridgely, Elizabeth D. 1850, 122
Ridgely, Greenberry, 11
Ridgely, Henry, 24
Ridgely, Henry 1728, Major, 31
Ridgely, Henry, Colonel, 14
Ridgely, Katherine Greenberry, 8
Ridgely, Nancy Anne 1771, 93
Ridgely, Priscilla, 23
Ridgely, Sarah 1745, 14, 15
Ridgely, William, 46
Riggs Hills, 40, 157
Riggs, Aaron, 68
Riggs, Amelia 1834, 121
Riggs, Amon 1808, 41, 180
Riggs, Amon Edwin 1748, 40, 180
Riggs, Amon, Jr. 1776, 41
Riggs, Anna, 89
Riggs, Annie E. 1860, 123
Riggs, Annie H. 1870, 123
Riggs, Antoinette 1811, 41, 180
Riggs, Artemus, Doctor, 101, 119
Riggs, Avolina 1838, 44, 101, 119
Riggs, Benjamin C. 1871, 122
Riggs, Catherine Augusta 1850, 44
Riggs, Charles 1774, 41
Riggs, Chloe, 68
Riggs, Douglas, 68
Riggs, Douglas Howard, 122
Riggs, Douglas Howard, III 1944, 89
Riggs, Douglas Howard, Jr. 1913, 89
Riggs, Eleanor M. 1784, 41
Riggs, Elisha, 43, 132
Riggs, Elisha 1810, 43, 101, 119
Riggs, Elisha 1845, 85, 122
Riggs, Elisha 1881, 123
Riggs, Eliza 1817, 41, 180
Riggs, Eliza A. 1830, 88
Riggs, Eliza H. 1875, 123
Riggs, Elizabeth R. 1891, 123
Riggs, Emanueleta 1850, 123
Riggs, George Thomas 1847, 44
Riggs, Georgia R. 1888, 123
Riggs, Gilbert 1838, 121
Riggs, Henry 1772, 41, 180
Riggs, Henry 1796, 41
Riggs, Howard Griffith 1805, 41, 180

—V—

—W—

Woodland, 69, 71
Woolf, Catherine, 12
Worley, Curtis, 195
Worley, Dorsey Waters 1872, 194
Worley, Dorsey Waters, Jr., 194
Worley, Edgar Brewer 1883, 195
Worley, Edith May 1871, 194
Worley, Helen James 1877, 194
Worley, Joan Roberta, 194
Worley, John William 1875, 194
Worley, Marion, 195
Worley, Nathan Maynard, 194
Worley, Sue Waters, 195
Worley, Sue Waters 1885, 195
Worley, Virginia, 195
Worley, Wilbur Moorman, 194
Worley, William Nevins 1834, 194
Worley, William Nevins, Captain, 194
Worley, William Nevins, III, 194
Worthington, Achsah 1836, 39
Worthington, Ann, 39
Worthington, Ann H. 1791, 39
Worthington, Bradley, 126
Worthington, Catherine, 24
Worthington, Catherine 1810, 39
Worthington, Charles, 24, 39
Worthington, Elizabeth, 24, 40
Worthington, Elizabeth 1843, 40
Worthington, James 1772, 39
Worthington, James 1850, 40
Worthington, John Griffith, 24
Worthington, John H. 1793, 39
Worthington, Joshua D. 1845, 40
Worthington, Lavinia 1847, 40

Worthington, Lloyd Anna 1839, 40
Worthington, Mary H., 39
Worthington, Nicholas 1733, Colonel, 24
Worthington, Nicholas Griffith, 39
Worthington, Sarah 1800, 39
Worthington, Susan 1803, 39
Worthington, Thomas, 24, 39
Worthington, Upton 1810, 39
Worthington, William, 39
Worthington, William B., 126
Wotthlie, Judith Ann 1948, 89
Wotthlie, Margaret Ann 1939, 89
Wotthlie, Mary Estelle 1945, 89
Wotthlie, Patricia Ann 1942, 89
Wotthlie, Richard William 1912, 89
Wotthlie, Richard William, Jr., 89

—Y—

Yate's Contrivance, 31
Yates, Edwin Langhorn 1903, 233
Yates, Ella O. 1848, 232
Yates, Paul, Reverend, 232
Yingling, David G., 163
Young, Angelica C. 1830, 181
Young, Isaac 1828, 188
Young, John 1790, 182
Young, Linda 1864, 188
Young, Margaret R. 1829, 188
Young, No given name, 64, 81
Young, Verlinda Catherine 1864, 188
Young, William E., 158

2086335

Made in the USA